A SPIRITUAL ODYSSEY

For
Sadie

Brian O'Hare

A Spiritual Odyssey

DIARY OF AN ORDINARY CATHOLIC

the columba press

First published in 2005 by
the columba press
55A Spruce Avenue, Stillorgan Industrial Park,
Blackrock, Co Dublin

Cover by Bill Bolger
Origination by The Columba Press
Printed in Ireland by ColourBooks Ltd, Dublin

ISBN 1 85607 512 5

Table of Contents

Give thanks to the Lord, give praise to his name!
Make his mighty deeds known to the people.
Canticle: Isaiah

Acknowledgements

This book describes a journey, two journeys indeed, which I never could have travelled had I not leaned heavily upon the shoulders of some significant others. To them I owe a huge debt of gratitude. I therefore wish to place on record my deepest and most sincere thanks to:

Sadie, my wife, who taught me the meaning of love; Father John Bermingham whose first gentle push propelled me on the Way; Father Niall Sheehan, spiritual guide, constant friend, and companion on the Way; Sister Briege and Sister Joan, my sisters, continuous source of advice and support; Sister Briege McKenna, friend; only God knows what I owe to her; Father Martin, long-distance friend, whose occasional interventions are timely and much needed; Father Andrew McMahon and Sister Julie McGoldrick, Father Matthew Despard, friends, and strong influences on my spiritual life; George Johnston, Stephen Wigmore, Tom Diamond, surgeons, to whose skill and dedication I owe my life; and finally, to the Unknown Lady whose death has given me life.

That said, however, I still have to accept full responsibility for what is written in these pages; no one else is to blame.

Preface

Given its personal nature and its somewhat conservative theology, I had reservations before undertaking this diary, reservations during its writing, and reservations even after it had been completed. So why write it? It was something William Barclay said:

> The Christian life is based on the twin pillars of discovery and communication. No discovery is complete until the desire to share it fills our hearts; and we cannot communicate to others until we have discovered him for ourselves. First to find, then to tell, are the two great steps of the Christian life.[1]

Shortly after I read this, I came across a similar message from Vincent Travers OP:

> At times we are tempted to think there is little we can do to advance the cause of Jesus in the world but that is a temptation we must resist … God needs us to co-operate with him in making him more known, loved and served … we are called to be witnesses.[2]

I have been favoured beyond the ordinary, beyond any deserving, and beyond any doubt as to the source of my blessings. I am compelled, therefore, despite any diffidence that I might feel, to add my own small witness to the magnitude of God's goodness. My prayer is that this book will reach out to someone somewhere, that it will touch a few hearts, that it will offer support and fellowship to one or two pilgrims who recognise in its pages a stage in their own journey. If this prayer is answered, then despite my littleness, I will have served God.

1. *The Gospel of St John,* Vol 1, St. Andrew Press, 2001
2. *On Song with God,* Dominican Publications, 2002

PART ONE

The Return

CHAPTER ONE

Impulses to Grace

March 1998

Today I drove past the cemetery where my father and mother lie buried. I said a prayer for them. Nothing out of the ordinary there, you might think. You would be wrong. I have not said anything remotely resembling a prayer for almost thirty years. So why today? I am sure there is nothing of grace in me. Can one pray and not be in a state of grace? I am reminded of Claudius' dilemma after Hamlet pricked his conscience with his 'play-within-the-play'. Claudius knelt before an altar and tried, vainly, to pray:

'My words fly up; my thoughts remain below.
Words without thoughts never to heaven go.'

Did my prayer go to heaven? What was I even thinking about? I have no idea. I was passing the cemetery and I said, aloud if you can believe that, 'God bless Daddy and Mammy.' I didn't plan it. I didn't have any notions in my head about how holy and how wholesome it is to pray for the dead. I was heading towards the golf course, no doubt with golf on my mind, and suddenly I said, 'God bless Daddy and Mammy.' I drove on, mystified, trying to remember some of the elementary theology I had studied in Canon Sheehan's *Apologetics* some forty-five years earlier in St Colman's College, Newry. I vaguely remember being told that if we are not in a state of grace, our prayers don't reach heaven. However, they can be put 'on hold', as it were, until such time as we go to confession (none of us had ever heard of the 'Sacrament of Reconciliation' in those days) and thus become restored to God's grace. Confession? What prompted that thought? I have not been to confession for more than thirty years and I have not the slightest intention of going now. Why am I even thinking about this? It is all very odd.

May 1998

Oddity piles upon oddity. Because it was forcing me to contemplate things I would have preferred to ignore, that first entry deflected me from any further thoughts of continuing this diary. But it was only the start of a very strange pattern that was beginning to emerge in my life. Every time I pass the cemetery, I say without fail, 'God bless Daddy and Mammy!' It is extremely puzzling, even discomforting. My life has been about career, money, material comforts, nice house, nice car, golf, holidays, television, reading and, ultimately, I suppose, self-indulgence – all the standard idols. God has not fitted into it anywhere, at least, not to my knowledge. Now every time I pass the graveyard I wonder if he hears me; I wonder what he is thinking. My prayer has to be meaningless! Given the materialistic life I have been leading, it cannot be anything else. Yet this whole business has me constantly thinking about God. In fact, every time I walk past the cathedral in Hill Street I now stop and go into it. I have not done that since I was young. I don't pray when I go in, however. I do not even go in as far as the pews. I stand at the back. I tend to hide behind one of the pillars there and do nothing, say nothing and, as far as I can figure out, think nothing. I stand there, blank, puzzled, ill at ease. After a few minutes I go out again. Inevitably I think about the Pharisee and the Publican, but I do not say, 'God be merciful to me, a sinner.' I don't say anything. I do not even know why I go in there.

But I return to my diary because today something strange has happened. I need to write it all down and have a look at it. I want nothing to do with it but somewhere in my heart-of-heart I think (I know this will sound crazy) that God is sending me a message, something he wants me to think about. Actually it was three messages ... or was it the same message three times? It came in the oddest juxtaposition of three ... three what? Three entirely different and unrelated ... poetic verses, I suppose I would have to call them. The first definitely is from a poem.

I was searching through an old poetry book this morning, looking for a quotation I couldn't quite remember. I thought I would find it in one of Wordsworth's reflective or philosophical poems. The line I sought is something like: 'The past is part, and a necessary part, of the man I am today.' (Obviously there are some peculiar reflections going on in my own head when I am seeking the genesis of an idea like that.) In the event, I couldn't find the quotation I was looking for but I did stumble across an old poem by Francis Thompson that I had studied at school – 'The Hound of Heaven'. The first lines hit me with extraordinary force, infused in that first instant with intense meaning, meaning that I could never have apprehended in my schooldays regardless of how much study and effort I might have put into them. But now – heart-stopping!

> I fled him, down the nights and down the days;
> I fled him, down the arches of the years;
> I fled him, down the labyrinthine ways of my own mind …
> Up vistaed hopes I sped …
> From those strong feet that followed, followed after.
> But with unhurrying chase
> And unperturbed pace …
> They beat – and a Voice beat
> More instant than the feet –
> 'all things betray thee who betrayest me.'

I stared at these lines then, and I am staring at them now. They are extraordinary but they echo so loudly in my head – like a loudspeaker turned on at full volume – that I have to turn away from them. I am afraid to follow where they lead. I don't want to follow where they lead.

Further into the poem I find yet more lines that seem aimed at the centre of my soul:

> For though I knew his love who followed,
> Yet I was sore adread
> Lest having him, I must have naught beside.

Lest having him I must have naught beside! So much meaning packed into so few words and, right now, a dagger in my soul. Almost my entire adult life has been a choice of earthly things over God, the material over the spiritual. It never bothered me before. I read a few lines from a poem and … I'm bothered! What is going on?

The second message I would not even have noticed were it not for the fact that Thompson's lines were running through my head. I was working in my study and I had slotted a Chris Rea cassette into my tape-deck. Rea is something between a rock-star and a pop-star. I have to be honest; I haven't a clue what he is. I am not a great follower of music fads. Classical and opera I like, but 'pop'... well ... if I was on a quiz show and had to answer a question about 'pop' music, I would lose the sixty-four thousand dollars. Chris Rea's gravel voice and haunting melodies, however, have great appeal for me. I was working quietly away when I heard him sing:

> I can run
> In your eyes there's no place left to hide.
> You've seen my every mystery
> Just show itself and die.
> So I will fly before you ...
> And I will always fly
> Like a seabird.

I had heard the song (the poem?) before, of course. But it did not particularly register on my consciousness, other than as some plaint to a girl he wanted to be with but felt trapped by. Right then, however, with the words of Francis Thompson fresh in my mind, Rea's words suddenly assumed a deep and spiritual significance. Comparison was inevitable:

'I fled him' – 'I will fly before you'
'I sped' – 'I will always fly'

Struck both this amazing coincidence and a hazy but insistent memory (or, in a phrase I noted in Wordsworth this morning, a '... recognition dim and faint'), I pulled down a small prayer-book from my shelves (echoes of the year I spent as a clerical student in Maynooth in 1956) and found Psalm 138. Here I found the third verse:

> O Where can I go from your Spirit
> Or where can I flee from your face?
> ... If I take the wings of the dawn
> And dwell at the sea's furthest end,
> Even there your hand would lead me,
> Your right hand hold me fast.

These three verses on the same day – can simple coincidence be the answer? I have a brother who sometimes talks about the reactions of petitioners who, having prayed for a favour and find it granted, tend to attribute the desired outcome to coincidence. Few, he said, will actually attribute it to the prayers they said. My own problem is not precisely the same but the issue of 'co-incidence in the spiritual realm' is similar.

I have written down what has happened and I have read and re-read it. I am affected by it; that I cannot deny. My reason is urging me to plump for coincidence. I can imagine the mockery I would receive if I tried to divulge the story and my uneasiness about it to my friends. And indeed, why would God go to all this trouble to catch my attention? Is it rational to imagine, even for an instant, that God would set up something as complicated as this? And yet, the old cliché 'God works in mysterious ways' is humming in my brain. I'm embarrassed even to write that down. None of this makes any sense. And what about that other Christian notion – 'impulses to grace'? I have experienced many times in the past number of years, dimly and at a distance but consciously, little promptings that might be described as 'im-pulses to grace' – the notion that I should bring Christian values into my teaching; the feeling that I should become a little more detached from ambition; the desire to help young teachers who are pursuing post-graduate qualifications. I have responded to a degree to such promptings but always I've been able to file them in my subconscious as some kind of social justice or a develop-ing maturity. But what is going on now, and what has been going on for the past several months, is not 'dim and at a dis-tance'. It is very much real, in my face, and challenging me. But what is the challenge? I am still the errant Christian I have been for a long time; I have no conscious need to change. Indeed, 'lest having him I must have naught beside' is a strong argument for maintaining my spiritual *status quo*. Except, a voice immediately sounds in my head, 'Your *status quo* is not spiritual.'

I was at a wedding of a nephew in Dublin some months ago. I remember a conversation I had with my brother, Sean, and my sister, Joan, who is a Poor Clare nun. We were talking about liv-ing the spiritual life, or finding one's way back into it. Sean is an inveterate attender of study groups. A Jesuit priest had once told one of these groups that 'to become a Christian and to live in grace, all one needs to do is to say "Yes" to God.' My brother laid this on me at the dinner table. Only the three of us were seated there at that point in the evening. I said, 'That is rubbish.' I knew the life I was leading. I knew the pull that life had on me. I knew the changes I would need to make, the time I would need to devote to prayer, the selfishness and self-seeking that would have to disappear, the grace that would be needed to clean, and then to reside in, my soul.

'All I have to do is say "Yes"?' I scoffed. 'Have you any idea of what one has to commit oneself to, the internal promises and vows one has to make, the radical changes one has to make in one's life before one can even remotely begin to think of saying "Yes" to God?'

My brother was adamant and, while my sister supported him in principle – 'there has to be a commitment in the "Yes" but God's grace will take care of all those other things you are worrying about' – she understood my point of view. I, however, could not even begin to understand theirs. My carefully constructed existence, built to suit me (selfish and self-centred though it may be) would be blown apart. Yet I could not say 'Yes' to God and carry on living in exactly the way I am doing. That makes no kind of sense. So, despite my brother's conviction, I remain convinced that it is not simply a matter of saying 'Yes', it is far more a matter, at least to my currently disordered thinking, of *doing* 'Yes'. So there was no 'Yes'. There was nothing. I am still the same. My life hasn't changed. And yet today the echoes of Thompson, Rea and Psalm 138 are loud in the corridors of my mind. I keep trying to ignore them, to dismiss them, but I am constantly drawn back to them.

One thing is clear. Either the entire episode is simply a series of coincidences or it is not. If it is coincidence, I can simply dismiss it from my mind. If it is not coincidence, then it must be something ordered, something meaningful. If I leave my rationality to one side for a moment, if I 'suspend disbelief', as Wordsworth suggests in another context, then the 'logic' of the 'message' becomes clear: 'You have fled me long enough; you have flown before me far enough; you can no longer hide from me. I have come to retrieve your soul.' No, that cannot be right. Written in cold print like that, this interpretation looks absolutely ludicrous. It has to be coincidence.

Reviewing what I have just written brings to memory something my sister, Briege, also a Poor Clare, once told me about 'synchronicity'. 'Carl Jung,' she said, 'did not believe in coincidence.'

If I remember correctly, she explained that Jung had a conviction that when unrelated events in life coalesce in some synchronous fashion the hand of God is there behind such congruence, the Divine Plan is in operation. For Jung the conjoining of events in a way that draws significant attention to them is simply the Spirit working in the world and in us. So where does that leave me?

CHAPTER TWO

An End ...

June 1998

I have always loved my job. I never stinted in the energy or the effort that I devoted to it. As a young teacher I gave late afternoons and evenings to the pupils; as an Assistant Director in a large Institute of Further and Higher Education many years later, I gave everything I could to organising, managing and building. I was so busy that I could not walk from one place to the next, yet as a Senior Manager it was undignified to run. I developed a kind of loping gait that was akin to that of an Olympic walker – but without the exaggerated arm and buttock movements. In my latter years I still dashed constantly between our two campuses – East and West –both of which have several floors and lifts. I never use the lifts, no time to wait.

Recently, however, I have noticed a slowing down in myself; more than that, a draining of energy and motivation. I stay in my office for much longer periods, devoting my time to paperwork where before I would be meeting with Heads of School or Section Heads. I am fatigued much of the time and bring very little paperwork home with me in the evenings.

The problem took me into the Director's office – a friend as well as my boss. We discussed it and considered the possibility of stress. The Director (Raymond Mullan) said that he could not imagine, given my nature, that stress was really the cause. Neither could he accept that I might be suffering from what used to be called 'executive burn-out'. There had been no warnings or symptoms that might permit such a diagnosis. In the end we agreed that if the condition, whatever it might be, deteriorated, we would meet again to consider the possibility of early retirement. I am touching sixty and have only two years left to complete my statutory forty years service. Thirty-eight years in the profession! I started when I was twenty-two. Twenty-two!

What an extraordinarily callow age. What could I have possibly known about anything at that time? Yet there I was in September 1960, fresh, eager, and totally unaware of the depth on my ignorance, unleashed upon a school full of unsuspecting teenage boys.

As the years went by, I became painfully aware of my ignorance and finally returned to university for further study – eight years in all, between 1978 and 1986. This study helped my teaching a bit and gave me, perhaps, a little added knowledge of psychology and of the nature of inter-relationships. It did not, however, put a great dent in my ignorance. But with the passing of the years, I think, I did grow a little in understanding of my profession. Sadly, in the spiritual sphere I remained not only in ignorance but also in splendid unawareness of that ignorance.

A few weeks ago I felt that I was no longer able to do my job. I have for years insisted to my wife that only wild horses will drag me out of my office on my sixty-fifth birthday, yet here I was, back in Raymond's office, asking him to use his influence to secure early retirement for me. Nowadays, in 1998, it is becoming increasingly difficult to 'get out', to use the profession's vernacular, and fewer opportunities for early retirement exist. But my boss is a man of considerable influence and this morning I was informed that my bid has been successful. I retire officially at the end of August. Notification and forms to be completed will be arriving in a few days.

I am not sure how I feel about it. I certainly am not particularly jubilant or excited. Indeed, I am somewhat depressed that my career should be 'fizzling out' as damply as it appears to be doing. Owing to my managerial responsibilities, I have not been teaching much, barely three hours a week, during the past decade. But I look back beyond that and see how much better my teaching might have been, how much more effort I could have put into 'character formation' as much as 'knowledge building'. It is sad – all we get is the one chance. Mine began at twenty-two and, my goodness, what did I know? Oh! I had my share of praise and did some noteworthy things. I made friends with Inspectors and got to work alongside many of them as colleagues in various projects. But did I really achieve anything or was I simply working for money, promotion and glory? I think I can say, I hope I can say, that I did the best I could with the skills and knowledge I had at the time. But now that I am older – and, perhaps, a touch wiser – I find it easy to stare into the embers of my dying career, to spot the mistakes, the omissions, the inadequacies of both temperament and understanding and to feel the onset of regret. These regrets appear to be influenced, too, by what I am beginning to suspect is a burgeoning spirituality, though where it might becoming from, or why, is a complete mystery to me.

I now see so many ways I could have used my teaching, especially through the great poets, the great novelists, the great dramatists, to establish a much more values-oriented focus on what I taught. I talked to my sister Joan a while back about this very point. She had once attended, with a group of nuns from her convent, a series of evening literature classes I was teaching. Her recollection was that my teaching not only had a Christian orientation but that I was charitable beyond the call of duty to one particularly recalcitrant student in the group. I hope she is right. I have no recollection of what or how I taught. I do remember the student she referred to, however. He tested my patience to the limit. Students like that you remember always.

Well! After August all I will have are memories. As I said, I am not sure how I feel about that.

CHAPTER THREE

'... and a Beginning'

November 1998

Retirement is fine. My brother, Sean (who has also retired), two friends and myself have now made up a regular four-ball which meets every Monday and Wednesday for eighteen holes of golf. It is very enjoyable although I notice that I now have to take a couple of painkillers before I go out because of abdominal pains with which I wake up each morning. I also tend not to play during the other days of the week because I seem to need them to help rebuild my energy. I am wondering if I am getting old but the men I play with are in the same age-bracket and they do not appear to suffer from any of these problems. I am not too concerned, however. Of course, I could do without the pains but they do not appear to be all that serious – more of an inconvenience than anything else.

What is more remarkable is that my prayer as I pass the graveyard has changed. I have added the names of a close aunt and uncle who also lie buried near my parents. Then, later, other names, for various reasons, were added to the list which has now become quite long. When I go into the cathedral I no longer lurk behind the pillars at the back. I go on into one of the pews and sit there. This situation has become quite extraordinary. I do not actually pray but sometimes I might say:

'Lord, I know you can see me. I know you are there. I know you know what is going on in the innermost recesses of my brain and heart. But I don't! I do not know what I am doing here. Is it you who is constantly calling to me or is there something in my psyche bringing me in here to seek answers to questions I don't even know I have?'

Then I might sit a while longer in silence, shake my head a bit at the mystery of it all, and leave. That is what actually happened today and has triggered another entry, among an already extremely erratic series of entries, in this strange diary.

Lent, 1999
Your new birth was not from any mortal seed but from the everlasting word of the living and eternal God. (1 Peter 1:23)

The mills of God grind slowly. Autumn and winter have come and gone since my last entry. All has been as it was. My life in retirement has rolled calmly along now-firmly-established tracks and nothing of any note has occurred to warrant further contact with my diary – nothing, that is, until a few days ago. Something truly amazing has happened and, while I am still trying to come to terms with it, I think I can now make an attempt to write about it.

My wife, Sadie, is a very Christian woman. She was a radiographer at the local hospital and was noted for the charitable and caring manner with which she treated patients. She is a regular communicant and often goes to Mass during the week as well as Sundays. She never passes a church, at home or abroad, without going in to pray. Perhaps it was she who inculcated that recently developing habit in me.

A couple of weeks ago, at teatime, she informed me that a group of Redemptorists were to conduct a 'mission' in Newry cathedral the following week. It is really a kind of public 'retreat' but for as long as I remember it has always been known in Newry as 'the mission'. I have no idea why. I suspect that the retreat may have been conducted by missionary fathers in earlier times. In any event, Sadie said that she would be attending each evening. I passed little remark at the time but some time later I spoke to her about it.

'That mission business ... I think I'll go with you.'

It is hard to describe the expression that appeared on her face. When I was a child our family used to say: 'He looked at me as if I had two heads.' Sadie's expression reminded me of that. I am sure she thought I was not well but finally she said,

'Certainly! Why not? It can't do you any harm.'

The mission was interesting. As usual, however, I sat to some degree aloof, as I have done all my life. I watch people. I examine them. I make assessments of their skills, their sincerity, their weaknesses, their tendencies. I do not believe I do this in any malicious way. Sometimes my conclusions are negative but

equally, depending on what I see, my conclusions can be lauda-
tory. I look; I see; I analyse. It is who I am; it is what I do.

When the missioners were preaching, I was watching and
analysing. I noted the one who spoke loudly, who moved
around in the pulpit as if he was pacing, who waved his arms
and continually made the grand gesture. I listened to what he
had to say and I filed it. I watched, too, the priest who spoke
earnestly and with great force, who relied on the eloquence of
his words and the strength of his gaze rather the punctuation of
emphatic hand movements. I listened to what he had to say and
I filed it. I watched the young, dark, slight, sincere priest who
spoke quietly, who placed no reliance whatever upon the customary dramatics we have come to expect from retreat preachers over the years. Father John, for that was his name, was one of
those rare people who do not deliberately do anything, who do
not adopt any particular kind of stance yet who, despite their
modest bearing and self-effacement, exude holiness. I listened
each time to what he had to say but I did not file it. I pondered it
... nightly.

Thursday evening came. Part of the planned ceremony was
the Sacrament of Reconciliation. When this was announced, it
didn't quite register with me. I think I vaguely imagined that
later in the devotional programme there would be some sort of
general blessing. What in fact happened was that a large procession of priests from all of the parishes in the diocese emerged
two-by-two from the sacristy and located themselves at various
points around the cathedral. Father John, who had been in the
pulpit at that time, announced that he himself would greet peni-
tents on the high altar. There occurred in my pew (what I described later to my sisters as) a 'kerfuffle'. I was sitting at the
extreme inside end of the packed pew. I can remember clearly
some noise, awkward movement, a series of suddenly startled
features (some slightly irritated) ... just faces, clear in my mind.
Nothing else! Without having the slightest clue how I got there, I
suddenly found myself at the foot of the main altar, well ahead
of any queue, making straight for Father John. When I realised
where I was, I realised equally that I had absolutely no idea of
what I was going to say. I had not had any intention of going to
confession. I had made no preparation of any kind – no exami-

nation of conscience, no Confiteor, nothing! I had been sitting in my seat calmly surveying the priests emerging from the sacristy. I noted that one priest had made to genuflect when passing the altar but, because his colleagues before and behind made no attempt to genuflect, he stopped himself, mid-obeisance, and walked on. I remember the incident clearly. I remember thinking that the priest should have gone ahead with his deferential gesture no matter what the others did. Then suddenly I was at the bottom of the altar steps. (I have just re-read this last section. It seems totally unbelievable that anyone could act in such autonomic fashion ... and yet, it happened exactly as I describe.)

I moved up the steps towards Father John. He stood waiting, calm, serene, an expression of ... what appeared to me to be ... kind interest upon his face. My mind, obviously, was now whirring at massive speed, mostly trying to figure out what I might say, now that I had taken (what I totally and absolutely knew to be) an irrevocable step. I framed in my mind something like 'Father, it is thirty years since I have been to confession. I do not know quite how to go about this. I forget the words, the formula ...' and I stepped forward.

'Father,' I said, and stopped, surprised at the weakness of the croak that emitted from my mouth. My throat was totally constricted; saying anything was a supreme effort. Somehow I managed to say, 'It's thirty years ... I don't know ...' and that was it! Tears began to course down my face. I looked mutely at Father John, desperately pleading for assistance. I tried again to speak but my mouth simply opened and closed, opened and closed, like that of a goldfish in a bowl. I kept looking at Father John, maybe wondering with part of my mind if he was going to become impatient and tell me to get on with it. No impatience – just complete kindness. He stepped forward and, in a gesture that I had seen many times in various depictions of the meeting of the Prodigal Son with the Father, he placed a hand on each of my shoulders and said, 'Don't worry that you can't speak. Are you sorry for all the sins of your past life?' I could only nod dumbly. 'Well, know this,' he continued. 'God now forgives you every sin you have committed since the day you were born.'

The tears continued to flow unabated but the enormity of what Father John had just said startled me into a brief and amazed response, 'All of them?' 'All of them,' he replied. 'I'm going to give you absolution now and you can return to your seat in the full knowledge that you are filled with the grace of God. Try now to say an act of contrition while I bless you.'

Was there ever a moment so magical? Is this how the woman about to be stoned for her sins felt when Jesus said, 'Since none of these has condemned you, neither will I condemn you.'(John 8)

I returned to my seat, blinded with tears. I stumbled, inevitably, on the steps but a kindly male hand supported me. What did I feel when I got back to my seat? I have no idea. I was stunned, that much is certain. I have a vague notion that the phrase 'Thank you, Jesus', was echoing over and over in my brain but there were no coherent thoughts. I was not aware of any of the relief that would seem almost a mandatory response. I was not aware of any need to prostrate myself humbly before the Lord and express my gratitude. I should have done – but I didn't. What did I feel? I would like to say I felt joy, delight, but I truly can't remember what I felt. I have tried and tried over these past few days to recall the emotions of that moment – a moment that shall be forever precious to me – but I can't. It seems to me that I might have been experiencing a total absence of feeling ... or was it a feeling so deep that my brain could not apprehend it, an emotion too deep for thought? I know I kept thinking, 'I should be praying! I should be thanking God!' But even this refrain was distant and vague. I simply sat in my seat, unmoving, unthinking, stunned ... in a state of ecstatic numbness. Ecstatic numbness? Where did that idea come from? I wrote it instinctively just now, without thought ... and yet, felicitous phrase, it explains exactly how I was feeling.

Despite some intense reflection over the past few days, I have been unable to find any explanation for what I have come to term 'this extraordinary epiphany'. What suddenly motivated me to rush to the altar? When did the notion of seeking forgiveness first enter my head? The obvious answer is that the grace of God was working in me. Of course it was. But does the grace of God usually operate with such suddenness, such force? This moment of love and forgiveness was, is, an immense gift but where did its intensity come from? My mother, God rest her, died when I was twenty-one. (She never got to see me get my first teaching job although she had been looking forward to the idea of being a teacher's mother.) Did she plead with Jesus' mother to do something? Did Our Lady then go to her Son, like she did at Cana, and ask him to sort this man out? I do not know but I do know that the miracle at Cana is no more incredible for me than this miraculous epiphany. Sadie, certainly, was pleased. She did not say anything but as we left the chapel she took my hand and we walked to the car in awed silence.

Lent 1999

It will probably come as something of a surprise when I say, given what I have already written about myself, that I had actually attended Sunday Mass without fail all during my years in the spiritual wilderness. I still had a faith of sorts. I still believed in God and his love. It was a kind of Augustinian thing – continued attendance at Mass would help me to cling to some shreds of my faith until such time as I was ready to commit myself to a true Christian life. I still believed totally in the Divine Presence in the Eucharist, a belief that explains why I, a sinner, would never present myself at the altar as a communicant. That, I felt, would be a horrendous sacrilege. Writing this makes me realise that having faith as I did I should have reformed my life long ago. Having been given the gift of faith and ignoring it so callously makes me a worse and more wilful sinner than those who sin in ignorance. This is a hard truth to face; nonetheless, I lived as I did.

In all that time I do not remember a Mass I attended when I did not feel regret at not being able to receive Holy Communion. I remember at many Masses, especially at funerals and weddings, watching people presenting themselves for Communion who had not been to Mass or confession for many months, even years, and feeling something between distress and anger at this terrible insult to the Lord. Even as I write this, St James's words echo in my ears, 'Who are you to give a verdict on your neighbour?' I had no right to judge – a weakness in my character I must now work hard to eliminate – but I truly envied those who received Communion sincerely, as I resented those who, in my opinion (an opinion that was probably biased and worthless, I see now) should not have approached the altar.

I record this because it will help explain the joy and anticipation with which I attended Mass the morning after my absolution at the hands of Father John. Joy and anticipation, yes, but wonder, confusion, deference, some disbelief, a little concern, and residual guilt all vied for equal space in my consciousness. One thought, however, burned more strongly in my mind than any of the others; it blazed in my brain before Mass, and during the Mass, with undiminishing brightness –'I am finally going to receive Jesus in Holy Communion again.' The moment came. Jesus and I were conjoined in a most intense and physical way. I talked and talked; I listened; I felt. I remained transported long after the rest of the congregation had left the church. There is much I could say about these moments but, open and honest though I want this diary to be, there are some moments that are too precious, too intimate, to share. This first re-union with my Saviour was a period of personal and private happiness that, quite simply, is beyond telling.

Wordsworth found God in his abiding love of nature. In a moment of ineffable affinity with the beauty of nature, he once saw deep into the heart of things and was moved to exclaim:

To me the meanest flower that blows can give
Thoughts that do often lie too deep for tears.

The smallest flower can induce emotion beyond tears? Can there be any wonder that I have been struck dumb in the face of this momentous union with the Son of God?

March 1999
I want to write only a short entry today. I am so affected by the news I have that I have no inclination to talk about anything else. On the Saturday night that the Novena ended, lines of people were waiting to speak to the 'missioners'. Father John's line was as long as any but I joined it. When I finally reached him, I began to say, 'I know, Father, that out of the hundreds of people who have spoken to you this week, it is completely unlikely that you will remember me, but I …'

Father John reached out a hand and placed it on my shoulder. 'Of course I remember you. How could I forget a moment so precious?'

He remembered! He, too, had been aware of the unique nature of that moment. I was overcome, yet again, thanked him briefly, and left.

Some days later, still deeply affected by what had happened, I was moved to write to Father John, not only to express a gratitude that I could scarce contain but also to tell him 'my story' which I truly believed he should hear. This morning I received his reply, a reply inevitably filled with the Christian love and encouragement that, despite my brief acquaintanceship with him, I knew to be characteristic of the man. His words will always remain with me and I quote the last three paragraphs, not for what they say about me but for what they reveal about Father John:

... It made me so happy to know that the grace of God's love and mercy have so entered into your heart.

I wish you now nothing but peace, joy and an ever-deepening knowing of the love which Jesus bears for you. I am so grateful for your sharing of this experience through your letter. That alone made everything in Newry worthwhile.

God bless you, Brian, in your life of faith wherever that may lead.

> *Thank you so much,*
> *Father John Bermingham*

Again I am struck dumb. Father John's words must speak for themselves.

PART TWO

The Search for Answers

CHAPTER FOUR

Father Niall

March 1999

Shakespeare once famously said (in one of those King plays, Richard the Third, I think): 'Hope to joy is more enjoyed than joy enjoyed.' In the past couple of weeks I have realised that I can turn that phrase on its head and coin a parallel one: 'Anticipation of fear is more feared than fear feared.' I keep thinking about Thompson's line, 'Lest having him I must have naught beside.' This has to be one of Satan's most cunning deceits. Lord knows, the apostles tried hard enough and often enough in their letters to tell us that there is nothing to be feared in turning to Jesus and to the Spirit. James says: 'The man who looks steadily at the perfect law of freedom and makes that his habit ... will be happy in all that he does.' Peter tells us that '... you did not see him, yet you love him; and still without seeing him, you are already filled with a joy so glorious that it cannot be described.' But we do not listen! And I believe that we do not listen because we fear that we might lose more than we want to give. And yet, after so many years in this very fear, I am beginning now to see, in wonder and amazement rather than in anger, the poisoned honey in the devil's lie.

My life, on the surface, has changed little since that remarkable Thursday evening. I still play golf twice a week with my friends. I read. I watch television. I can still be grumpy at times. I can still neglect my household chores. And I can still watch, and judge, and criticise. These are personality defects that I can try to correct, that I will try to correct. But my inner life has experienced a radical change. Radical – a sometimes misunderstood word. It hints at left-wing politics, iconoclasm, youthful rebellion. In fact, it pertains to change at the very root of things. My perception now of how my life should be lived has changed beyond all imagining. The 'loss' I feared has, in fact, become totally irrelevant. The wonder of God's grace working in me (I am sure there is nothing of my will in what has happened) has had the most amazing effects. So much of what seemed important or attractive before bears no interest for me at all. I am not even susceptible to the wistful glance backwards that got Lot's wife into so much trouble. I grow increasingly mystified as I become aware of the superficiality and aridity of what once I deemed so important. How could I have been so blind?

And I begin to have some dim understanding, too, of what saying 'yes' to God might mean. I still believe that saying 'yes' is not simply a matter of 'deciding' to. It cannot derive from a direct and deliberate act of will. That much I do know. The 'yes' must stem from an invitation from God; it is a response to his gift of grace. We say 'yes' because we cannot help ourselves, and from that 'yes', however slowly and reluctantly we arrive at it, emerges a commitment to change our lives. The 'yes' is impossible without the commitment.

There is an obvious pattern, or order, here. 1. God knocks, and no matter how subtle or gentle that knocking may be, we hear it. 2. When we hear, we have two choices – we can ignore the knock or we can listen. 3. If we ignore, we do not progress; if we listen, we respond, in however shallow or unsophisticated a fashion. We may simply say 'What?' or, as in my own case, 'What is going on?' 4. The listening, the questioning, inevitably leads to further grace and, ultimately to a response, to a beginning of understanding, to a tendency to prayer. 5. It is at this point, perhaps consciously but perhaps also unconsciously, that the commitment is made. When the commitment is made, does God's grace, as Joan said, take care of the rest? To a degree! No sacrifices have to be made because suddenly one's aspirations have become truly different. Prayer becomes a need, not a duty. Sin is avoided, not because of fear but because of love.

But saying 'yes' is only the beginning. To say 'yes' and then passively wait for God's grace to work in us is 'quietism' and is really indicative of a certain spiritual indolence. The Spirit expects us to co-operate actively with him and I believe that the more we co-operate, the more grace we are given. St Peter tells us that while we are waiting for the new heavens, we should do our '... best to live lives without spot or stain so that he will find you at peace.' (2 Peter 3:14) 'Do your best ...' clearly implies a personal effort, an active involvement in our spiritual growth. Jesus himself said much the same thing, demanding an active self-discipline from us: 'Try your best to enter by the narrow door because, I tell you, many will try but will not succeed.' Again we find that same implication that a significant element in our hope for eternity lies in our own hands, in our own efforts.

And yet there remains in all of this the most wonderful of paradoxes. The 'efforts' we have to make become, through God's grace, 'effortless'. Jesus says, 'For my yoke is easy and my burden light.' The same paradoxes are here. 'Yoke' implies restraint, but 'easy' implies lenience and forbearance; 'burden' implies encumbrance and impediment, but 'light' implies insubstantiality and manageability. To that degree, God's grace definitely takes care of the rest. It is, quite simply, a force that is irresistible.

I find it quite amazing, and in some ways amusing, to have had my entire world, and my focus on it, turned upside down and inside out and yet to note that my friends and various acquaintances see exactly the same man they always knew. It must be something to do with the idea that each of us is specifically and uniquely loved by God, that each of us privately and individually responds to that love. To me the change feels wonderful, extraordinary, inexpressible, and yet I know that externally I am little changed. I now, of course, go to Mass and Communion every day. People may well mark that but, if they do, they show no sign – apart from Sadie who now accompanies me to Mass every day as well. Not, of course, that it matters one jot whether people remark on my change or not. It is just a little mysterious that the spiritual earthquake that exploded in my soul should register zero on the body's Richter scale.

I am reminded by this of Prince Hal's remarks in Henry IV, Part 1. Prince Hal was rather disgracing himself by carousing nightly with the Shakespearian equivalent of 'lager-louts' in the local pubs. Left alone on stage at the end of a scene early in the play, he soliloquises about his 'loose behaviour' in a way that makes it clear that he is quite unlike his debauched companions and that it is his intention to tolerate this lifestyle for a brief period only. And then he says:

And like bright metal on a sullen ground,

My reformation, glittering o'er my fault,
Shall show more goodly and attract more eyes
Than that which hath no foil to set it off.

For his own reasons he has chosen to hide his true nature, like the sun behind clouds, so that when he does chose to break through the mists 'he may be more wonder'd at.'

Perhaps he feels that when he ascends the throne and assumes the mantle of maturity, the contrast will make him all the more respected.

Thinking about Prince Hal's assumptions about how people will respond to the changes in him, has given me pause. Initially I thought that seeking to 'be more wonder'd at' smacked of egotism and pride. But one of the readings at Mass the other day contained the phrase, 'by their fruits shall you know them.' Maybe my newfound glorious but internal relationship with Jesus is not quite as it should be. Perhaps there should be some 'fruits' of which my friends and family should become aware; maybe my reformation should glitter o'er my fault. This quite disturbs me. My mind fills with thoughts of example, service, charity, love of neighbour and the good of others. It is a sudden and confusing mix. Where are these virtues in my new life? There comes the thought that there is no room for selfishness, for self-centredness, in the life of the Spirit. Clearly this is something to which I must give deep and earnest thought. I need help!

March 1999
Either Jesus read that last line or it came to him as a prayer. Mass this morning was celebrated by one of our parish curates, Father Niall Sheehan. Where Father John is slight, Father Niall is stocky; where Father John is dark, Father Niall is fair. There, however, the dissimilarities end. Each is young, each has the same gentle manner, the same easy smile, the same affable approachability. Father Niall, like Father John, does not say or do anything overtly spiritual but his whole mien has an aura of holiness. I watched him pray at Mass this morning. I watched the diligent manner in which he followed the rubrics, the sincerity of his prayers, the devotion in his attitude. When Mass was

over I was moved to follow him into the sacristy. I introduced myself and asked him if he had time to talk to me for a little while. 'Sure,' he said. 'Come over with me now to the Parochial House and we'll talk.'

I accepted the invitation gratefully and when we were settled in one of the rooms I told him my story. It was a strange and liberating experience for me to sit with a priest (for a couple of hours as it turned out) and speak with total and heartfelt candour. Father Niall expressed himself pleased that I had asked him to hear my story, along with my confession (a much longer and infinitely more detailed version than the one Father John heard). I was thus emboldened to ask if he would consent to be my spiritual director, for a while at least, until I was no longer sailing rudderless on this new sea. His response was typically generous. He invited me to continue to visit him for guidance and confession every couple of weeks. I look forward immensely to my future sessions with him.

CHAPTER FIVE

Accident or Design?

March 1999

I had another meeting with Father Niall today. He is only in his mid-thirties but he has an amazing grasp of life and its difficulties as well as an impressive knowledge of matters spiritual and theological. He is also an avid reader and has already lent me some of his books to help slake my own increasing thirst for theological awareness. Today we spoke of the will of God. I have a vague recollection of studying Cosmology at UCD in the mid-fifties. I recall some discussion about whether God intervenes to any great extent in the affairs of the world or whether he created it, gave it a push to start it off, and then sat back to observe the natural flow of cause and effect, of accidents and inevitabilities. Obviously, since I have given no thought to matters such as this for more than thirty years, my thinking about it is woolly in the extreme. Father Niall actually laughed when I broached the subject. 'Do you know any easy questions?' he asked.

He told me an interesting anecdote about St Teresa of Avila who, one wet evening, stumbled and fell out of a horse-drawn cart. Looking heavenwards, she said, 'If this is how you treat your friends, Lord, is it any wonder you have so few of them?'

The story is amusing but the implications of her remark are far-reaching. Was St Teresa sincere in her assumption that God is the initiator of all of the events in this world or are some things merely accidents? Hamlet, musing over old Yorik's skull which he had come across in a freshly dug grave, said, 'There is a special providence in the fall of a sparrow', implying that even the slightest of events in the world are a direct result of God's will. The priest who taught us literature at St Colman's College told us at the time that Hamlet was wrong, that his comment was a form of 'fatalism'. All of us dutifully underlined the quotation and studiously wrote 'fatalism' in the margin of our texts. It

makes me laugh to think about it now. We were so earnest, yet
how many of us (at age fifteen or so) had a clue about what we
were noting?

Father Niall says that God 'allows rather than causes' things
to happen and then uses them as part of his divine plan for all of
us. God doesn't starve the poor Africans in such huge numbers;
it is not his will that they should starve. Their starving is an effect of the broken world in which we live. It may well be that he
is waiting for the rest of the world to waken up to its responsibility to help and support them. But who knows? There is a beautifully poetic passage in the Book of Wisdom that encourages us
to try to accept God's will but not to try to divine it:

Who can divine the will of the Lord?
The reasonings of mortals are unsure
And our intentions unstable;
For a perishable body presses down the soul
And this tent of clay weighs down the teeming mind.

Free will inevitably features in the context of God's will. Many
things that happen in this world, good or bad, are a direct result
of man's deliberate intention. God cannot be said to be the cause
of such events. If he were, then where is man's free will? But
where, then, is God's will? How does it manifest itself? How can
we know it? There are the commandments, of course. There is
no doubt that they are a specific statement of God's will. But
there are more esoteric areas where his will is not immediately
visible. Father Niall used the example of someone who has a
vocation to the priesthood. The vocation, clearly an urge from
God's will, can often be easily sensed. But less easy to determine
is whether service as a priest may be carried out in a parish of
one's own country, as a missioner in foreign fields, or even as a
monk in a contemplative order.

I remember once at university reading about St Thomas
Aquinas. The writer was relating an incident that occurred
while Thomas was studying at a seminary before he was or-
dained. He was playing chess with a friend in the common-
room during the recreation period. A few other students were
there, reading, chatting, playing some games. The Head of
Novices (or some such, I can't really remember) entered the

room and surveyed those who were there. 'Gentlemen, ' he announced. 'Consider this. If you were informed that the world was to end in ten minutes, what would you do?' (The exact words I can't remember; the dialogue is mine though it remains in essence what I read.) One student responded: 'I would go immediately to my spiritual director and ask him to hear my confession.' Another said, 'I would go to the Oratory and prostrate myself on the altar and try to establish such close affinity with the Lord that, when I die and meet him, I will already be in the middle of a conversation with him.' Others offered suggestions in similar vein until the priest turned to Thomas and asked, 'And you, Thomas? What would you do?' Thomas, who had been reflecting quietly on the matter, replied slowly, 'The programme of studies planned for us in the seminary at this stage in our formation, our timetable, is for us a precise statement of God's will. This particular period is scheduled for recreation. I would therefore continue playing this chess game with my friend. What better way to die than engaged in an activity which is God's precise will for us?'

Admirable certainty there! Father Niall liked the story when I told it to him and said that it gave him an added perspective on something that was going on in his own life. Sadly, however, most of us do not go through life with God's timetable in our hands. We might think, 'Well, it is God's will that we be Christian in our actions and in our attitudes to our neighbour.' The two great commandments – love God and love our neighbour – are the whole of the law. But how do we manifest that love? To what extent are we aware of negative or hostile actions or attitudes towards our neighbour? To what extent are we aware of any deficiency or neglect in our love of God? And when we move away from these direct instructions into areas more vague, how do we know what is and what is not God's will?

A child is killed in a horrific accident. Someone in the family later crosses herself and intones, 'Ah well, it was God's will.' But was it? I have great difficulty in accepting that God would deliberately will a child to be killed. I can accept that he could foresee the series of circumstances that would culminate in the child's death. I can also accept that, because he has given us free will, he has limited his ability to intervene in our lives. Occasionally he does intervene – witness the miracles in the gospels, the miracles at Lourdes and other Marian Shrines, the miracles attributed to various saints throughout the world over the past two thousand years and, indeed, the previous two thousand years of the Old Testament. But miracles are a rare and clearly supernatural occurrence. Ordinary life does not and, for the most part, cannot rely on miracles. Although, having said that, I must confess that there are far more miracles around us than we truly realise – the daily miracle of Transubstantiation, the many miracles of spiritual and physical healing, the miracles of lives changed radically for the better. I believe my own reformation was some sort of miracle. Nonetheless, miracles, i.e. God's direct intervention in our lives, are rare. Sickness, disease, hunger, poverty, are all around us. People who live questionable lives attain great riches, power, talents, fame and adulation. How difficult it is to discern God's will in these circumstances? We look at the increasing violence and evil in our society, the terrible moral decline in television and cinema, the drugs culture, the impact of technology upon man's view of himself and his decreasing need for God, and we ask why God is allowing these things to happen. Why doesn't he stop them? What, or where, in all of this is his will for us? For the world? I do not know. I think it is all bound up in man's free will. The mess is his; it is up to him, to us, to clear it all up. And it has to start with our prayers, our charity and our love.

As I said, Father Niall and I had a most interesting discussion about this but I know that, given my current confusion about it, this is a topic to which we will return again and again.

It will be a while, however, before I see Father Niall again. Sadie and myself are going to Portugal for the next three weeks with Sean and Sally (his wife) to play golf. Sean and Sally have been going there each spring for the past twenty years (Sean owned his own business and could take his holidays whenever he liked) but because of my job we were never able to join them. This year we have accepted their invitation. I am looking forward to it. Sean's descriptions of the weather, the golf courses, and out-of-the-way country restaurants they have discovered, paint a picture that sounds idyllic.

CHAPTER SIX

All Is Less Than Well

May 1999

What was it Robbie Burns said about the best-laid plans of mice and men? Our much anticipated sojourn in Portugal ganged totally agley. I must explain that on a few occasions during the winter of 1998 I was forced to abandon golf because of quite severe abdominal pains, nausea and a general weariness. On such occasions I could only loll most of the day in my armchair until the misery passed. But always it did pass, never lasting much more than a day. A few days before our departure date for Portugal, I fell foul again of these same symptoms. Sadie was not too happy. 'Are you sure you'll be all right for Portugal?' 'Of course! Don't worry! I'll be OK tomorrow. This always goes away in a day or two.'

It did not go away the next day, however, nor the day after that. I grew increasingly ill. The abdominal pains got worse, the nausea got worse and fatigue left me virtually incapable of effort. I remained in the armchair, eschewing vehemently any impulse to take to my bed. That would be an admission of failure. Sadie could see, wriggling and restless on the armchair, an increasingly pale, damp-haired specimen who, she fully believed, should be in hospital. 'No way you're going to Portugal!' Stubborn as ever, I replied, 'It's only a temporary thing. I'll be right as rain in a day or two.'

Packing for Portugal was a torture. The night before we were due to leave I put on my bravest face and, sick, exhausted but determined, I lugged our suitcases down from the attic and packed. Golf bags, and other equipment that we would need, had to be ferried in from the garage and squeezed into special carrier bags. Sadie wasn't fooled at all by my 'don't worry' smiles (or what I fondly imagined were smiles). I could tell this by the way she kept shaking her head and tightening her lips. (Observant or what?)

This episode is not, of course particularly noteworthy or significant. I write about it because it helps to explain subsequent events. What bothers me now about it, as I reflect back, is that I do not recall offering my discomfort to the Lord for his intentions for souls or for sinners. I remember reading once about a man who was about to die. Asked by a friend if he had any regrets about his life, he replied: 'I regret wasting my suffering. I could have done so much good with it.' I feel the same now. I am sure I said my morning offering each day but I do not recall marrying that offering with what was actually happening. I seem to have been saying that little prayer with blinkers on, and at one remove from '… the sufferings of this day'. Prayer and involvement in it – I am finding it a huge subject, and one that has been exercising me of late. I am going to have to think about it, write about it, and see exactly where I am in my prayer life. But that is for another time.

The morning we left for Dublin airport I was bent almost double. Sadie had to drive while I lay on the passenger seat, tilted back as far as it would go. We had agreed to meet Sean and Sally at a large roundabout near where we live and travel on to Dublin behind them. They were waiting for us when we got there. Sean got out of his car and came to ours. His surprise at seeing Sadie behind the wheel was nothing to the expression on his face when he saw what was lying on the seat beside her. His comments were predictable; Sadie's comments were predictable; I sang the same old refrain.

We had to change flights at Gatwick. My condition was not helped by an unexpected four-hour delay. There are some nice restaurants at Gatwick Airport. The others went to have a meal in one. I lay on one of the hard airport seats eating Paracetamol and groaning. I still did not pray; I still offered nothing to God. I may have found my way back to Jesus but there are some technicalities in this relationship that I still have not quite got a grasp of.

That evening I saw nothing of Portugal. I went straight to bed with a cup of tea, a biscuit, and a couple of painkillers. Sadie, Sean and Sally went out for a meal (Again? Where do they put the stuff?) but I was quite happy to be alone. The following morning Sadie took one look at me and said, 'Right! That's it!

We're going straight to the doctor.' Sean drove us there. I had a distant impression of blue sky, bright sun, low cream and white buildings – straight walls, straight roofs, occasional round bits – architecturally uninspiring. The doctor poked, prodded, hummed, haa'd, and muttered. Clearly puzzled, he eventually ventured, 'It might be a pancreas problem; you're going to have to go to hospital right away, either here or at home.'

We opted for the latter. In less than an hour we were driving back to the airport at Faro. Sean and Sally would be staying in Portugal, of course, but Sean, the group's organiser, was going to try to arrange for Sadie and myself a speedy return flight.

Something odd … strange … mysterious (when you hear the story you can pick your own adjective) occurred at Faro. Our first attempt to arrange a flight resulted in an offer that was extremely expensive. I reached for my credit card but Sean, ever the businessman, stopped me. 'We can do better than that. I'll go and talk to somebody about stand-by.'

The rest of us found seats. I lolled back, in a great deal of pain and misery – but still wasting it in self-pity. I must have dozed off. When I wakened a while later, I could hear Sally saying to Sadie, 'A family of five has just phoned in a cancellation. You should be able to get two of their seats.'

I opened my eyes. Sadie was sitting alone doing her cross-word.

'Where's Sally?' I asked.

'She's gone to look for Sean.'

'What was that about a family cancelling?'

'What? What family?'

'I heard Sally telling you just now that a family of five had phoned to cancel their flight.'

Sadie looked at me … questioningly, I could say, but more truthfully, as if I was not fully lucid.

'Sally's been away for almost twenty minutes,' she said. 'You must have been dreaming.'

I lay back but I was convinced that I had heard what I had heard.

A short while later Sean and Sally returned. Sean said,

'You're on a BA stand-by. If you get seats, it'll cost you a quarter of what that other group was charging.'

I said to Sally,

'Were you talking about a family of five cancelling?'

She was every bit as mystified as Sadie had been.

'No, I never heard anything about that.'

We all sat there, me drifting in and out of awareness, the other three talking quietly. About half-an-hour later, a young lady in a BA uniform approached us.

'Mr O'Hare?' she said to Sean.

'Yes?'

'A family of five has just phoned in a cancellation. There are two seats available for your party.'

We all looked at each other.

'When did they phone?' Sadie asked.

'About five minutes ago.'

When the attendant left, Sadie said to me,

'This is giving me goose-bumps.'

I was too sick to be affected much by the incident at the time and, though I have reflected on it a number of times since, I simply cannot fathom it. I cannot for the life of me perceive anything in what happened that might be deemed spiritual. Getting seats so handily might be considered a blessing (if one leans towards synchronicity rather than coincidence) but why the forewarning? Like I said, it was definitely odd ... strange ... mysterious. ('Inexplicable' also works for me.)

The flight home was not uneventful either. My golf clubs (which included a recently purchased and quite expensive set of irons) were lost at Gatwick. An hour and a half of searching, dealing with officialdom, filling-in lengthy claim forms, tested to the limit what little endurance I had left. (The clubs did arrive at my home a week later.)

I was in hospital for two weeks. A diagnosis of total dehydration was a bit of a surprise but the real reason for my illness should not have been a surprise to either of us. How easily we dismiss possibilities from our minds when their import is, in all probability, dire!

CHAPTER SEVEN

Antecedents

May 1999

To explain that last remark I will have to go back nearly thirty years. One night, early in 1972, I woke up with troublesome stomach pains. As the night progressed, the pains became more and more severe, reaching around to my back as well. At one point I was in such agony that I could not lie on the bed because the very pressure of my weight was unbearable. I recall pressing my heels into the bottom of the bed and the back of my head into the pillow, in an effort to raise the rest of my body into the air and away from contact with the bed. Sadie, obviously, was extremely worried and towards dawn phoned for a doctor who arrived surprisingly quickly. He gave me a painkilling injection and some strong tablets (Pethedine, if I remember correctly) and promised to call again later in the day. True to his word, he returned around lunchtime and found me groggy from the Pethedine, not quite in as much pain but, in truth, not really any better. He did not like the yellow tint that had appeared in my eyes and arranged to have me admitted to the local hospital right away.

A couple of days later I was recovering from a six-hour operation. The surgeon confessed to Sadie that he was baffled, that he could find no reason for my illness. He had had 'to close me up' after six hours without being able to do, or even to discover, anything. He did say that my '… bile-ducts looked a bit narrow' but he did not think that that was significant.

During the course of the next two weeks, I remained in hospital, suffering recurrent abdominal pains while my skin began to adopt a strong yellow hue … some kind of jaundice. A day or two later the surgeon came into my room (I had been left in a private room in case I had a variety of infectious hepatitis) and told me that he was a bit worried about my symptoms and was arranging to have me transferred to the Royal Victoria Hospital in Belfast. In those days, one did not go to 'the Royal' unless there was something seriously wrong. I confess I went into something of a panic, distressed not only at the implications of the transfer but distressed, too, at being far from home and friends.

I look back at the evening of that announcement. I remember well how I felt – scared, lonely, tearful. I did not pray then; I did not have a prayer life at all. From my present perspective, I cannot imagine how I got through that traumatic episode without prayer, without being able to turn to Jesus and discuss the situation with him, without having the grace to ponder, without the panic I was in, the role of God's will in this, and the purpose of my suffering (my terribly wasted suffering!). I am not sure, even now, what kind of thoughts I might have had but it seems to me that if I could have had conversation with Jesus (even one full of questions, pleas for help, and poorly-formed assumptions about what my response as a Christian should be) I would have found the experience infinitely easier to cope with.

My next memory is of lying on a narrow, hard leather table, wired to a TV monitor, with a doctor nearby pumping a dye into my system. The pictures on the screen were incomprehensible to me. Shortly after that, while I was still on the monitor, a smallish man in a white coat, brisk, competent, entered the room and went straight to the screen. He stood staring at it for a few minutes, turned to me, and said.

'Sclerosing cholangitis. It's quite serious. I'll have to operate more or less right away.' And he left the room.

I thought he was hard and abrupt. But I didn't know him. George Johnston, later to become Professor Johnston, is one of the kindest and most competent men I have ever met. What I took initially for abruptness was his characteristic forthrightness. He never attempted to colour hard facts; he spoke only truth. We were to become firm friends and that was one of the traits that I came most to admire in him. I still correspond with him, albeit only occasionally. He likes me to, as he once put it in a Christmas letter, '… keep in touch and keep me informed.' He's retired now but I still keep in touch.

Sclerosing cholangitis? What was that? I had never heard of

it. Neither, as it was to emerge, had many of the people in the medical profession. It was a rare disease then; I was one of about four known cases in Northern Ireland. It is more recognised nowadays, of course, and many more cases are being detected as a result. George once showed me a huge medical tome, about four inches thick, and pointed to a little paragraph of about seven or eight lines. 'That,' he said, ' is all that is known about sclerosing cholangitis. We don't know what causes it; we don't know how to cure it. We can only describe it.'

Hardly surprising, then, that the surgeon at my local hospital was unable to make a diagnosis. George, on the other hand, was to become a foremost expert in it, lecturing on it during the 1970s and 1980s in America and Europe.

I did pick up a little about the disease I was … am … suffering from. It is a liver disease. The technicalities are complex and, for the purposes of this diary, not particularly relevant. The disease, however, is. The liver, apparently, is a 'factory' in the body that removes from the blood the poisons and other dangerous substances that drift through the body via the bile-ducts into the liver where they are neutralised. (I would really need to check this out; I think I am guessing a bit here.) This works fine so long as the liver is not abused, e.g. through alcohol or drugs or too much medication. By good fortune (or was it again the deliberate grace of God?) I have been teetotal all my life, having joined the Pioneer Total Abstinence Association when I was a teenager. Oddly enough, this was one of the few religious aspects of my life that I had deliberately clung to. I used to think that if I could just remain true to this promise, it would stand me in good stead in the future. The 'good stead' I was thinking about was the hope that through the 'faith' connection I might be helped one day back to God. George told me something that gave me a different interpretation of the 'good stead', something that convinces me yet again of the deliberate and constant hand of the Lord in the affairs of my life. 'You are extremely lucky you chose to be teetotal,' he said. 'If you'd even been a moderate drinker, your liver couldn't have coped with it. You wouldn't be here now.'

It appears that in 1972 my liver was not in good condition. I had had the disease most of my life. It just had never been diagnosed. This explains the mysterious bouts of tummy ache that used to confine me to the Infirmary a couple of days at a time when I was at boarding school.

Sclerosing cholangitis is a rare disease that results in a narrowing of the bile-ducts due to some kind of growth that appears inside of them. The ducts into my liver were blocking constantly, causing the muscles of the stomach to spasm violently in an attempt to unblock them so that the bile could resume its flow. George once told me that whatever was happening (and he did not know the cause) was akin to the body rejecting its own tissue.

In 1972 my bile ducts were in bad shape. Parts of them were 'squashed together like a chewed biro tube', as George colourfully explained. He told me that there was nothing he could do to unblock them, that there was no cure, that all he could do was to cut away the bad bits and try to join what was left to the ducts on the edge of the liver. All very technical; all very complicated; and all just a little bit scary.

The operation went ahead within a day or so. It took something like six hours. George later professed himself satisfied with what he had done. As far as he could tell, 'all the bad bits have been cut out and the bile is flowing again.'

I should have taken a couple of weeks to recover and then have been allowed home. It did not quite happen like that, however. George had elected to enter my abdomen through the cut already made by the Newry surgeon a couple of weeks previously. Unfortunately the second slicing of this area made it more difficult for the wound to heal. One morning, shortly after the second operation, I was violently sick and my wound split open like an old pyjamas jacket that had lost a few buttons.

That was the beginning of a period of the most agonising suffering I was ever to experience in my life. The edges of the wound turned red, raw and excruciatingly tender. All along the nine or ten inches of the wound were several holes which were caked ... there is no need to go into that. What happened was that I had to go into the Treatment Room each morning to have the wound washed, sanitised, and dressed. Sounds simple! But it involved pushing plastic tubes down into the holes and pumping some kind of saline solution into them. The slightest pressure of any kind on the wound was agony; the pain caused by those hard plastic tubes was searing.

How I made it through the next few weeks I do not know. The wound was making absolutely no effort to heal. The Treatment Nurse was efficient and kind but relentless. I had to resort to a kind of insane humour to get me through these sessions, asking her if she done courses in sadism and assuring her that I already knew that she had got an A grade. George called in a few times during these sessions, poking and prodding and finding himself accused of patient abuse. He seemed amused; I thought he was heartless.

May 1999
The French have a saying: *'Plus ça change, plus ça même chose.'* 'The more things change, the more they remain the same.' I never quite understood that. I imagine if my grandfather were whisked from his own time into the present, he would believe he had come to an alien world. Massive technological advances, linguistic changes, attitudes that he would inevitably perceive as moral degradation, would leave him simultaneously amazed, mystified and horrified. A case could be made, I suppose, for claiming that the 'essence' of things never changes – people still need shelter, nourishment, clothes, regardless of how much fashions or tastes in these material essentials may change. People love, hate, feel envy, seek riches, search for truth, ignore truth, fight for survival, procreate ... the list is endless.

But given the situation in which I found myself in 1972, I was infinitely more drawn to the philosophy of Heraclitus, a Greek who, a few hundred years before Jesus was born, proclaimed that the entire world was 'in a state of constant flux', that everything was invariably in a state of change. His famous analogy, by which he chose to exemplify the fluid nature of the times and tides of humankind, is still oft-quoted today: 'One cannot step into the same river twice.'

It was belief and hope in this inevitable change that kept me relatively sane during my seven or eight week sojourn in Ward 16 of the Royal Victoria Hospital. If old Heraclitus was right, then things had to get better. Gradually the angry red suppuration at the edges of my wound eased to bearable pain. The vari-

ous slots and holes in it were closing up (much to the chagrin of
the Treatment Nurse, I imagined, who now had fewer places,
during her daily ministrations, to dig into with those hard, unre-
lenting plastic tubes.)

I began to achieve a degree of independence, walking without human aid, though I did require the support of a couple of
those metal things with the black rubber tips on them. I could
not fully straighten up, of course (if memory serves, it was quite
a few months before I regained full uprightness), but I was beginning to feel confident enough to drop the odd gentle hint to
George, when he and his cohort made their daily round, that it
might soon be time to send me home. At least, I thought they
were 'gentle hints' but he did say to Sadie on the morning of my
release, 'I figured that if I didn't let him go soon, he'd find his
way up to the roof and jump off.'

This was said with a smile and a twinkling eye. I have read
many times over the years about 'twinkling eyes' but I do not recall ever having been confronted by any. I can definitely aver,
however, that when George Johnston smiles his eyes assuredly
twinkle.

The hospital arranged for a district nurse to call at my home
every day to change the dressing on my wound and to keep an
eye on my general condition. It was fully six months after the
night I first experienced those dreadful abdominal pains before I
returned to work. I regret now, and I suppose I shall always regret, having wasted (what I referred to in a conversation with
Father Niall as) 'all that good suffering'. I feel that it might have
helped a lot of souls.

Life returned to normal. I began to play golf again, although
my brother, Sean, found it distinctly difficult to come to terms
with my initial approach to playing each shot. I would first hit
the ball as hard as I could, drop the club, grab my tummy with
both hands, groan, 'Aaarrrgh', and set out after the ball to repeat
the process. Thankfully this pattern of play faded and soon I was
a hundred per cent again … or so I thought.

In the summer of 1974 the pains returned. I soon regained
that sickly, deep, yellow colour. The whites of my eyes turned
pure yellow as well. I was quickly back in the Royal Victoria and
subjected to the usual battery of blood tests, X-rays, and other

investigations. I was back in Ward 16 and lay there, thoroughly miserable. It was as if I had never left.

Yet again I have to relate an incident that many will claim can easily be explained by natural and spontaneous bodily functions. Nevertheless, the contiguity of events, the way things fell into a synchronous time pattern, has often caused me to reflect on the manner in which events slightly-beyond-normal have affected my life. A couple of days after my return to Ward 16, an important Professor, accompanied by a substantial retinue of housemen, nurses and a Registrar, stopped by my bed. He had my file in his hands. After greeting me quite pleasantly, he said,

'Your condition is quite serious, Mr O'Hare. I think we'll have to operate right away.'

Innocently I asked,

'Will Mr Johnston be doing the operation?'

'No! Mr Johnston is on holiday. He is not due back until August. I will be operating myself.'

Again in total innocence, and perhaps with a touch of desperation, but merely stating what I was feeling, I said,

'With the greatest respect to you, Professor, I am sure you are quite brilliant at what you do. But I have developed an enormous trust in Mr Johnston. I really would prefer to wait until he returns.'

It was only when several of his retinue recoiled in horror, while others stared at each other aghast and looked as if they wanted to dive under the various nearby beds, that I gathered that what I had said might have been deemed untoward. In those days Consultants and Professors were the nearest things in hospitals to demigods, especially in a significantly famous hospital like the Royal Victoria. Mere mortals such as myself rarely spoke to, much less questioned, one of these deities. Nonetheless, ignoring the consternation around me, I gazed in placid expectancy at the Professor as I awaited his response. He seemed somewhat nonplussed and, a touch uncertainly, he said,

'As I said, Mr O'Hare, your condition is very serious and Mr Johnston will not be back for a month. An immediate operation is almost certainly necessary.'

I was becoming quite frightened now. I could not tolerate the idea of anyone other than George operating on me. I had little technical knowledge of my condition other than what I had gleaned from my conversations with George but, grasping a little desperately at straws, I asked,

'Supposing the bile starts to flow again and the jaundice recedes, would it be OK then to wait for Mr Johnston to return?'

I can still see the Professor's face. He wasn't doing anything but I knew he was metaphorically pulling at his hair and wondering how he could possibly have allowed this discussion to occur.

'But ... but ... there's no justification for ...'

'Theoretically, sir?' I pressed. I had no idea why I was asking these questions. They were in my head and they seemed important. The Professor wanted away from this. He said,

'We'll check with you again on Sunday evening. If your condition hasn't changed, we'll have to operate.'

A man of his hauteur could never allow himself to be seen to run but, I have to say, his departure did not have the same regal pace as his arrival.

What happened after that was a little odd ... strange ... mysterious – as I have had occasion to say before. I had heard somewhere that with the application of sufficient mental force we can affect and influence the way our bodies function. There was something of this in my head as I questioned the Professor. That was on Friday. All of that night and during the next couple of days, I willed my bile ducts to unblock themselves and to allow the bile to flow. I did not say any prayers nor ask for divine help. It did not occur to me to do so. I just lay interminably on my bed, concentrating on my condition and mentally willing something to happen.

The Professor returned on Sunday evening. I had had blood tests a couple of times a day and he was reading my most recent results. He expressed surprise at them, quoting some numbers relating to 'enzymes' and stating that my 'biliruben' count had dropped remarkably. On top of that, he could see for himself that my jaundice was clearly receding. Given the fact that there were no bile ducts left outside my liver to work with and that any operation would thus be experimental at best, he felt that 'the most appropriate course of action would be to do nothing'. They would observe my recovery over the next couple of days and if my spontaneous recovery continued to progress I would be sent home.

I recall feeling no surprise at this. It was exactly what I had expected would happen. I did not question it at the time. I was relieved that no-one other than George Johnston would be poking around in my insides. I did not consider that the event had anything of a spiritual dimension. In fact, I had been telling the story for years as testament to the power of the mind over matter. But reflecting on it now, I am not so sure, particularly when a week after the date I was told that George would be back from his holidays, I was back in Ward 16 in worse state than ever. Did something in me, or outside of me, hold my condition in abeyance until George would be there to decide what to do about it? I fully believed at that time that the hiatus was due to the power of my will. Now I believe that divine intervention was the cause because what George Johnston was to do after that was new, inventive, remarkable, and was to have an immense and far-reaching impact on the rest of my life. I have little doubt that the Professor, given the originality and novelty of what George was to do, could never have dealt with the problem.

It was at that time, too, as I remember, that my sister, Joan, taught in a convent in a small village near my home town, around the time she and some nuns from her community had been coming to one of my literature courses. I remember Joan phoning me between the two illnesses to tell me that she had been in touch with Sister Briege McKenna (later to become famous as 'the miracle nun.') She had been a friend of Joan's and Briege's since their early years in the Poor Clare Convent in Newry. She told me that Sister Briege had returned the call detailing some of the spiritual exercises and prayers she had offered on my behalf. I may not have thought so at the time, but from my present vantage, I can see that these would have been powerful prayers indeed. A line from an old black and white movie from the 1950s seems apropos: 'Somebody up there likes me.' Amazing thought! I am 'the Beloved!' This is a theme to which I shall return when I have come to a better understanding of it.

May 1999

I did, of course, need a second operation. On the night before I was due in the operating theatre, George visited me in the ward. He sat beside me on the side of the bed, pencil and paper in hand, drawing diagrams and explaining what he was going to try to do. He explained that the absence of any length of bile duct outside my liver was giving him serious problems. The previous night he had taken my notes and X-rays home with him and had finally devised a technique that might help me. (He stressed the 'might'. Typical George!) I have little recollection of the technicalities of what he told me – something about having to move my whole stomach to the edge of my liver (he called that something like an 'anastimosis') and the using of a small tubular section purloined from my bowel to create a new bile duct. Something of what he was about to do had already been done before but other bits and pieces of ideas were his own. He called the whole operation a 'Rue-en-Y' (I think this is how it is spelt; I have never seen it written down.) He then finally admitted that a lot of this was new, experimental, that he had never done it before and that, at best, he could only promise a fifty per cent chance of success. I felt surprisingly calm when he said that; perhaps I had such trust in him that these odds did not register. I simply asked,

'What is the alternative?'

'There isn't one.'

'Well then, we'll have to go with your Rue-en-Y. If I wake up dead, I won't blame you.'

He gave my shoulder a friendly pat and left.

My next memory is stark, clear, and one that I will never lose. I am lying on a hard table. Someone is hitting my cheek. I am a bit annoyed. I open my eyes. George in theatre scrubs, a surgical mask hanging loose from his neck, is smiling down at me. Totally clear-headed and aware, I ask,

'How did it go?'

'Fantastic!' he said. 'Unbelievable!'

I offer him my hand and we shake. I am deeply grateful and relieved, so I press enthusiastically. He blinks a bit and says,

'My goodness! What a strong grip for someone just coming out of a six-and-a-half hour operation.'

In my head I form the reply, 'It's the golf!' – just two old friends having a pleasant chat in the park on a Sunday afternoon – but before my lips can form the words, the lights go out.

I came to in the ward some time later, stiff, sore, sick, my belly wrapped in tight bandages. Recovery this time was much easier. George had decided to avoid the previous cuts and had come in from the side. My tummy looks like an ordnance survey map but other than that I have suffered no lasting damage.

In little over two weeks I was ready to go home. On the day of my release, George accompanied Sadie and myself down in the lift. In his customary direct fashion (with which I was by now familiar and totally comfortable) he said,

'Remember now, you do not have a normal life expectancy, so make the best of the years you have left.'

Unruffled by this, I said calmly and with genuine interest,

'Care to hazard a guess as to how many years we are talking about?'

'I'll guarantee you ten. After that you are in the hands of God.' (Not, I point out, 'in the lap of the gods.' George was, and is, a Christian and a good man.)

'What happens, ' I continued, 'if the new duct fails?'

'You better make sure it doesn't; there's nothing more I can do for you.'

'Do you mean …' I asked, (and I used a daft phrase which I don't remember using. It was Sadie who reminded me about it later. She had been standing silent during the conversation, trying to appear unconcerned. She told me that she had been, in fact, clinging to the walls of the lift, trying to neutralise her shock at this casual discussion about my possible demise.) '… that it might be a coffin job?'

'Probably, but who knows? No need to worry about that now.'

I report this episode because both George and myself failed totally to take into account the possibilities in the power of prayer – and not any prayer but, who knows, my mother's prayers (God rest her), Sister Briege McKenna's prayers, Sadie's prayers, Saint Joseph's, Our Immaculate Mother's – I don't know! But I will return to that later, including a remark by an incredulous American surgeon that would seem to confirm that George's comments, under normal circumstances, would have been perfectly valid. Right now, however, I do not want to lose the chronology of my recollections.

I had to report back to George on a regular basis, initially once a month, later every three months and finally, for a long time, every six months. The ten years he promised me passed uneventfully. My life became totally normal, filled with the usual pursuits, ambitions and concerns of the middle-class professional. Sadly, as I reported earlier, it was not filled, at least not consciously, with the Spirit.

More time passed. During one visit, it must have been fifteen years after my operation, George said,

'I'm amazed! You're a total bafflement to me. I can see no signs of degeneration anywhere. It looks like you're going to live as long as I will.'

That interested me. In an effort to assess what time I had left to me, I asked,

'Is that good? How long are you going to live, George?'

He laughed, and muttered something unintelligible as he wrote notes in my file – probably as fair a response as the question deserved.

May 1999

I have only one small incident more to recount and I can leave this period – not a particularly significant event but one which adds to the total impression of a man singularly blessed, however undeservedly. Undeservedly? How I have come to recognise, with never-ending amazement and deep gratitude, that the love God has for us, the blessings he showers on us, bear no relationship whatever to what we 'deserve'.

The incident I refer to stemmed from a quest made by an American named Ed O'Hara to find his roots in Ireland. The first attempt, when he and his wife, Rita, visited the area around Newry, '… hit', as Ed was later to tell me, 'a brick wall.' Ed, however, is nothing if not persistent. He applied to his search that same persistence that had enabled him, in his early career with an oil company, to purchase large tracts of land from Native American Indians who did not particularly want to sell. Ed's further research led him to customs records and to some American cousins whom he had not known about. He learned that his grandfather, a brother of my own great-grandfather, had emigrated from Ireland to America over a century before. Whether through the thickness of his Irish brogue or poor handwriting, it transpires that Ed's grandfather was recorded on the initial immigration documentation as Mr O'Hara. When he later protested that his name was O'Hare, an imperious customs official informed him that his papers had now been stamped and that he had to accept that his name would henceforth be O'Hara. Hard to believe, but I am assured that it is true. As our American friends might say, go figure.

Armed with this new information, Ed returned to Ireland and soon struck up acquaintance with a close cousin, my father. Inevitably, Sadie and I too became acquainted with Ed and Rita and several years later, after many letters, phone calls and a number of invitations, Sadie and I arrived one July in the mid-90s, at Lakewood, near Denver in Colorado. It was a wonderful month. Ed and Rita were superb hosts. We spent time exploring parts of Colorado in the shadow of the magnificent Rockies, attending baseball games in the huge stadium in Denver, cheering at a kids' rodeo in Boulder and playing golf at the beautiful Lakewood Country Club.

It was at this golf club that I met a friend of Ed's, a gentleman of Italian extract named Oreglio. Having heard so often many of his American friends claim Irish descent, Bill (I think that was his name) decided that he, too, would make equal claim. With a straight face he informed me that his forebears had emigrated from Ireland to Italy during the famine and that, through time, the family name, O'Reilly, had metamorphosed to the Italian Oreglio. Totally apocryphal, I am sure, but I nodded, equally straight faced, and we said nothing more about it.

During our round of golf I discovered that Bill was a surgeon who specialised in problems with such organs as pancreas, kidneys and liver, an inevitable invite for me to tell him my story. When I told him about the Rue-en-Y in 1974, he was astounded. He told me that about five per cent of his own annual schedule included versions of this operation and informed me that they had an eighty-five per cent mortality rate, while those who did survive rarely lived beyond ten years. And he stared at me with an expression of sheer disbelief.

'What on earth are you doing walking around twenty years later in the rudest of health and fitness?'

His remarks and sheer disbelief have stayed with me, a potent reminder that my acceptance of life has been overly casual, that my lack of tangible gratitude to my Maker bespeaks an attitude of extraordinary complacency. Thank God for the line in a little prayer that I now pray with the utmost sincerity every morning:

Thank you Lord for the grace of being alive today;
thank you for this chance to make a new beginning.

God gives us limitless chances, limitless opportunities, to make new beginnings. How wonderful it is to be able to take advantage of that infinite generosity, to acknowledge but equally to forget the ingratitude and infidelities of the past and to start each new day in the embrace of his forgiveness and his love!

CHAPTER EIGHT

Back To The Present

September 1999

Given the experiences of the early 1970s, it seems surprising that we did not immediately jump to the conclusion that the problem in Portugal was liver-oriented. It may be that Sadie and I both subconsciously remembered George's remarks about my not having a normal life span and that once the condition returned there was nowhere for me to go, and found ourselves blocking out any possibility of a return to that scenario. Whatever about our subconscious, the Newry consultant suspected quite quickly that the problem did, in fact, stem from a liver dysfunction of some kind. What bothers me most, as I reflect on my reaction to this news, was the emptiness I felt. I had come, I thought, to some understanding of prayer after several chats with Father Niall about it. I continued experimenting with ways of praying, of talking to Jesus, almost definitely achieving some kind of rapport but for some reason never alluding to or praying about this hugely fearful event going on in my life. During the two weeks in hospital I dutifully read my Morning and Evening Prayer (a 'mini-office' that Father Niall gave me), said occasional rosaries and a few other prayers as well. When I think of it now I am mystified. What kind of relationship was I having with Jesus? Did I know how to pray at all? Was I 'babbling as Pagans do'? Why was I not spending every second talking to him about what this new liver problem might mean and asking for the support I needed to cope with it? To tell the truth, I think I may have been employing the same evasive mental tactic I had employed in Portugal, something like, if I don't acknowledge the problem, maybe it won't exist.

I have never really given a great deal of thought to final things and was not then, and probably am not now, quite ready to face any discussion about them. That reminds me of a little story I heard recently. At evening devotions one Sunday, a priest asked his congregation if they wanted to go to heaven. All he got in reply were a few murmurs. He tried again. Still only a few inaudible murmurs.

'Right,' he said. 'Everybody who wants to go to heaven, over to the right hand side of the chapel.'

When all the movement died down, there was one little man sitting alone on the left. The priest glared down at him and thundered,

'Do you not want to go to heaven?'

'Oh! I do, Father, but I don't want to go this evening.'

I may have felt something like that at this time although I had not articulated thoughts as specific as these in my mind. I feel, however, that my attitude was spiritually cowardly. And I still don't understand it.

The Newry surgeon told me he had a friend in the Mater Infirmorum in Belfast who was a noted expert in liver problems. He promised to use his influence to get me an early appointment with him. In the meantime, I spent two weeks in our local hospital, most of that time on a drip until I was re-hydrated – or whatever the proper term is –and able to eat properly again.

Actually, I recovered quite quickly after that. We went to France for three weeks in July, a holiday we enjoyed with no repercussions of any kind. I am back at golf with 'the boys' and life has resumed is even tenor. It is as if Portugal had never happened. But I am a little edgy. What if it happens again? Next week I have that appointment with the consultant at the Mater. I am curious, and more than a little anxious, as I wait to hear what he will have to say.

September 1999

'Babbling like the Pagans' is something I thought … well, Pagans did. Lately I notice that I could enter 'babbling' contests and win. When we have conversations with people it is nothing but good manners to focus on them, to talk to them with attention, and listen to what they have to say. (This latter skill is one I have yet to develop.) Sometimes I see people gossiping in town, their mouths flapping incessantly, their eyes and their heads swivelling this way and that as they note and examine everyone who appears within a 360° range of the immediate vicinity. I often think that this is scant courtesy to the 'friend' they are 'conversing' with. But how easily do I fall into the same trap when I am conversing with Jesus. If I am analysing some event of the day or simply talking about things (probably things of direct interest to me) I seem to manage well enough. But when I turn to the formal prayers I feel I need to say, I often find that I have left Jesus at the door while I have wandered away off up the street.

Part of the problem, I believe, is the speed with which we tend to pray our formal, if familiar, prayers. We seldom stop to savour their meaning. I was praying the Credo during my rosary today and I was struck by the phrase 'the Communion of Saints'. I have never meditated on it nor, indeed, have I given any real thought to it. But every day in my rosary I declare my firm belief in it. Do I ever think, when I pray that line, that I am part of the Mystical Body of Christ, that through him I am linked to the sick, the lonely, the hungry, the suffering, the dying, the dead in heaven and in purgatory? Do I realise that through this link my prayers, for the major part, should always be in the plural, even if I am in a room by myself. Because I am not by myself; I am part of the huge Communion of Saints. When we pray in the plural we inevitably pray for each other and, if we pay attention to what we are saying, we will be drawn more and more into the love of God, into the love of all that is God's, into the love of his church, and into the love of his creatures. We begin to see in our suffering fellow the suffering of Christ; we begin to see in the companionship of others, the companionship of Christ; and we begin to see in the needs of others, at home, abroad, an obligation to do what we can to answer that need because it is Christ's need. David Torkington says that the whole point of prayer is that it takes believers out of themselves, 'for you are praying with the whole body of believers who are alive in Christ and not just by yourself, and you are praying for all humankind, not just for yourself.'

I write all of this as if this is what I am experiencing. Far from it, sadly. But sometimes, when I find myself drifting into these sorts of meditations, I begin to 'see through a glass darkly' where I should be heading on my spiritual journey. Am I *en route*? Hardly! But I feel that if I can get my hands on a map (and

that is what meditation offers) I can trace the route with my finger so that I will know where I am supposed to be going. If I step
out now, knowing the Way (Jesus), I have a chance of reaching
my destination one day. At least, that is my hope.

This morning I did not get to the five mysteries for quite a
while because I got caught up in this reflection about prayer.
And I realise now that my prayers are becoming shorter in
length but much longer in time because I am finding that to
'babble' the words is really quite pointless. I am finding that no
matter how familiar a prayer is, it is possible to pray it with a
kind if earnestness and sincerity as if we are saying the words
for the first time. I know of no formal prayer that cannot be
prayed as if the words are fresh and new, interesting and absorbing. I am drawn to the analogy of human love. Lovers meet
time and time again and, in breathless emotion, repeat endlessly
words and phrases that they have used so often before yet never
tire of repeating, never tire of hearing. And as long as the love
survives, these same murmurings remain a fresh, absorbing and
necessary part of the relationship. And so it is with our prayers.
If there is real love, we can never allow ourselves to 'babble'
meaningless words. We will want to be sure that not only is
what we say meaningful and important but that we will say it
with sufficient earnestness and intensity to ensure that the loved
one, Jesus, really hears and understands us.

How fresh are my prayers? How absorbed in them am I? Can
I say my morning prayer, my evening prayer, each day and feel
that I am saying something to Jesus, or to the Spirit, or to the
Father, that is new and important, something that simply must
be said? I am not sure. I know that I am working at it. I was saying to Father Niall the other day that every morning, as I read
my missal at Mass, a line somewhere in the liturgy jumps out at
me, a line pregnant with meaning and implication, a line that I
never saw or thought of in quite the same way before.

David Torkington says that praying, like learning the piano
or some other skill, takes time and practice. He is probably right.
He says: 'Learning to pray, learning to open ourselves to God, is
like anything else; it needs practice and it takes time.'

But I am not conscious of any such practice although I do set
aside time every day for prayer. Or maybe that is the 'practice'.

But I do think that we will 'learn pretty good', as the Americans say, if we open our lives to God, if we sit before him in the evening allowing him to see our innermost thoughts, the desires that we have, the weaknesses that thwart us, the lacks we are ashamed of. If we can expose the lot and say, 'Here I am, Jesus; this is who I am; this is what I am. Help me!' we are at a good starting point because after that we can say anything, think anything, confess to anything … we simply have nothing to hide, no ps and qs to watch. In letting Jesus, or the Spirit, or the Father, whoever we are most drawn to, get to know our innermost selves, we get to know a little about him. And it is so liberating. Love grows, friendship grows, the relationship grows; prayer becomes a necessity, an essential. We can no longer 'babble'. The words and their meaning have become too important for that.

September 1999

I had a long meeting with Father Niall this morning. We spent much of the time talking about prayer. The discussion was prompted in part by the concerns I expressed a few pages back but also as a result of a chat I had with Sean after golf the other day. He told me about a method of prayer promoted by a Father John Main. Essentially, according to Sean, the person praying is expected to will his soul into conversation with God while the body remains still and repeats a mantra 'Maranatha' (which means, 'Come, Lord Jesus.') I probably have misunderstood what Sean was trying to explain to me. I have no wish to offend him, or Father Main come to that, but what I write in this diary has to reflect my own heart and mind, my own spiritual state. I tried the method, intoning the mantra and willing my soul to link with God. Try as I might, I could not avoid images of bearded fakirs and bald Buddhists, sitting cross-legged and humming. I truly did try but I felt totally lost, isolated from Jesus. I needed contact; I needed to ply Jesus with questions, talk about things, try to hear answers. As I said to Sean later, 'How can you develop a relationship with someone if you don't even talk to them?'

Father Niall was less dismissive of the mantra approach than I was. He said that this form of contemplative prayer was difficult and he did not believe that God was calling me to that type of prayer yet. He advised me to follow my instincts as I continued to try to develop my relationship with Jesus, instincts that almost invariably will reflect God's voice. He also told me that there are as many ways to pray as there are people praying and that at this stage in my development it would be best to pray as I can not as I can't. I am impressed by that. Not only because it makes total sense but because it contains within it the strong implication that Jesus will monitor the way I pray and help me to change it should that ever become necessary.

Having said that, there is something new going on in my prayer life that is having a remarkable effect on the way I pray now, on the way I relate to Jesus. I told Father Niall last Tuesday that I had attended a Mass celebrated by our bishop, John McAreavy, and a number of Benedictine friars who have now set up a new monastery in Rostrevor, a village about nine miles from Newry. One of the Benedictines preached the homily and I found myself immediately and deeply affected by something he said. I cannot remember the exact words but the friar quoted Cardinal Basil Hume, saying something like, '… a true Christian must learn to see the invisible', a paradox that appealed to the intellectual in me but also to something much deeper. Its impact upon me was momentous. I told Father Niall about it and recounted to him also a little story I had come across somewhere that contained within it the seeds of the method of prayer I am now developing.

The story concerned an old man who had become bed-ridden. He did not know how to pray. His parish priest lent him a book on contemplative prayer written by an eminent theologian. Unfortunately, the old man had to use his dictionary a dozen times in his attempt to read the first three pages. He tossed the book aside and gave up on it. He was talking to a friend about it a day or two later. The friend said,

'Maybe you should try what I do. I put an empty chair beside me and try with all my power to imagine Jesus is sitting in it. He did say that he would be with us always, so I'm sure he's there. Once I establish his presence, I can talk away to him.'

The old man tried it, liked it, and prayed thus for a couple of hours each day. Any time his daughter came into the room, she would tidy the empty chair away. She was always surprised, each time she returned, to find the chair back at the side of her father's bed. He never told her why. He died one day while she was out shopping. Later, talking to the parish priest, she said,

'He was in good form when I left so I think he died happy. It was weird, though. He always had this empty chair by his bedside and when I found him dead that day I came home, he was lying sprawled across it.'

I could not help the tears that came to my eyes when I finished recounting the story to Father Niall; I have tears in my eyes as I write it now. It is a moving story, full of the love of Jesus.

The night after I heard the Benedictine advise us to see the invisible, I placed a chair at an angle to my own in the study (where I go to pray) and tried to 'see' Jesus. I found it then, and continue to find it, an almost overwhelming experience. The effect of this approach is remarkable. Conversation flows easily, nothing is too intimate, too ordinary, or even too shameful to talk about. Someone watching might see a man waving his hands about, evincing facial expressions of interest, enquiry, puzzlement, peace – for all the world, a person engaged in animated conversation with an invisible friend. Something of the formality of ritual prayer is missing, perhaps something of the immense respect owed to the divine. But I feel so drawn to the approach, so close to and so at ease with Jesus, that I will follow where it leads despite these peripheral misgivings.

It does not quite work the same with the Father or the Spirit. Father Niall pointed to my heart –'You'll find them in there.' But I was reminded a while back, when I was trying to visualise the Father and the Spirit in my study, of the Euclidian Nomen. I actually know very little about it but what I do know, or think I know, is currently helping me with this visualisation even if my understanding of the theory is entirely erroneous. The concept was explained to me some years ago by a friend who was an avid student of William Butler Yeats. Yeats at some point in his philosophy of poetics analyses such concepts as 'the centre of things' and 'inner space'. Somewhere in his searchings, he propounded his theory of the Euclidian Nomen. It is an odd theory of space within space. I tried to explain it to Father Niall by asking him to imagine that in the centre of the room where we were talking a large statue of St Joseph used to stand.

'Imagine you have been so accustomed to seeing that statue there that even though it is now gone, you almost tend to walk around the space it was in rather than walk through it. That space in the room is somehow different from the space in the rest of the room. It is almost as it that space isn't entirely empty.'

For me the visualisation of the Father and the Spirit is something like that. I have an idea what Jesus looks like; I have no idea what the Father or the Spirit look like. I imagine, therefore, that there are two spaces in the study that are not quite empty. They have no form, shape or substance. They are simply there. In that way I can contact and feel close to God in the persons of the Father and the Spirit as well as of Jesus.

Currently, however, it is Jesus with whom I am most in touch. When I 'stare' at him, I see a kind face, calm expression, still body. There is, perhaps, a touch of a smile at the edges of his lips, perhaps the expression of a parent listening fondly to the incessant chattering of a favoured child. Indeed, that may not be far from the truth. Sometimes I engage in conversation that is, to me, serious and weighty, an attempt to examine, analyse and re-solve issues of import. But Jesus is beyond time. He can see the beginning, the end and the middle of my life simultaneously. In the vastness of that massive scope, how truly significant can my problems really be? I have taken to wondering lately if, on the intellectual scale of the infinite, the level of my theological mus-ings transcends at all the teenager's slang-ridden mumblings. Hard to say! But being detached, I can see that there is a certain naïve and breathless 'nattering' in much of what I deem to be prayer, an inversion of (as a nun friend once pointed out to me) 'Speak, Lord, for your servant is listening.' to 'Listen, Lord, for your servant is speaking.'

But if there is a childlike quality in this method of praying, I do not feel, for the time being at least, that it is a matter for con-cern. To be able to 'stare' with total trust into the loving face of Jesus, to have not the least worry about the value of what I am saying, to expose to his soft gaze, without any reservation, the deep and innermost parts of my mind and soul that for years were never permitted to see the light of day, to experience (albeit ingenuously or unconsciously) the child's faith that nothing in its babblings will engender the remotest censure – how extraordinarily liberating! It brings to mind Jesus' own dictum: 'Unless you become as little children ...'

Oh dear! I have re-read the last few lines and I can find nothing in them that even resembles the virtue of humility. I remember reading, at the urging of a priest friend, St Thérèse de Lisueux's *Story of a Soul*. Hundreds of thousands of faithful the world over have read and loved this book. Its message is quoted *ad infinitum* in other writings. And yet, on first acquaintance, I could not accept what I thought was her ego-centredness. Try as I would, I was unable to quell a growing impression that here was a person of little humility. How wrong I was! I could not see that what I took for self-centredness was her effort to describe her innermost feelings. What I took for ego was searing honesty. It took time and effort but I gradually began to understand her own quest for humility, her perceived 'littleness', the extent to which her awareness of God's greatness, and the intensity of that awareness, made her own ego so irrelevant. What I had been doing was confusing 'style' with 'substance' and I had to spend some time explaining and apologising to St Thérèse for my own vain and sniffy intellectualism. We are great friends now and I have enlisted her aid in praying to Jesus that I, too, may be given the virtue of humility. I have other saint and blessed friends, each of whom is urged to pray for specific spiritual qualities that I lack and need. St Thérèse is assigned exclusively to secure for me 'humility'. I tell her that hers is by far the most difficult task. Sometimes when I find myself plagued by a vain thought, I will say, 'St Thérèse, we're getting nowhere. I warned you that this would be difficult. Even with your great influence over Jesus, your efforts will have to be compelling indeed to persuade the Lord to pry me loose from my stubborn and wilful ego.' But Thérèse is resourceful. That much is evident in her *Story*. So I remain hopeful.

I can't help but wonder, however, if my own words give that same impression of egoism that I initially disapproved of in St Thérèse's writing. I was tempted to go back over what I have written, check for questionable passages and erase them. But if I did that, I think I would be erasing myself. I am who I am; the Diary is what it is. I do not believe that there is very much I can do about either.

Basil Hume writes about humility, pointing out that none of us enjoys being criticised, misjudged, snubbed, written-off. But he also says that for some of us:

> … it is when we realise how little we are regarded by others that we begin to realise how highly we are esteemed by God. We have ceased to wonder what others think about us; we have discovered our worth in the eyes of our Father.

And it is in discovering this esteem, this worth, that our urge to connect, to communicate, grows. We just want to touch base, to 'be' with God. Ego, modesty, pride, vanity – when we talk with Jesus, none of these are of any relevance. We are who we are. Jesus knows us inside out:

> Before ever a word is on my tongue
> You know it, Lord, through and through.

We do not need to make any kind of impression. We become souls thirsting for God:

> Oh God, for you I long, for you … my soul is thirsting like a dry, weary land without water.

And that is why we pray, and that is why we keep trying to find better ways to pray. Some ways work; some ways do not. The key, I think, is to keep trying … when we try, we pray. Sometimes I make a total mess of my rosary, but when I say, 'Lord, please accept it, bad and all as it was, for you know I tried', then I feel secure. Bernard O'Connor OSA, has comforting words to say about this:

> However dissatisfied one feels with a session of prayer, the effort to pray is itself a prayer … it is a cry of greeting , through the haze of distraction and preoccupations, to the unseen God who always sees and hears and cares.

PART THREE

In the Shadow of the Cross

CHAPTER NINE

Early Warnings

October 1999

Despite my experience with George Johnston, I still tended towards the common impression of surgeons and consultants as men of eminence, probably distant and difficult to communicate with. I had some such similar anticipation when Sadie and I visited the Mater Infirmorum for my first meeting with Mr Tom Diamond. I need not have worried. He is a very pleasant man, medium build, glasses, quiet-spoken, and down-to-earth. His demeanour would inspire confidence at any time but when I learned that he had worked under and alongside George Johnston for several years, my confidence level, and my heart, lifted enormously. That led to a happy conversation until the time came for me to broach the real reason for my visit.

He had some notes from our local surgeon, a Mr Brian Cranley, but he still had to retrieve George Johnston's files on me from the Royal Victoria. However, he would be doing his own tests anyway, and basing his opinions on them. When he heard my own less-than-technical version of the 1974 operation and my description of my recent illness, he surmised that the problem could well be inside the liver.

'I'll take some blood now,' he said, 'but I am going to have to arrange for a transhepatic cholangiogram to have a proper look at what is going on in there.'

'A what?'

'A transhepatic cholangiogram! It's an X-ray but it involves a needle being inserted into your liver – usually from the back – through which a dye is released into the ducts and around the liver. The dye shows up on the screen and gives me an idea of what the ducts are like.'

'Is it a big needle?' (Getting the important issues out of the way first!)

A laugh. 'It's about nine or ten inches long, but you'll be

given a local anaesthetic and some valium injected into you during the process. Usually it doesn't take much longer than fifteen minutes. It shouldn't hurt much.'

'Hmmm!'

I was not really convinced but I turned to something else. Sadie and I were naturally concerned about the comment George had made in 1974 about there being nowhere else to go if the ducts failed again. We had had a worrying couple of weeks since we heard that the liver was involved. I tentatively asked Mr Diamond for an honest assessment of the situation.

'Well ... it's hard to say anything of real accuracy until I have had a look at the X-rays,' he hedged.

'But supposing the Sclerosing Cholangitis is acting up again,' I pressed. 'What then?'

He looked at me over the top of his glasses and made a small grimace.

'Well, it depends on what's going on in there ... the kind of blockages you're suffering ... it could be serious ... but right now, it's ...' He straightened up and continued briskly, 'But we're jumping away ahead of ourselves. Let's wait until we see the X-rays.'

'Just one more question,' I pleaded. 'If the liver is in serious trouble, can nothing further be done? Was George right?'

'Ah no!' he replied, shaking his head positively. 'George was right in nineteen-seventy four but we've moved on a lot since then. He would never have heard of a liver transplant, for example, in nineteen-seventy four. We've been doing them with good rates of success for over a decade now.'

I brightened up at that (as one would). He saw my mouth beginning to open again and held up his hand with a smile,

'Don't let us even go down that road. The question might never arise.'

Still, we arrived home that afternoon a lot happier than we had been when we set off. Regardless of how things turned out with the X-ray, we were no longer at a (literal) dead end. Did I thank the Lord for this new development? Not yet.

November 1999
The transhepatic cholangiogram took a lot longer than fifteen

minutes; it also hurt … a great deal. I turned up for my appointment as arranged and was soon lying, stomach down, on a flat
X-ray table. The attendant nurse was inserting a tube into a vein
in my arm while the radiologist was wiring me up to a television
monitor. They worked calmly and efficiently but their total,
probably professional, silence was unnerving. Somewhat appre-
hensively, more to break the silence than anything else, I asked,

'Is everything OK?'

'Oh yes!' came the calm reply. 'Just getting a few preliminaries out of the way. I'll explain in a minute what we're going to
do.'

There was some conversation after that. A few minutes later I
felt the prick of a local anaesthetic in my back while the nurse
said she would be injecting some valium through the tube in my
arm to keep me relaxed.

The first entry of the needle was probably not as bad as my
imagination caused it to be. I certainly felt it; but the realisation
of what was happening was harder to cope with than any initial
pain. The calm tones of the radiologist were reassuring, however,
as he quietly muttered meaningless comments such as, 'This
spot looks promising …' or 'Maybe we'll try over here …'

The problem for me became twofold. First, I was beginning
to realise that the procedure was not going as smoothly as it
might. Second, the needle going in and out was starting to hurt –
a lot. Not only could I feel increasingly each sharp initial prick
but my innards were reacting as if I was receiving a heavy blow
each time the needle penetrated into my back. After about half
an hour I was distinctly uncomfortable. I asked if anything was
wrong. The same unruffled voice replied,

'Just a little problem finding a duct. Usually we hit one more
or less right away … just a little while longer.'

Another fifteen minutes passed. I was extremely uncomfortable by this time. I told the doctor that I was in a great deal of
pain.

'I'll try to hurry,' he said, and told the nurse to inject a little
more valium. It made little difference. More time passed. I was
gasping with pain now and getting irritated rather than scared.
In the end, about an hour after we had started, I had to say (quite
crossly, I am ashamed to admit),

'Look, you're going to have to do something about this pain or pack the whole thing in. I am not tolerating this any more.'

The radiologist was a little taken aback.

'OK!' he soothed. 'We'll take a rest. Maybe we should syringe some morphine into your tube.'

He asked the nurse to get some. She injected it into the tube. In a few minutes I felt better.

It took another hour and a half before the doctor could find a duct. Not his fault; the ducts were so narrow that it was like trying to spear a fish in a running stream. He did not say much but I was in something of a state wondering about the extent to which my liver had deteriorated when a process that should have taken fifteen minutes took almost two and a half hours. By that time I was too groggy with morphine and valium to ask any questions. Sadie was with me, of course, to drive me home.

Some weeks later we were standing in Tom Diamond's office looking at the X-rays in a lighted compartment on his wall. He pointed to what looked like two small tubes, not quite as thick as drinking straws.

'These are your two main ducts,' he said.

'They don't look too bad,' I said. To my inexpert eye there seemed plenty of room for liquid to flow. He shook his head and pointed with his biro.

'Do you see this pale grey shadowy area?' He pointed to an area near the middle of the upper duct. I peered more closely.

'Yes?'

'This is a growth inside the duct and it is what is causing the blockages. Bile, unfortunately, changes from time to time. Sometimes it can run like water, other times it can be thick … er … gooey! Just here …' he pointed where two pale grey areas in the upper duct seemed almost to touch, '… this is where the trouble is. The gap is very narrow here. You'll survive a while longer with it … but if the bile should thicken any time …' He trailed off.

'Is there anything we can do about minimising bile viscosity?' I asked, sounding very grown-up and professional (the exact opposite of what I was feeling).

He laughed. 'If I knew the answer to that I'd become a millionaire.'

However! He did not seem particularly pessimistic and suggested that we carry on with our lives as normal and he would
arrange for us to see him every three months for blood tests and
examination. I told him we were thinking of going to France in
July. He saw no problem with that. He noticed that I was staring
again at the X-ray.

'Don't worry!' he soothed. 'I've seen ducts in worse state
than that and yet those people were able to go about normal living for years.'

November 1999

I really must have some kind of spiritual blind spot. Despite
daily Mass, despite daily prayers, despite having berated myself
several times before about this very tendency, I still do not think
to turn to Jesus during these episodes of uncertain health and
even more uncertain future. Now again, in moments of quiet reflection, I simply cannot understand why I choose to bear this
growing anxiety alone (apart from the comfort and support
Sadie provides, of course), denying myself the spiritual and, deriving from that, the psychological sustenance which communion with Jesus would offer me. Knowing now that the liver is
definitely involved, that unthinkable eventualities are now possible, that mad considerations such as transplant have entered
the picture, why don't I discuss them with Jesus? They are in my
mind, even when I am in his presence, but somehow I simply do
not talk about them. It seems to be something that I deliberately
avoid doing. Can it be that despite my Masses and my prayers, I
have not really found my way to the Lord, that what I have is a
series of daily rituals that don't actually reach my heart – even
worse, my soul? I cannot accept that that is true. The Jesus I talk
to in my study at night is so close, so real, so visible. But why am
I so reluctant to bring this series of health 'hic-cups' before him?
Is there a clue in the word 'hic-cups'? My first impulse had been
to write 'health scares'. Do I have some kind of fear that if I talk
to him about what are little more than vague threats, they will
become real and I will have to face possibilities that my subconscious currently denies? Or can it be that I feel that Jesus has protected me throughout my life with an extraordinary generosity
and love of which I have been so totally undeserving that, again

subconsciously, I avoid the topic because I am unwilling, or feel that I am not entitled, to ask for anything more? Or perhaps it is something more straightforward than that. Perhaps I have no conscious need to turn to Jesus, that I just do not feel that this is something I should be talking to him about. If that is truly the case, then I am no kind of Christian at all.

December 1999

I am no kind of Christian at all. How that judgement reverberates across the spectrum of my behaviours. Today, yet again, I have been presented with cause to question the depth of my re-formation.

When I was a young classroom teacher, and later a senior manager with disciplinary responsibilities, I developed and perfected what I used to refer to as my 'basilisc glare.' Generations of adolescents have experienced its force. Like the Medusa of Greek mythology, my gaze could turn the most recalcitrant student to stone-like stillness … and that is when it was tempered with some restraint. At full blast, it could turn a pupil to ashes. A useful tool in my profession but one which, unfortunately, has followed me into retirement. When I am even mildly irritated – by inefficient service in shops, by queue jumpers, by other road users (invariably less expert that myself), by someone moving when I am in the middle of my back-swing, by perceptions of ineptness in any situation – the glare will sear into life. More than once I have heard my children remonstrate with their own offspring, 'If you don't behave, I'll get Granda to glare at you.' (I am not fully certain that this particular duty features in the manual of 'Grandfatherly Responsibilities'.) A lifetime's exercise of this of this faculty has apparently stamped something of a residual shadow upon my features, even when in repose. Sadie herself has often been deceived into assuming that I am fulminating internally when my reflections are, in fact, benign.

I love to sit in the front pew at Mass. I feel close to the tabernacle, to God and, in particular, to the consecration. This morning after Mass I was kneeling in this seat saying my after-communion prayers when a group of people stopped in front of the altar and began to engage in a loud and, to my mind, utterly pointless conversation. The very use of these adjectives reveals to me now, in after-thought, how immediately lacking in charity my thoughts became, at a time when I should have been absorbed in Jesus. I really should have tried to ignore the distraction; I should have burrowed more into my companionship with the Lord. Instead, irritation seeped in and, inevitably, I 'glared'. I have become aware, in a way that I have not been aware before, that it is impossible to 'glare' without feeling and transmitting an attitude of considerable hostility. Nothing in it reflects Christian charity. I tried to return to Jesus, upset with myself, knowing that the calm and peace that I had earlier been feeling had now been shattered. And whose fault was that? Only my own! Regardless of what other people do, it is only I who can allow my peace to be disturbed.

I seem to recall something Anthony de Mello once said about allowing people to live their own lives, about training ourselves to be so unaffected by what other people do or say, that we could live out our lives without ever again having to feel annoyance, resentment or anger. I remember reacting negatively to this. If we dismiss the behaviours and opinions of others so completely from our lives, are we not denying ourselves the gifts of reciprocated love, affection and companionship? Do we not, from the reflection of ourselves in the eyes of others, see faults and deficiencies that we can learn to adjust and correct? Is this not how we grow and develop as human beings?

Having said all of that, I can now perceive that there is something of truth in what de Mello says, that by distancing ourselves from the perception of faults and foibles in others, we can enhance our own inner peace. It is probably obvious that I have not yet arrived at that level of maturity.

Father Niall had celebrated Mass that morning and when he came out of the sacristy, I walked over to the Parochial House with him. 'Where is the love?' I asked him. In response to his quizzical look, I explained that I am supposed to be a Christian, that the second great commandment is to love our neighbour as ourselves. Why is it, I then asked him, that despite having traces of the Divine Body and Blood of Jesus still in my system and my mind reasonably focused on him, I practically burned holes in five innocent people, such was the animosity of my gaze? The Lord loves each of those people with a singular and unique love.

They are his. I profess to love him. Should I not therefore love them? How could I have allowed myself to react like that? Where is the love? What kind of Christian am I?

Samuel Taylor Coleridge wrote poetry in the early 1800s. Some of it was weird and fantastical and, in order to stimulate his imagination to inconceivable strangeness, he used to smoke opium. Indeed, one of his drug-riddled dreams resulted in the wonderful *Rime of the Ancient Mariner*. In this strange tale a mariner shot an albatross with his crossbow, a 'hellish thing' to do. It resulted in his ship being cursed. It was becalmed on the huge ocean, no wind, no water, and one by one his shipmates dropped dead from thirst. The mariner was cursed to live on among the carcasses of his dead companions, a kind of death-in-life, with the corpse of the albatross tied around his neck. Once or twice he tried to pray but instead

A wicked whisper came, and made
My heart as dry as dust.

All around him was the rotting sea where 'a thousand, thousand slimy things lived on.'

A long time passed and one moonlight night he noticed the creatures that had so disgusted him coiling and swimming in flashes of glorious colours in the shadows of the ship. Without realising it, he stared at them in delight:

O happy living things! No tongue
Their beauty might declare:
A spring of love gushed from my heart,
And I blessed them unaware.

In this moment of love, the albatross dropped from his neck, the wind came up and he sailed home to safe harbour. Even in the midst of Coleridge's opium-fuelled dream, this nugget of Christianity shines out. Love can rescue us from death-in-life. In gospel terms, how many of us are living in spiritual death because we have not learned to love? And hence my concern over my behaviour in the chapel and my question to Father Niall, 'Where is the love?' Father Niall, kind heart that he has, tends to be much less critical of my uncharitable behaviour than I am myself. I do believe he even chuckled. He told me not to be so hard on myself, that my respect for God's house and his presence in the tabernacle had caused me to over-react.

Nonetheless, there is much here to ponder. Father Niall did explain that Christian love does not necessarily mean liking people. It means having a desire, because of love for Jesus, to help people, never to do anyone an injury, to be unselfish and sharing. I can understand that. But Father Niall does not have a basilisc glare; Father Niall has a kind and benevolent gaze. There is love there. Jesus had such love in his eyes that all who knew him were totally captivated by him. I think the love should be there, in the heart, in the mind, in the eyes of all who profess themselves Christian. When Sadie worked in the hospital, and even now, the sight of anyone hurt or in trouble had her literally running to help. That essential charity is there. I see it, too, in the men and women who selflessly devote their time and energy to bring the ill and the disabled to Lourdes, in the brothers and sisters of the St Vincent de Paul Society who do what they can to alleviate the hardship of the local poor, in the Legion of Mary members who visit the sick in hospitals – so many examples of remarkable charity and concern, so much Christian love. And what do I do? I glare!

But I'm trying to change. I'm praying for the grace to answer the commandment to love. I do what I can; there is no need to write it down but there is slight evidence of improvement. But I doubt if I will ever achieve the level of true Christian love that is so evident in the attitude and demeanour of these truly Christian people.

December 1999
I ruminated on this several times during the evening and night. I felt unhappy at what I saw in the mirror that the episode held up to me. By a stroke of good fortune, I met Father Niall in town this morning. During our chat I told him that I was feeling a bit depressed at discovering how lacking I am in Christian charity and how I feel that my efforts to generate it are bearing little fruit. Father Niall's focus, however, was rather different from mine. He warned me to be careful about being too scrupulous and pointed out that if I were trying to sort myself out on my own, I would never succeed. He told me quite simply to turn it all over to Jesus and let him deal with it. We can do nothing for ourselves, he told me, but for Jesus nothing is impossible. There

are echoes here of my earlier thoughts about saying 'yes' to Jesus … my own conviction that I, personally, have to be doing something, a conviction that conflicts with Sean and Joan's contention that God's grace will do the work. I still know that the process is not as simple as that, just as I know there is more to Father Niall's remark than I am at present able to comprehend. It is part of the whole business of placing all our trust in the Lord. I understand the words but I have no idea how to do it. Still, the very fact that Father Niall talked to me about it and was, in the main, positive about how I am doing, has eased my anxiety.

I read once that Jesus told some saintly person that if we would find ourselves a spiritual director and open our hearts, our minds, our souls to him (or her), the Lord would ensure that our spiritual guide would always have the right words for us. I once told that to Father Niall. He looked at me over his glasses and laughingly shook his head as if to tell me that, in his case, the mystic might be a bit off the mark. However, the wise words that he spoke to me this morning are evidence enough for me that the good Lord is, indeed, working through him.

CHAPTER TEN

Relative Calm

January 2000

From time to time in these pages I have mentioned my sisters, Briege and Joan, and my brother, Sean. I suppose I should also mention that I am the oldest child of a family of eight, four boys and four girls. Sean, the second child and thus nearest to me in age, shares with me my passion for golf, as well as the more than occasional tussle over a chess board on a winter's evening. Similarity of temperament, shared interests and the fact that we are both retired, have ensured that we remain close and generally spend our recreation times together even though we live in different towns. The other two boys, Willie and Paul, still earn their daily bread, also in different towns, and thus our paths seldom cross although since Paul, too, is a golfer, I would see him from time to time on the golf course. My other sisters, Sadie and Kathleen, married with their own families, also lead lives distant from my own. Our occasional meetings are familial and friendly but they are infrequent, tending to occur only on special occasions. I remember once meeting my ex-boss, Raymond Mullan, at the funeral of a colleague a couple of years after I had retired. 'Weddings and funerals,' he said. 'People can be close for twenty or thirty years and then they never see each other except at weddings and funerals.' It's true, and something of the same truth has entered into the lives and relationships of the family of my childhood.

Circumstances and age-differences, however, dictated that I would never be close to Briege and Joan during their childhood. I was sent off to boarding school at the age of eleven when Briege was only four or five and Joan had just been born. I came home only for holidays, later to go on to Maynooth, from there to University College, Dublin, and finally, to St Joseph's Teacher Training College in Belfast, all those years coming across my youngest siblings only infrequently.

I do remember as a student in my second or third degree year at UCD receiving a letter from my mother informing me that Briege, at the age of fifteen, had entered the novitiate at the Poor Clare Convent in Newry, a strict enclosed order at the time. I recall penning an immediate and long response, detailing several reasons why this course of action was madness and advising my mother to go and talk to her. Big brother, age twenty-one, who thought he knew so much and who knew nothing. I still remember how angry I felt the following year, however, when mother died of cancer and Briege was not only forbidden to attend the wake, she was not even permitted to attend the funeral and make her farewells. How much harder must that have been on Briege?

My only childhood memory of Joan is of coming across her once in one of the many rooms of the large three-storey house in which we spent our childhood. She was wearing a towel over her head, in the shape of a veil, had a stick in her hand, and was happily hammering a line of dolls that were seated, pupil-like, on a row of chairs in front of her. She was teaching them what she had learned at school the day before and it was clear, judging from the severity of the punishment being meted out, that the dolls were being singularly recalcitrant and stupid beyond the pale.

'Who are you? I asked
'Sister Alphonse.'
'Sister Alphonse? Are you a nun?'
'Not yet, but I'm going to be.'
She was about six at the time.

But the age gap of eleven or twelve years did not really allow much in the way of communication, particularly with so many other siblings and an exponentially increasing number of young friends milling around the place. Joan followed Briege into the Order of Poor Clare when she, too, turned fourteen.

I was not to see them very often after that. I remember a couple of family gatherings in the garden of the convent, I presume in the summertime because the sun was shining and the weather warm. Briege and Joan, I recall, were holding court, explaining things and, once in a while, introducing us to other nuns who might appear. I remember little more than that.

Their lives, however, were not destined to be spent permanently at the Newry convent and, indeed they were soon to go
their separate ways. Occasionally, when they came back to
Newry on rare holidays, they would do the rounds of family
members, including me in their itinerary. Our conversations
then, since teaching was a common denominator for us, tended
to focus on issues professional. If I recall correctly, and with not
a little embarrassment, 'conversations' might be something of a
misnomer since most of our discussions consisted of my pacing
the living room floor delivering long monologues while my sisters dutifully nodded wisely and made soothing noises in all the
proper places.

Spiritual matters, I presume, did not feature on our agendas
in those days although, having said that, I have a sudden recollection of Briege making me a present back then of a book entitled, *Has Sin Changed?* by Sean Fagan SM. Some kind of serious
discussion must have prompted this gift. (Since I wrote this last
sentence I checked my study shelves and found the book. A note
in the flyleaf reveals that Briege gave me the book in 1982.)

There were, of course, the conversations I had with Joan and
her colleagues after class each week during the two years they
attended my courses. But if memory serves, these too were the
kind of affable conversations a teacher might engage in with a
group of favoured students.

February 2000
We have been back to see Mr Diamond. The 'hic-cup', or the
'scare', has receded. There is little in the blood tests to disturb
him unduly although the 'ensymes' and the 'bilirubin' counts
are higher than those of a normal person's. That, however, is
only to be expected. My health is fine again; energy and fitness
are fully restored. Despite the fact that we are in winter, our
Monday and Wednesday golf games are little affected. We are
fortunate indeed this winter that rain, snow or storms do not
seem to fall on our golf days. Occasionally we are obliged to
commence a little later than our usual 11.00 am start because of
frost on the greens but this tends not to delay us much longer
than noon.

So confident are Sadie and I that some kind of watershed has been passed that only yesterday, with Mr Diamond's blessing, we phoned our usual hotels in the south of France to reserve rooms for July. In addition, we have been introduced to a gentleman in Newry who organises, each year, tours of the Marian Shrines in France. We have arranged to join his September pilgrimage, one that will take us, we are informed, in a huge circle from Paris to Lourdes in the south, and back again via places like Ars and Lisieux ... something special to look forward to! Sadie tends to mutter vague aspirations like 'You never know!' (She's obviously thinking about miracles!) but I have to admit that I am rather more pragmatic or, perhaps, sadly lacking in the faith needed to even contemplate such utterings.

Or is it truly a lack of faith? Prayer, as a concept, continues to absorb and fascinate me and not simply for its spiritual purposes. I continue to intellectualise about it, about its methodologies, about its effects, about how its value might rise or fall, adjust or change, in accordance with the individual who is doing the praying. Somewhere along the line, quite unconsciously and without any real awareness of when it happened, I have found myself occasionally talking to Jesus about my health situation. So often nowadays I say to Jesus, 'Lord, I know you can see me; I know you can hear me; I know you know what is going on in my head; I can't hide it from you. I know you have said, "Ask, and you shall receive." But what am I allowed to ask for, Lord? Your will has to have some bearing on things. Lord Jesus, dear Friend, take a mad scenario! Suppose I were to say, "Lord, take away this liver problem. Make me whole. If you want to, you can." Heavens, Lord, you did it often enough during your ministry on earth. If I have enough faith, like the centurion or the woman troubled with the issue of blood, can I legitimately expect to be fully cured? Or is it your will that I now have to suffer a little bit? Lord, I know you have looked after me all my life in ways that are far beyond anything I possibly could have deserved. How can I seriously sit here and ask for yet more when, like nine of the ten lepers, I do not believe I have ever thanked you for what you have already done?'

When I pray, or talk, (or whatever it is) in this vein, I am invariably pursuing a line of secondary thoughts that seem to run parallel with the reflections on the surface of my mind, thoughts about the millions of petitioners whose prayers are not answered; thoughts about the way I am withholding myself, not 'storming heaven', as my mother used to say; thoughts about how the miracles in the New Testament were also 'signs' that confirmed the truth of Jesus' message, signs for which there is not the same necessity today. Perhaps all of this does bespeak a lack of faith. Perhaps there is a streak of rationality in me that inhibits a full, untrammelled demand for God's intervention. A while back one of the readings at Mass related an episode in which Abraham, I think it was, was concerned about God's threat to wipe out a couple of sinful towns (Sodom and Gomorrah). Abraham pleaded with the Lord:

'If I can find fifty good men in these towns, will you relent?'

God thought about this for a while and then agreed. Abraham, however, began to worry that he might not be able to find fifty good men, so he set about working on God, beating him down to forty-five, to forty, then thirty, twenty and even to ten. Here is a perfect example of God being persuaded to change his mind, change his will. And there are other examples, similar to this, in the Old Testament. Is there a message here that we should keep on trying? Are we being told that God's will is not fixed in stone? Or is it that we simply have no idea what God's will is and that we should ask for what we think we need, irrespective of God's will?

There is a very strong message here and one that is reinforced in Luke eleven – a message about the power of persistence. God wants us to keep on trying and not to give up after one attempt. Luke tells us that Jesus spoke to his disciples about a man who wanted to borrow some bread from a neighbour in the middle of the night. The friend was understandably reluctant to get up out of bed, get dressed, light lamps, unbolt the door – it was all very bothersome. But Jesus said (and, maybe it's me but I can't help feeling that there was quiet humour in his voice when he said this), 'I tell you, if the man does not get up and give it to him for friendship's sake, persistence will be enough to make him get up and give his friend all he wants.'

In other words, if you make enough of a pest of yourself, your neighbour will give you what you want in order to prevent you from annoying him further. There is more to the parable than that, of course. Jesus is telling us that true friendship will bear persistence, is tolerant of continuous demands. Rather the opposite of something I heard about someone the other day: he, too, was in dire straits and, in desperation, turned to the Lord. 'Lord, ' he said, ' you know very well I have not asked you for anything this past thirty years. If you give this to me now, I won't annoy you for another thirty years.'

Not quite how Jesus sees it … he wants us to keep on asking. Maybe it is another of his ways of persuading us to stay in touch with him. Even if we are only asking for favours, a fairly basic form of prayer, at least we are acknowledging his existence, and more, we are acknowledging his power and majesty.

So, when we are praying do we take literally, 'Ask, and you shall receive.'? I read somewhere in a little brochure (I cannot remember the source) a sentence that struck me as deep: 'Whatever you ask for, the Holy Spirit will be the answer to your prayer.' The writer is not saying that we will get exactly what we ask for but what we will get will be what is for our good and the effort we make in praying will be blessed with the ultimate good – the Holy Spirit in our hearts.

Pray with faith and confidence, we are told time and time again, and the Lord will grant you all you ask. But Jesus himself prayed with faith and confidence in Gethsemene – and what a disaster for Christianity had the Father granted that request! Thus somewhere in the back of my head there will always be reservations about the likelihood of my prayer being granted, not because I do not believe, or because God is not prepared to grant what I ask, but simply because what I ask may not be for my good, or again, unlikely but possible, the denial of my request may be for a greater good.

These kinds of reflections are not easy; they are complicated. Because of what I have just written, I am immediately drawn to think: Can I pray to God with total fervour and faith for my liver to be healed? Clearly, I cannot assume that this is his will for me … but should that in any way inhibit my prayer? Equally, I cannot assume that it is God's will that I am not to be healed, that my liver is to be allowed to continue to degrade. If I were to make that assumption (presumption, really), then logically I would have to assume that there is no point in praying for a miracle and simply forget about it. And my response to that? It sounds most un-Christian!

So what am I to do? Given the nature of these reflections, it seems to me that I go ahead and pray for what I need, or think I need (provided it is for my spiritual good and not something material or selfish), and take my chances with God's will. But there again – 'take my chances'! Is there not in this simple phrase a clear weakness of faith, a lack of the total belief that was so evident in the prayers of those New Testament supplicants that Jesus was moved to admiration as well as to mercy.

Faith! It gets even more complicated. Although this is winter, the American professional golf tour continues in the sunshine states of Florida and California. This weekend, an unknown golfer who has been struggling to make ends meet for years, suddenly won a tournament and a great deal of money. His wife, speaking to a journalist afterwards, reported that some of the responsibility for this victory rested with an Irish priest whom she had met on the plane *en route* to the tournament. She had told the priest something of her husband's story and aspirations and the priest, as she was leaving, called out, 'I'll pray for your husband's success.'

When I read that in the newspaper yesterday, it sparked an immediate train of thought. God loves each of us equally. Why would he favour one golfer over another? Is this not a situation, remembering something of what I wrote earlier, where the normal ebbs and flows of life's events simply follow natural, perhaps accidental, patterns without direct intervention from God? Sometimes, in Newry, when our county team is in an all-Ireland final there are prayers said in our church that cause me to lift my eyebrows and wonder why God would favour Down over Kerry – especially when, in all probability, priests in churches all over Kerry are making equal but opposite demands? Levity aside, it does raise questions about what we can legitimately pray for.

And yet again, does it? What little I know of Jesus, what little experience I have of him, talking to him in the evenings, persuades me that we can talk to him about anything, ask him for anything. Father Niall has told me on more than one occasion that no prayer is wasted, that something good will always come from our prayers, even if the specific requests we make do not appear to have been granted.

Wise words – again. But somehow I know that I am still not finished with this particular line of thought. For the present, however, I come back in my heart and mind, time and time again, to Jesus' own prayer in Gethsemene, '... yet not my will, Father, but yours be done.'

April 2000
Last Sunday we went to Mass at 3.00 pm instead of our usual time of 10.00 am. We were led there by a marvellous devotion that I have only recently discovered, a devotion much beloved by Pope John Paul II, and known worldwide. Yet, until very recently, I had never heard anything about it. All to do with selective perception, I suppose, because now that I am familiar with it I am finding evidence of it everywhere I go. Indeed, I might never have got to hear about it were it not for the fact that I came across a little holy picture with the face of Jesus on it. Something about it appealed to me, so I wrote to the address on the back of the picture and thus I learned about Helen Kowalska, a Polish girl, born in 1905. She became a Sister of Our Lady of Mercy at age twenty and lived her life in humble service, performing duties of cook, gardener and doorkeeper.

It was to this uneducated but deeply spiritual young nun, who took the spiritual name Sister Faustina, that Jesus chose to appear in a number of visions, entrusting her with a mission to promote a devotion to his Divine Mercy throughout the world. In one of her visions she saw Jesus

> ... *clothed in a white garment. One hand was raised in the gesture of blessing, the other was touching the garment at the breast. From beneath the garment, slightly drawn aside ... there were two large rays, one red, the other pale. After a while Jesus said, 'Paint an image according to the pattern you see, with the signature: Jesus, I trust in You. I desire that this image be venerated, first in your chapel and then throughout the world.*

The story of the difficulties she faced in carrying out this mission, her efforts to get the Divine Image painted (she was disappointed at the final result), her failing health and heroic sufferings (she died at age thirty-three), all make fascinating reading in her diary *(Diary of Blessed Faustina)*. She was beatified in a very emotional ceremony by her fellow countryman, Pope John Paul II, in 1993 and canonised a few years later. Her name is known today in every continent in the world and devotion to the Divine Mercy is drawing more and more followers with each passing year.

Jesus requested that the feast of his mercy should be celebrated on the Sunday after Easter. On this Sunday every year the Dominican chapel in Newry celebrates the feast with great ceremony. The chapel is invariably packed to the doors, standing room only for the tardy. What is significant about the feast, according to Canon Ignacy Rozikyi, is that the extraordinary grace promised by Jesus to those who venerate this feast and who carry out certain small but solemn obligations,

> *... is a gift of grace comparable only to the grace of Holy Baptism. This means that on this day your soul can be renewed as on the day of baptism, so that if you died immediately after receiving this grace you would go straight to heaven with no purgatory to serve at all.*

What an immense and wondrous gift!

Needless to say, I was first in line, with Sadie in tow, to venerate this feast which fell last Sunday. The obligations required were not difficult to carry out. They include:

– confession on the day (or as close to the day as possible); the Dominicans hear confessions in the chapel early on the Sunday afternoon;

– Communion at Mass;

– an act of mercy should take place in our lives as part of our preparation for the feast. (This can be a merciful word – forgiving and comforting; a merciful deed – any of the corporal works of mercy; or a merciful prayer – prayers for mercy for someone);

– the Chaplet of the Divine Mercy has to be recited for nine days before the feast, beginning on Good Friday; and

– a sermon on the Divine Mercy has to be preached by the celebrant.

The preliminaries, the reciting of the Chaplet, the Mass, the sermon, were all very moving. To leave that church convinced that I was reborn as if baptised anew was an indescribable experience. This time every year from now until the end of my days will find me returning to the Dominican chapel to honour St Faustina and to venerate this great and extraordinarily generous feast.

June 2000

My stepmother, Mollie, died some days ago. She was eighty-seven and died peacefully in a hospital bed. She and Sadie were great friends. Each week Sadie would go to visit her in Banbridge and take her out. Mollie's eyesight was bad and her heart was suspect so she was generally confined to the house, something she found difficult to accept because, despite her years, she was fit and sprightly and loved to go shopping in the nearby towns of Lisburn and Dromore. When she died, most of the family were gathered around her bed. There were tears everywhere … almost everywhere. My own eyes were dry. I was fond of Mollie and sad that she had died but I kept thinking, 'She's in heaven, now – bad eyesight, questionable heart, both irrelevant. Whatever her life was, it is infinitely happier now.' So, no tears. But I had to question myself. Am I lacking in compassion? Am I cold?

These were questions I put to my sister Joan at the wake. (Briege was delivering a series of lectures on Franciscan spirituality to a group of priests and nuns in Rome and was unable to be with us.) The day was bright and warm. Joan and I went off for a long walk and, as it transpired, for a long talk. As well as a life spent in prayer and contemplation, Joan has also acquired skills and qualifications in spiritual counselling. I do not know if she actually used these skills on me but our conversation was deep, personal and focused much on matters spiritual. She dismissed my fears about lacking compassion, preferring to believe that my faith in Mollie's present happiness rendered the need for tears pointless. My faith in her present happiness is, I truly believe, genuine, but again, lurking away in the back of my mind is the question, 'Where is the love?'

When we returned to the others a couple of hours later, Joan's final remark to me before we entered the house was,

'Do you know something? We're brother and sister; you're in

your sixties; I'm in my fifties; and this is the first real conversation we have ever had in our lives.'

I was deeply affected by that and, indeed, by our talk. I hope it was only the first of many.

July 2000
This morning I stubbed my toe. Even as I write this, I find myself pondering the responses it might engender. I have long enjoyed the twists, turns and originalities of our living language as it evolves and develops. Nowhere are its ingenuities more evident than in the ever-changing vernacular of youth culture. When I wrote that first sentence, I immediately found myself envisioning the archetypal adolescent, complete with the one-hundred yard stare and the aura of bored detachment, 'And this is interesting because ...?' A superior put-down, by the cool over the square. You gotta love it! Well ... maybe not!

My wife has suffered puzzlement for years over that peculiar aspect of my personality that I call my 'sense of humour'. I cannot number the occasions when, doubled up with mirth, I tried to share with her a cartoon in a journal or a sentence in a novel, only to be met with blank mystification. We had a conversation the other day. We were on the beach in Menton, Sadie sunning herself while I sat under an umbrella reading.

'Shakespeare was a wise old bird,' I said.

There was silence. After a while, I asked,

'Did you hear that?'

'I did ... but I didn't know I was supposed to say anything.'

'Ah, you weren't. He was a brilliant psychologist, you know.'

'He was?'

'He was. He knew that human emotion was too dynamic, too fluid, to remain stable for any length of time.'

'I'm supposed to know what you're talking about?'

'He knew that nobody can stay exhilarated all of the time, or deeply depressed all of the time. Specific emotions might dominate but they invariably give way to others from time to time.'

'He said that?'

'No, he didn't. But look at the great tragedies ... he knew his audiences' emotions could not be kept focused on the tragic events of the play for the entire three hours. So he introduced humour to give their emotions a change, a rest. There was the old gatekeeper in Macbeth, for example, or the grave-digger in Hamlet. And, of course, you had the jester in Lear.'

'Of course you had.'

'That way he ensured that, when he brought back the tragic events, he could always maintain audience engagement. Not like some of those modern horror films – one shock follows another without let-up and with such rapidity that after a time all shock value is lost.'

A pause.

'And this is interesting because …?' (Actually, she didn't say that. I couldn't resist it. But it does paraphrase what she did say.)

'Well … I've been thinking about this diary I'm writing. I was wondering if too constant a focus on the spiritual might be making excessive demands upon anyone who might read it.'

'So?'

'So … from time to time I have been tossing in the odd humorous aside … to relieve the intensity a little bit.'

Another pause.

'Is it your usual brand of weird, obscure humour?'

'What? Well … I suppose so … yes.'

'I've got news for you.'

'What's that?'

'There's no humour in your diary.'

Go figure!

Anyway! This morning I stubbed my toe. I had been swimming in the Mediterranean just off a stony beach on the south side of Menton on the French Riviera. I was making my way, barefoot, to one of the freshwater showers fastened at various intervals to the shore wall. I had not noticed a large jagged rock sticking up out of the stones and, as I was walking past I smashed the little toe of my left foot against it. The pain was excruciating. I had to sit down, groaning and grunting through clenched teeth as I tried to massage the pain away. In the middle of all of this I found myself saying inwardly, 'As I understand it, Jesus, there were angels appointed to make sure you didn't dash your foot against a stone. Sadly, it seems that I am on my own. But, for what it is worth, I offer this wee bit of pain to you. Maybe between us we can help a needy soul or a sinner somewhere.'

Offering up minor pains is a little habit I seem to have picked up lately, a response, I think, to the many times I have had opportunities in the past couple of years to offer up pain and discomfort and did not use them. What invariably happens, though, is that after I make my prayer, I go on moaning, resisting, wishing the pain away. There is no sudden calmness, no resolute or heroic acceptance of the pain for the sake of sinners, just me continuing to suffer and hating it.

I have often wondered exactly how I am supposed to behave in these situations. I always imagine that, after the offering, I should behave differently. But I don't. I never do. Jesus himself, faced in Gethsemene with the full and awful realisation of the suffering to come, was compelled to try to persuade his Father to arrest it. That was only his human side talking, of course. His divinity bowed, even as his humanity demurred, to his Father's will.

I once talked to Father Niall about suffering. He suggested that these little episodes are already taken care of in our Morning Offering. I told him that I believed he was right but that something in me wanted to be involved with further offering and some kind of commitment as these opportunities arose. As gently as he could, for he is always kind, he said that he understood these urges but asked me to reflect upon the extent to which pride or ego might be involved. He reminded me that I am still human, that the pain is always going to be a problem and, as before, he suggested that I hand it over to Jesus and try to deal with it the best way I can. We talked about this for a while. There is, apparently, quite a theology on suffering. I am not sure that I understand it. Suffering *per se* is an evil in the world, something that God permits but does not cause. How we deal with it is what is of interest to God but we are not necessarily expected to embrace it. If we can get rid of it, then we should do so. As Father Niall matter-of-factly suggested, if an aspirin or something helps me to get rid of pain, then I should take the aspirin. God gave it to us for that purpose.

There is depth in all of this, and meaning that I have not yet fully grasped. What Father Niall says seems to make the offering up of pain a deal easier than I think it should be. However, something of what he says is echoed by St Thérèse of Lisieux although I have to confess that while I have an intellectual understanding of her words, they are underpinned by a level of such deep humility that I have far still to go before I reach empathy with them:

Of course we should like to suffer generously and nobly; we should like never to fall. What an illusion! What does it matter if I fall at every moment? In that way I realise my weakness, and the gain is considerable.

It is clear from my reaction to this morning's event that this is a topic that still leaves me much to ponder about.

Although I feel that it is not something I should be talking about in the same breath as my own petty discomforts, I try to learn something about accepting suffering from the manner in which Jesus dealt with it. The gospels do not tell us what he was feeling or thinking but there were certainly moments of immense heroism. Even the very act of taking up the cross, when his body was exhausted and torn to pieces by the cruel scourging, was an act of extraordinary courage and will; his struggling to his feet every time he fell was indication of his determination to suffer for our sakes; his gentle advice to the crying women to weep for themselves and for their children showed that he could look outward and away from the self-absorption the rest of us feel when racked with pain; and even at that moment of horrendous agony which is beyond anything we can comprehend, the driving in of the nails, he could still pray for his tormentors. Can we ever hope to respond to suffering in a way even vaguely similar to that? Not I!

But there was one moment when Jesus was lost, a little boy crying for his Father. It was one I had never given any thought to until Sean mentioned it a year or so ago. For some reason I can remember clearly where we were; we were on the fourth fairway of the Warrenpoint golf course. Sean had been telling me about a study-group meeting he had attended the previous evening. The Jesuit who had addressed the group told them that Jesus' cry on the cross, 'Lama! Lama! Sabacthani?' was, in fact, a cry of victory. I could not see this at all and said so. Sean said that it was actually the first line of a victory hymn from the Old Testament.

A couple of holes later, when I had had time to think about it, I said to Sean, 'I don't think your priest is making much sense. The prophet in the Old Testament would have known, as we do, that Jesus' sufferings would result in victory – victory for Christianity, victory for sinners. But there was no victory at the precise moment when Jesus cried out in despair to the Father. Think about it! Jesus suffered and died to save us from our sins. He took on to himself the burden of the sins of all humanity and the punishment due to them. But what is sin if it isn't ultimately a separating of ourselves from God? When we sin we go somewhere love can't follow, where God can't follow. If Jesus took on to himself the sins of the world, inevitably he had to take on to himself, for a time at least, the consequences of that sin ... that awful and total separation from God. During the pains of his physical suffering, he was probably in touch internally with the Father, to whatever degree, and deriving some comfort from that. When there came that awful moment of separation, when he found himself abandoned in a dark and terrible place, he cried out in desperate loneliness and loss, 'Father! Father! Why have you forsaken me?' No victory hymn there!'

Sean actually agreed with me for once and thought my theory made sense. He also wondered why no one had brought it up at the meeting.

I have thought about this from time to time since. I am not sure of its theological accuracy. Did Jesus actually find himself in that awful dark where sinners go? I tend to think he might have. I have often found myself deeply moved by his sufferings as I meditate on the Sorrowful Mysteries but I never grieve more deeply, as I contemplate those terrible moments, than I do when I think of Jesus, a little boy lost, crying aloud in pain and fright for his Father. And in those moments, I imagine, Jesus was probably lost to the purpose of his suffering. He was just suffering. Maybe that is what Father Niall is asking me to do ... just to suffer. The Lord will be able to use it as he wills if I say, 'This suffering is for you, Lord.'

St Louis Marie de Montfort offers some advice on suffering:
God loves you; he knows what he is doing; he has experience; each of his blows is skilful and loving. He gives no useless blow unless you make it useless by your impatience.

There is, in these lines, more than an echo of what I have been thinking about. There is also, for me at least, something of the same vagueness that keeps me pondering on the issue. For example, '… unless you make it useless by your impatience' seems straightforward until I try to quantify my level of impatience and, by extension, the level of uselessness in my suffering. Then I am back, going around in circles.

But for now I am quite content to go on thinking about it. I have discovered that, as with most of the things I meditate on, I am not going to solve this overnight. I may never solve it, or any of the other issues. But at the present stage of my spiritual development I am content just to be working at them. I like Catherine of Sienna's observation: 'God does not desire a perfect deed but a perfect desire.' That I can live with!

This morning I stubbed my toe. What a tiny and irrelevant little discomfort to have led to reflection on the terrible sufferings of our dear crucified Lord.

CHAPTER ELEVEN

Service

August 2000

Not long ago, at a Sunday Mass, our bishop, John McAreavey, preached a homily on 'Service'. During his talk he quoted a little prayer. I was so impressed by it that when I went home, I immediately tried to write it down so that I would not forget it. However, in the attempt to write it down I discovered that I had already forgotten it. The following morning after Mass, I followed the priest, Father Brendan (with whom I had conversed before), into the sacristy. I mentioned the bishop's prayer and asked him if he knew anything about it. He rummaged in a corner of the sacristy, found some photocopied pages, and handed one to me. He said, 'I think this is what you are looking for.' And so it proved to be.

The full text of the prayer is:

Lord, I want to serve you;
I want my life to include your concerns at a deep level of my being.
I want to give generous love in return for your wholehearted love.

I don't know where and how to serve –
Help me to know your plan for my life.
Help me to know where my personality and talents
might be used in your service.

Help me to know and really to believe
That you work also through my weaknesses
Which sometimes make me despair and become mistrustful.

Lord, I desire to be your servant,
In suffering and in joy;
Show me how, please Lord, show me;
Teach me your path.
Be with me
light in my questioning,

comfort in hard times,
companion in joy.

The bishop's homily was preached at a time when I was beginning to feel that something was missing in my prayers, that there was something ... selfish ... about them. My prayers on the surface seemed laudable, fully in tune with the injunction that we must do everything we can to save our own immortal souls. And so I pray for the graces I need to be a true and holy Christian, for tolerance, for faith, for love, for compassion, for trust in God's will, for purity, for health in body and soul, for the grace of true repentance for my sins – but these prayers are all about *me*. Should there not be something more, apart from the prayers for friends in trouble or in need, for the souls of recently deceased relatives?

A reading at Mass the other morning has added to my concern. The Lord had asked Jeremiah to preach to the people at the Temple Gate and say, '... put no trust in delusive words like: This is the Sanctuary of the Lord, the Sanctuary of the Lord, the Sanctuary of the Lord.' (That is, do not babble pious and meaningless word as if they were prayers). He told Jeremiah also to say: 'Amend your behaviour and actions ... treat each other fairly ... do not exploit the stranger, the orphan and the widow ... yet you are here, trusting in delusive words to no purpose ...'

Jeremiah goes on to accuse the people of murder, adultery, perjury, following alien gods – none of which, I sincerely hope, I can be accused of engaging in – but the basic message of babbling prayer without accompanying good actions and love of neighbour remains. Now I am beginning to wonder if, in choosing simply to go to Mass each day and say a few prayers each evening, I am not making things rather too comfortable for myself. It is easy to sit in my warm study and say loving things to the Lord but what am I doing to prove it? How am I, in accordance with the second great commandment, 'loving my neighbour'?

I am probably being, as Father Niall so frequently tells me, 'a bit hard on myself'. If I am granted answers to some of these prayers, the grace to be a good Christian, for example, or the gift of compassion, I might well be moved through these graces to do things, to enhance my spiritual life through Christian action. And so these prayers might ultimately be deemed unselfish rather than selfish. (This argument sounds vaguely sophistical; I hope it isn't.)

But the bishop's prayer set me thinking. Is there something I can actually do that might make my Christianity more real, more alive? I have to say that, being in my mid-sixties and with health that, despite my optimism, can best be described as questionable, I was not inundated with a rush of ideas. However, I began to think about something St Thérèse of Lisieux said. She had wanted to be a missionary and convert the world but, confined as she was to a small convent at Carmel in France, she was somewhat limited in terms of the extent to which such aspirations could be actualised. So she decided that her mission would be to pray for the world in her room.

I stood at Our Lady's altar after Mass one morning and talked to her about this. What kind of things, I asked, should I be praying for? I came away with an impressive list – souls in purgatory; sinners; aborted and miscarried children; the starving in the world; those suffering imprisonment, torture and abuse for their faith; the old; the sick; the lonely; the dying and their immortal souls, especially those in terrible danger of eternal damnation; peace in the world and in the hearts of men; friends in trouble and in need; the salvation of my family; priests – at home, or abroad in distant mission fields … and so much more, not the least of which was the almost whispered injunction to show more love and attention to my wife and family.

I am almost overwhelmed by this, so much so that I have had to pattern my day around different types of prayer and even to enlist a virtual army of saints and blesseds to help me cope with the load. There is a kind of service in this and, however good or bad I am in the doing of it, I am pleased I have been given the grace to make the effort and even more pleased to know in my heart-of-hearts that the effort is not coming from myself alone.

One aspect of this particular form of service has seized my attention – prayers for poor sinners. I began simply by praying for sinners in a general way but I found that I was forced to actually think about what I was doing. I realised quite soon that 'sinners', in my mind, was a meaningless amorphous group. Recently, however, I was reading a newspaper account of the death of an eighteen-month old boy due to neglect and the most terrible physical abuse. The doctors doing the post-mortem found old fractures, recent fractures, new fractures, cigarette burns, bruises old and new … it was absolutely horrific to read and simply broke my heart. I should say (because I have forgotten, or perhaps had no reason, to mention it) that for a long time now I pray earnestly for abused children. I find I can scarcely bear to read these reports and praying for a cessation of such terrible violence to little children is some comfort. It does test my faith, of course. More than once I have asked, 'God, are you listening to me? Are you doing anything to stop this dreadful sin?' and then I remember Father Niall's words, 'No prayer is ever wasted.'

The report I referred to above carried a photograph of the couple charged with the abuse and murder. They were a wretched looking pair. I stared at them, filled with judgementalism, distaste, and distress at what the child must have suffered. And suddenly I realised, 'These people are "poor sinners". These are the people I pray for, whom I offer my Holy Communion for. Hate the sin but not the sinner. Pray for them.' Pray for this pair? And Jesus whispered, 'Yes! They need help. God loves their immortal souls and if they do not turn to him, they will die and that will sadden him.'

So I stared at the photograph.

'Dear Lord, I was a sinner and you brought me back to you. I am still a sinner but I am in your love now; we are together. These poor misguided sinners are lost in evil. Lord, touch their souls, their hearts, their consciences, and bring them back to you. You did it for me; do it for them, Lord, please.'

This was such a hard prayer to say. I could only say it from love of God, from awareness of the great love he has for all souls, from awareness of the hurt he feels when souls he loves are mired in evil. I have not yet progressed to love of the sinners, except in so far as I wish their souls to be saved from damnation. Since then I pray ever more and more for sinners. I try to offer up pains, disappointments and even petty irritations for sinners. God wants them back; that is all I need to know. But how hard it is to separate the sinner from the sin. Television coverage of rioting, muggings, thieving, murderous acts, and all kinds of sinful rage, fills me with immense anger at the perpetrators – and then I remember, 'These are poor sinners. Pray for them. Do not judge them.' And I try. It is not easy. But I, too, was … am … a sinner in need of help. So I try.

Lately, however, I am considering other options in answer to the bishop's prayer – nothing, I hasten to add, that might be deemed significant or in any way praiseworthy – simply enough to help me feel that I am making a little contribution outside of my room as well as in it.

The first opportunity came when Sister Magdelen Doyle of St John of God, who reads at Mass on Tuesday mornings, asked me to fill-in for her because a health problem was making it difficult for her to continue in the role. Although I was sorry to hear of Sr Magdelene's problem (she has since become a friend) I was delighted to agree, realising that here was an opportunity to serve, to have some direct involvement in passing on the word of God. I was fortunate, in some respects, that the actual standing in the pulpit and reading to a full congregation presented me with little problem. I had been teaching for thirty-seven years, many of which years saw me teaching large groups of adults in evening classes. But there was, nevertheless, in the early stages at least, a problem. I talked to Father Niall about it. Actually it was he who brought the subject up. He says Mass on Tuesdays (I must say that I do enjoy 'working' with him like this). One morning after Mass, while I was over at the parochial house with him, he complimented my reading. 'Will you quit!' I said. 'I'm having enough trouble holding on to whatever bit of humility I have left without you starting.'

So we talked about it. I told him that I could never go on to the pulpit without thorough preparation the night before. Too many times I have sat in the chapel listening to readers who, either through inhibition or lack of thought, read without clarity and, ultimately, without effect. I would study the passage, try to thoroughly understand and assimilate its message and, having done that, try to figure out where best to place emphases and make pauses, to ensure optimum possibility that God's word will not only be heard but also be understood.

'Where's the problem in that?' he wanted to know.

'Well … to be truthful, I'm wondering how much of vanity

there is in all of this. In the pulpit you're in the public eye. You're inclined to try to make an impression. If ego gets in, humility is out.'

So often during our conversations, Father Niall, when he responds to a point I have just made, prefaces his answer with, 'No ... No ... your thinking is wrong!' This time was no different. He wanted me to examine the issue from another perspective, telling me that I had a reputation for having been a good teacher and that clearly I am bringing that on to the pulpit. In a very matter-of-fact tone, one without hint of praise, he told me that this is a talent and that all talents come from the Holy Spirit. We are expected to do the very best you can with our talents. He referred to the parable of the talents and stated quite earnestly that I had, in my reading, an opportunity to promote God's message and that I should seize it. Vanity should not be a part of it but if it troubles me I should simply tell the Holy Spirit honestly about it and ask for his support.

I was greatly helped by that and I have learned from it. I no longer feel troubled by vanity and I enjoy the experience, reading some of the more dramatic passages with a great deal of spirit and gusto. A lady recently came to me after Mass and thanked me for 'an inspirational reading'. She said she had enjoyed it but had to admit to some little amusement as she watched my fingers trying to pry themselves loose from their clutch on the pulpit's edge as I resisted the impulse to make little gestures.

'One of these days, ' she smiled, 'your hand is going to break free and fly up. I'm looking forward to that.'
I hope not. For the time being at least, I continue to read with appropriate levels of earnestness and gravitas.

A second opportunity for service, one not yet realised and which is currently only an aspiration, has presented itself for consideration. During one of our talks after confession, I mentioned to Father Niall my concerns about 'living the commandment of love', a phrase that seems to have fastened itself in my brain and continues to resonate there, particularly when my behaviours tend to reflect the exact opposite of love. Father Niall, who had been listening quietly to what I had been saying, suggested that there are tangible ways in which I could find opportunities to 'live the commandment of love'. Making no prescription nor placing any kind onus on me, he asked me if I had ever considered joining the St Vincent de Paul Society. I baulked immediately. 'Ah, come on, Father. That's out of my league.' He smiled and shook his head as if to say I was being silly. He certainly did not think that I should run around to the offices and join up immediately but he did intimate that I might like to give the idea some thought. He told me to pray about it for a while, that it was not a decision I should rush into.

Even as he was speaking, I felt a tug at my soul. This is definitely something I will talk to Jesus about. There would be plenty of time to think about it anyway. As I told Father Niall then, I would be touring the shrines of France in a couple of weeks and there would be little point in my trying to do anything until I got back. In the meantime, I have agreed to give the matter further thought.

CHAPTER TWELVE

Pèlerinage

October 2000

A few times during August I had periods of fatigue and sickness, together with some aches and pains that were new to me. Naturally we were worried that there might be a replay of the events that led to our early departure from Portugal last year. There were a couple of times, indeed, in early September when I truly thought we would have to cancel our tour of the French shrines. But, thank God, I seemed to recover well enough to go. I was reasonably fit, suffering no nausea and, although stomach pains were now constant daily companions, there was nothing of any serious import to prevent us making the pilgrimage.

We had an early start from Newry, 5.00 am to be precise. In terms of travel, our pilgrimage involved a bus journey to Dublin, a flight to Paris, and further long bus journeys each day in France, apart from a three-day break in Lourdes. Stated baldly like that, the schedule sounds daunting. But the tour director, Michael McAllister, enlivened the various journeys with singsongs, talks, raffles for prizes he had purchased earlier (I won a little alarm clock), occasional rosaries, as well as videos about the various shrines we were about to visit. Then, of course, there was the beautiful French scenery, the little villages and towns that passed by the bus's windows. For Francophiles like myself and Sadie (we have holidayed in France every year since 1980 except for that one year we went to Colorado) there was little hardship in feasting our eyes on the changing landscape, all the way from the apple-trees and timber frames of Normandy to the red roofs and vine-groves of the south. The opening prayer at one of the Masses we attended could easily have been prayed in this context:

... open our eyes to see your hand at work in the splendour of creation.

101

However, the journeys themselves were irrelevant; it was the stops that mattered and, perhaps, the friendships that were formed. I developed a valued friendship, for example, with the priest who accompanied the group as spiritual director – Father Andrew McMahon. I knew him already, as a matter of fact, because he is a priest in my home parish but apart from one brief conversation, I had never formed an acquaintanceship with him. I remember one Sunday, about three years ago, being very impressed by a homily he had just preached, something, if I recall, about the small epiphanies that can awaken our souls and bring us to closer awareness of our need for God. After that Mass I spoke briefly to him, in the manner of a stranger, congratulating him on his sermon. Even as I write this, I am surprised to say that I clearly remember – and I am thinking about it now for the first time since that morning – saying to Father Andrew, 'I enjoyed your homily, Father, though I have to admit, I am speaking as one who is still waiting for one of those epiphanies you spoke of.'

I thought no more about it at the time but now, in view of all that has since happened and what I have written earlier in this diary about 'epiphany', I find the coincidence quite startling. This happened in the dark days before I began this journal. Was God's grace, to which I was totally oblivious, working in me even then? Was Father Andrew's choice of the word 'epiphany' back then, and my own unrelated choice of the word earlier in this diary, part of the circularity of things, that puzzling tendency for spiritual events to recur and to reflect and to re-echo in our lives time and time again?

Father Andrew is young, sincere and can speak eloquently without notes (clearly because what he says comes from the heart). He made a strong impression on the pilgrims and I was pleased, and fortunate, that the seating arrangements for meals left Sadie and myself sitting with him and his mother, Nancy, who was also making the tour. Sadie and Nancy became firm friends and are corresponding and telephoning each other even now when the pilgrimage is over.

I said 'fortunate'. I meant, of course, from my own point of view. How Father Andrew might have viewed it is another matter entirely. Each night at dinner, and again at breakfast, he was subjected to such a barrage of philosophical and theological questioning that Sadie, on considerably more than one occasion, felt impelled to urge me to desist. I think she felt, probably quite justifiably, that there was something of the fanaticism of the reformed alcoholic in my constant focus on religion. I tried to temper my conversation with forays into other subjects but I do not recall having had any great success in my efforts.

Nonetheless, although Father Andrew has the heartiest of laughs and likes a joke, he has also a serious side that responded to my importuning with grace and interest and we had many a long and complex conversation that kept us at the table after the others had left.

I do not recall that my health bothered me particularly but there are one or two little pointers which indicate that my tendency towards positivism may be making my memory somewhat selective. I recall, now, Sadie insisting on carrying the bags on a few occasions. At other times she and friends would go for walks while I had to take to our room with a couple of tablets. Nancy, too, once said something to Sadie about my being cheerful in spite of my suffering. I cringed at that and immediately thought, 'Oh no! I've been hamming it up again.' There is that in me that tends, generally unconsciously I will admit, towards the dramatic. I was talking to my boss in the college foyer once when a colleague, who was walking past, stopped and said, 'If you tied Brian's hands behind his back, he wouldn't be able to talk.' I think what prompted Nancy's observation was the fact that at table I would get the occasional abdominal twinge – nothing unusual about that, it happens all the time. However, despite the fact that I would be in the middle of a sentence to Father Andrew, I would tend to grimace, groan, jerk around a bit as if I had been prodded with something electrical, and then continue on speaking as if nothing had happened. Sadie is totally inured to that but Nancy, innately sympathetic and watching these performances with her unaccustomed eye, probably thought there was something heroic in it. There wasn't, of course! Rather there was in it something of the twitchy finger episode when my hands sought to free themselves from their clutch on the pulpit to punctuate my reading, and something, too, of the propensities in my very prayers which numerous times have forced me to appeal to the Lord in Francis Vayne's words: 'All powerful Lord, remove the affectations from me that make my prayers a ridiculous drama.'

The pilgrimage, or *pèlerinage*, as it is called in France, while physically demanding, brought many moments of spiritual uplift. Each of the various stages had something significant to offer. Our visit to Nevers jumps immediately to mind. The beautiful convent of St Gildard, memorable for its spacious grounds and grottoes, was even more significant because in a little chapel it housed, in a bronze and crystal casket, the incorrupt body of St Bernadette of Lourdes. I knelt for a long time before that casket, studying the calm, beautiful young face, pondering her sufferings while on earth and, for reasons I am unable to explain, establishing a rapport with her that will stay with me until my dying day. I have many saint and blessed friends to whom I pray daily and with whom I have established special relationships but somehow, when I come to speak to St Bernadette, something in me changes, something softens, something feels easy, comfortable and warm. So to kneel before her, to talk to her about the wonder of my being so close to her incorrupt physical body, was an experience of remarkable intensity and joy.

But I was able to take away more than joy from the moment. The search for answers, for that picture of sudden clarity to which we can point and say, 'I see it now!' seems to me an integral part of what it means to be Christian. Theologians explain, preachers preach, apostles write, yet in all of this expanse of knowledge most of us wander in cloud, in confusion and, sometimes, in unadulterated ignorance. Occasionally God lets the clouds drift briefly apart and we experience some shadowy intimations, apprehensions dim and faint, that allow us to touch the mystery if only for a moment.

When I prayed before Bernadette I had one such moment, a momentary glimpse ('… through a glass darkly', but a glimpse) of a 'totality' that I have heretofore missed and if I could only have grasped it for a second or two longer before the clouds reformed I would have understood so much more. I have been meditating on and off about God's will, occasionally about suffering, sometimes about humility, about prayer, about forgiveness, but I have been examining these concepts in isolation from each other! Talking to Bernadette and reflecting on some simple words that this uneducated little girl once spoke, made me realise how easily she had grasped immense complexities that continue to elude me. I was able to reflect on the uncomplaining and humble way she endured the most appalling suffering and, while my own insignificant circumstances pale in light of hers, I ponder with quiet admiration her own prayer of trust:

I felt that the Good Lord wanted it. When we think that the Good Lord permits it, we do not complain.

Here there is love, here there is service, here there is prayer, here there is suffering, here there is humility, here there is self-giving, here there is acceptance of God's will – all contained in these simple words. And in these simple words lies a heart and a soul that totally understands how inter-connected, how whole, how 'one', all of these things are. I write as if I, too, understand. I don't, of course! I simply recognise one who does. I stand in awe, even with a shadow of Christian envy (if such an emotion can be said to exist). All I can do is pray that the Good Lord will one day give me the strength and the love to pray that same prayer with that same conviction.

October 2000

I have mentioned St Thérèse of Lisieux in these pages and how my initial contact with her was tinged with reservations. We're great friends now – that happens when people talk openly about difficulties and differences of opinion. It was with great anticipation, therefore, that I found myself heading for Alençon and Lisieux. At Lisieux we visited the huge, majestic basilica with its vaulted ceilings and gloriously coloured mosaics. We wandered through the house and gardens at Les Buissonets where Thérèse and her family lived. We paused to admire the statue in the garden that depicts Thérèse asking her father for permission to enter the convent when she was fifteen years old and, indeed, we visited and prayed at the convent at Carmel where Thérèse lived and suffered as Sister Thérèse of the Child Jesus.

At the town of Alençon where Thérèse was born and lived her childhood we visited the little chapel where she prayed. The walls here are entirely covered in cream-coloured, square, marble plaques, each a gift from an individual or family in thanksgiving for some spiritual grace or miraculous intervention. The names of the donors and, in some cases the blessing received, are written on the plaques. As I knelt in the chapel and talked to St Thérèse about things, marvelling again, as I did with St Bernadette, about the wonder of this proximity to her life and to her, I observed a number of the pilgrims pressing themselves against the plaque-covered walls, arms spread, hands tracing the embossed lettering. I gazed at them somewhat askance, unable to suppress the uncharitable thought that they looked quite ridiculous. However, a little while later the group had moved on and I found myself alone in the chapel. Gazing left and right, a little furtively, and feeling idiotic, I, too, went over to one of the walls and pressed myself against it and tried, with spread arms, to incorporate within my reach as many of the plaques as I could. Suddenly I no longer felt embarrassed. I felt instead a sudden rush of the love and the gratitude of the souls whose faith had decorated those walls. I sensed in the plaques the presence of St Thérèse. I stayed there for quite a while, not saying much, simply absorbing … I don't know … grace, I think. It was an experience I will remember.

Our tour director, Michael McAllister, loves Ars. He has said on numerous occasions that if he could get a few pounds together he would retire and live there for the rest of his life. He is devoted to the Curé of Ars, St Jean Marie Vianney, and his enthusiasm for the saint and the little town had infected us long before we arrived there. Michel's talks about the Curé on the bus, and the video he showed us, ensured that St Jean Marie would be no stranger to us when we arrived at the large basilica that towers over the little town. Again we met a saint whose incorrupt body was encased in an ornate glass container above an altar in the nave of the basilica. There is also near the basilica a little chapel called The Chapel of the Heart because here, in a brass reliquary, above a famous kneeling statue of St Jean Marie himself, the saint's heart is preserved. These miraculous relics were inevitably impressive and, if they tested faith a little, they also inspired prayer and wonder.

I was unfamiliar with St Jean Marie before I came on this pilgrimage but I found a little booklet of his 'thoughts' – the simple reflections of a relatively uneducated country curate which, because they are inspired by a deep faith and love of God are, in fact, enormously profound. Reading through them in the chapel one afternoon I found myself getting to know, and tremendously admire, this humble saint who had given himself totally to his flock, who spent up to eighteen hours a day in the confessional, who lived a life of utter poverty (giving away what little he had to the poor) and who still was afraid that he might go to hell.

The 'thoughts' are wonderful, short and exact, and there are so many of them. More than once in these pages I have spoken about prayer, agonising over exactly how best I might pray. St Jean Marie deals with the issue in a few simple lines:

> *You can pray by putting yourself quite simply in touch with God. When one finds nothing more to say to him but just knows he is there – that in itself is the best prayer.*

He talks about humility and offers a marvellous analogy:

> *Humility is to the various virtues what the chain is to the Rosary; take away the chain and the beads are scattered; remove humility and all virtues vanish.*

And on suffering he says:

> *I have had crosses in plenty – more than I could carry almost! I set myself to ask for the love of crosses – then I was happy!*

Who could not want to know all there is to know about such a good, holy and saintly man? I have tried to learn about him, get to know him, and to win his friendship. He is now one of the saints to whom I pray every day and I never go to confession without first asking Jean Marie's help to examine my conscience and have true sorrow for my sins. A wonderful man and a joy to meet him!

October 2000

In one of the naves in Newry Cathedral is a little railed-off altar that houses two statues, painted in gold and skin-coloured tones, depicting the visitation of Jesus to St Margaret Mary Alaquoque. It is an altar at which I stop for a short prayer each day, asking St Margaret Mary to help me learn to accept God's will for me and to teach me to trust totally in the Sacred Heart.

Small wonder, then, that I was excited to visit, in the little French town of Paray-le-Monial, the very church where Jesus appeared to St Margaret Mary. The visit, sadly, was little more than a brief stop for a bite of lunch – in a grassy park nearby – so there was time for only a few prayers and a walk around the church. Sadie is always on the look out for subjects to paint and we quickly went to various vantage points in the town and took some striking photographs of the magnificent church sitting, with its three tall conical towers, on the bank of a wide river. Inevitably one of these photographs led to another of Sadie's paintings that now hangs above the fireplace in our lounge.

Our three-day visit to Lourdes has merged into a kaleidoscope of memories, some of which I will briefly touch upon. But first it has to be said that there are two Lourdes – the town of Lourdes itself and the Massabeille area where the true essence of the 'Lourdes concept' is to be found. Lourdes town, viewed dispassionately, is (or could be) a typical, lovely French town with its winding streets, distinctive architecture and pleasant location in the rolling southern countryside. Today the town seems to me to be composed of three types of buildings – hotels, restaurants and shops, so many shops that it seems that every building houses a shop. And what shops! Every inch of space – shelves, ceilings, windows, counters, walls – packed with religious artefacts of every size, shape and hue. And packed, too, with items that, while not being remotely religious, e.g. glassware, pots and pans, clothes of various kinds, are all emblazoned with religious symbols. And every single shop is selling precisely the same wares. The overall impression is one of crass commercialism of the tawdriest kind. Statues of Our Lady, three feet high, in garish colours with little lights flashing on and off over her head; large paintings of beautiful suffering madonnas and impossibly handsome, crucified Christs; thousands of candles, rosary beads, holy pictures, prayer-books, icons, crucifixes in every possible colour and every possible size. False, insensitive, tasteless, coarse – I cannot produce enough synonyms to express the dismay and disappointment I felt when I first left my hotel to walk through the town. Ornaments, baubles, plates, blatantly covered with gaudy portraits of Our Lady of Lourdes. There were even dozens of ashtrays for those who wanted to stub out their cigarettes on the sorrowing face of Our Holy Mother. I did not like it! Father Andrew was altogether more understanding than I was. 'People need these things, ' he told me calmly. 'They'll bring them home for themselves and friends and have good memories of Lourdes.'

I did not argue because there was, of course, merit in what he said. But I know that on the wall in front of my study desk are a couple of small crucifixes and some small pictures (the Divine Mercy Jesus, the Sacred Heart, St Jean Marie Vianney and St Bernadette) and, somehow their design and colour seem to me quiet and in good taste. But then, they are mine! Why wouldn't I think that? But this diary is my truth; I can only write what I honestly, however mistakenly, feel and believe.

My feelings about the other Lourdes are equally strong but totally opposite. At the outskirts of the town, manned by a kind of security guard, there are huge iron gates though which pilgrims must go to enter the Massabeille area. Just inside these gates is the Great Esplanade whose centre is dominated by a huge and glorious marble statue, in the centre of a large flower-bed, of Our Lady Crowned. This Esplanade radiates immediate and serene peace, a much-needed contrast to the frenetic avarice that pervades the town. For hundreds of yards one walks in the silence of a broad boulevard, bordered by trees and grass verges, towards the immense forecourt that fronts three great basilicas built one on top of another – the Crypt, the Basilica of the Immaculate Conception, and the Basilica of the Rosary. The Massabeille area, originally wild countryside, is still wide and open, with more than enough space to accommodate huge open-air ceremonies. Here is found the Grotto of the Apparitions, the Baths, the Churches of Pius X and St Bernadette and, beyond that, the great open-air, hilly and demanding Stations of the Cross. Bridges are built here and there to cross the beautifully scenic River Gave that meanders through the area. Green-clad hills nearby and snow-capped mountains in the distance lend additional beauty and enchantment to a place that already possesses its own tangible magic.

At night thousands of pilgrims gather here for the famous 'torch-light procession'. Everyone buys a candle in a wind-shielding holder (probably from one of the stores in town) and walks in procession all around the area. The rosary is recited and is led in many different languages, including Irish one evening we were there. A thundering Ave Maria is sung after each decade, at which point all of the thousands of pilgrims raise their candles arm-high in salute to Our Lady. To be there and part of it is extraordinarily moving; to observe it from the high railings above the Basilicas is to see a most amazing, a truly incredible, flowing river of light that stretches back for hundreds of yards and which illumines the whole Esplanade as it glides, ever tighter and brighter, to gather in a huge mass of flame in the forecourt at the steps of the main basilica. The feelings of spirituality are deep, very intense. I wondered if perhaps I might have been in the grip of some kind of crowd hysteria but I quickly dismissed that thought. Everyone was extraordinarily calm, smiling, friendly and anything but hysterical.

Lourdes is a place that demands the co-operation of the pilgrim. I did enjoy my time there; I did have several moments of spiritual awareness and peace. But I believe I 'didn't really do it right,' as I said to Sadie. I was examining too much, watching too much, maybe criticising too much. For example, there was a huge ever-constant queue moving slowly through the Grotto as each pilgrim sought to be near and to touch the base of the rock where Our Lady appeared eighteen times to the simple, peasant girl, Bernadette Soubirous. I joined the queue and trudged slowly towards the rock, praying my rosary and trying, with scant success, to offer up the irritation I was feeling at the pushers and prodders behind who, clearly unfamiliar with the concept of queuing, were unaware that a queue will only go as fast as the people at the head of it.

Eventually I arrived at the Grotto and that special place where my heart yearned to pause and share a sublime moment with my Blessed Mother. Instead I found, at both the entrance and the exit of the Grotto, four or six tired and impatient marshals who harried everyone through the Grotto with a deal of arm-waving and hissed instruction, in Italian, I surmised. I did not understand the words but I was left in no doubt about their meaning – 'Hurry! Hurry! Move along! There are others! Move along!' It pains me to relate (Ah God! Can I truly have progressed so short a distance on my spiritual journey?) that I responded more to the hassle of the marshals than I did to the aura of the Grotto. What began on my lips as muttered supplication to the Virgin, took on (God forgive me!) the altogether different hue of muffled imprecation. I would love to explain this spiritual disharmony by reference to my tummy pains and general fatigue but I am afraid the real cause is to be found in defects of character that I have yet to subdue.

Father Andrew's visit to the Grotto fared rather better – in spiritual terms at least. He had decided to wait until late in the evening, beyond dusk in fact, when the crowds had thinned and access to the Grotto was unhindered by marshals. He sat near the rock on one of the many chairs and recited a complete rosary, the fifteen-mystery rosary. He found that the peace and the location were inducing in him a great spiritual calmness and a wonderful closeness to Our Lady. So immersed was he in his contemplation that he completely lost track of time and space. When he finally returned to awareness of where he was, it was totally dark with only the odd distant lamp glowing here and there. He made his way to the huge Esplanade gates only to find them locked. It took him a considerable time to find a wall with a tree beside it that he could climb, but he still had to suffer some moments of concern about what kind of landing area lay in the blackness at the other side. He made it back to our hotel about 2.00 am and while the story he later told me emphasised the wonder of the time lost in the contemplation of Our Beloved Mother, I sensed in it just a hint of suppressed glee at the little-boy-escapade element of his tale.

A huge open-air Mass, which required an army of priests to distribute communion, followed by a bus-trip to the nearby village of Bartrès where Bernadette spent two separate periods of her life, ended our sojourn in Lourdes. My account of our days there sounds petulant and ungrateful – and there are some aspects of Lourdes (to my own thinking, of course) that seem to forget that the place is about faith, serenity and love – but there was much about the visit that wakened my soul. I did go back to the Grotto one evening and found great tranquillity there, a peace in my soul that came from a togetherness with my Holy Mother that I had been unable to find in the early days of the visit. And I did become caught up in the fervour and spirit of the candle-light procession to a degree that was almost charismatic. I also went to the Baths and was dunked in the famous (if freezing) waters and felt only awe and prayerfulness.

I did not really ask for, nor expect, a miraculous cure. I learned shortly after my arrival there that, despite its fame and its one-hundred-and-fifty-year history, Lourdes has fewer than a hundred authenticated miracles, only sixty-four, in fact. An innate rationalism, coupled with (I am saddened to realise) a weak faith, protected me from any unrealistic expectations. Sadie made it clear to me, however, that she intended to ask point-blank for the miracle I was refusing even to consider. What was it Matthew told us about the time Jesus returned to his home town and found that the people there gave him scant respect? Something like '… and he did not work many miracles there because of their lack of faith.'

Nonetheless, one of the most important 'signs' given at Lourdes is the grace that manifests itself in conversions, in the serenity of the spirit, in the purposeful redirection and renewal of lives, and in the peaceful acceptance of any suffering we might have. This 'sign', I truly believe, I did experience, perhaps not fully, but enough to know that I intend to go back again next year and 'do it right'.

October 2000

There was one final visit – or combination of two visits, to be exact – that I need to mention. We had finally circled all the way back to Paris on the day before our departure from France. Michael had planned two final visits for us, one to a church in which rested the body of St Vincent de Paul and the other to a nearby church at 140, rue du Bac.

St Vincent's body, apparently incorrupt as well as those of St Bernadette and St Jean Marie Vianny, was in yet another crystal reliquary but high above and behind an altar. The body could only be viewed by climbing a set of stairs on the right of the altar, crossing a short landing to where the body reposes, and exiting by another set of steps on the left. When it came my turn to stop before the body, I said, without any awareness that I had made any decision about it, 'It's good to meet you, St Vincent. I'm going to join the St Vincent de Paul Society shortly after I get home. I ask you, please, to pray that God will give me the graces I will need – and I am afraid, dear friend, that I will need an awful lot—to be a truly charitable, compassionate and sincere Vincentian brother.'

And that was it. The decision was made. I prayed a little while in front of the main altar and then joined the group as we walked the short distance to 140, rue du Bac.

For more than one hundred and fifty years the miraculous medal has been worn by Catholics throughout the world. Popes and saints, bishops, nuns and priests, have promoted a devotion to this powerfully sacramental medal. At the church in the rue du Bac we learned that Catherine Labouré, a Burgundy farmgirl, had a prophetic dream of an elderly priest saying Mass – a priest with a gentle face, short pointed beard and a black skull cap whom she had never seen before – who called her to follow him. She was later to learn that the priest was St Vincent de Paul, founder of the Daughters of Charity, an order she was one day to join. During her time in Paris, living in rue du Bac and caring for the inmates in a home for elderly men, she was visited by the Blessed Virgin who 'commissioned' her to design, and promote devotion to, the 'Miraculous Medal'. St Catherine's vision of Our Lady was slightly ... I suppose one could say ... indirect. What happened was that Catherine was awakened during the night by a 'shining' young boy who led her from the bedroom to the chapel where Our Lady was sitting waiting for her in a chair at the side of the altar, a chair that was normally occupied during various services by Father Aladel, Catherine's confessor. That chair is still there and I knelt before it for a long time trying to 'see' our invisible Mother as I talked to her. There was a time in my life when I would have dismissed such imaginings as superstitious but these 'connections' on the pilgrimage with the saints and Our Lady were very real to me and profoundly moving. That chair, a short time into my contemplation, became more than simply a chair. It became for me surrounded by an aura of awe and wonder, a seat in which Our Lady reposed, looking calmly at me as I prayed. My birthday fell a couple of days ago (sixty-four and I am sure George Johnston is scratching his head about it somewhere) and Sadie bought for me a gold miraculous medal with a gold chain. I have not recorded the story of its design, the difficulties Catherine faced in persuading anyone to mint it, that fact the no-one knew that Catherine, at the behest of the Blessed Virgin, was its source, and many of the other fascinating details of this story related to us at the rue du Bac. These facts are easily accessed elsewhere. But the story is wonderful, the medal's history amazing. I will treasure Sadie's gift and wear it around my neck for the rest of my life.

October 2000

A couple of years ago I fought my way into the third round of one of the golf club's match-play events. The man I was drawn against, Norman Bowden, I had met a few times before. Pleasant and good-humoured as he was, we had a very friendly and enjoyable match. That is not to say that we did not fight like tigers; it was, indeed, a hard-fought tussle that ended only on the seventeenth green. Modesty forbids me to reveal who emerged victorious; the result will remain forever lost in the golf club's annals. Anyway, it is irrelevant. The real point is that during the round Norman had talked about his job and had told me where he worked.

I mention Norman because over the years I have seen him outside the cathedral after Mass holding a collection box for the St Vincent de Paul Society. I pass his workplace every time I go to play golf and one afternoon, a few weeks ago, I called in to see him. I explained that I was thinking about joining the Vincent de Paul Society and wondered how I should go about it. He was pleased to learn of my interest and said there should be absolutely no problem, just a couple of basic formalities. He promised to propose my name at the next meeting and said that he would bring me along to introduce me to the group the week after that. All happened as he predicted. The members, composed of a group of men, three or four women and two nuns, (and their chaplain, Father Andrew, I was pleased to discover) welcomed me in the warmest of manners and thus I, too, became a Vincentian Brother.

The group is amazingly knowledgeable about the poor in Newry, as well as about the location of small streets and mews in older parts of the town that I am completely unfamiliar with. Not only that. Already they are thoroughly familiar with all of the huge profusion of avenues and crescents, groves and parks, springing up with ever-increasing rapidity in new housing estates all around the suburbs of the town. I have been a native of Newry all my life but when I go to these meetings I am filled with the impression that the group is discussing locations belonging to some alien land. Yet letters from troubled people are read out at the meeting by the President and always some of the members, many with over thirty years of service, will know the background, antecedents and current circumstances of the family involved. It is amazing to listen to. The depth of discussion, the desire to help, the sympathy for the various cases, and the sheer graciousness of the Christian charity that pervades the work, humbles me. I do not know if I will ever fit in, if I can ever measure up to the standards that these people set. Something of their aspirations can be learned from the prayers that are said before and after the meetings, prayers that ask the Lord to allow the brothers to share their communion with the Eucharist with those in need and to share their burdens as true friends.

I understand now why Father Niall wanted me to consider this kind of service and I equally understand why he suggested the I do not rush into it. I don't know if I can ever attain the spirit of my new friends but I can, and do, pray to Jesus and to Blessed Frederick Ozanam, founder of the Society, for the grace, charity and compassion I need to participate in this wonderful example of the corporal works of mercy.

One reflection always gives me comfort when I find myself inadequate or some way lacking in matters spiritual. I simply remember the precept of Jesus to Mama Carmella, an Italian mystic, that roughly paraphrased, says, 'Keep trying! As long as you are trying, I am content.' This is one thing I know I can do. No matter how badly I perform, I know in my heart that I am trying. Jesus knows it too. That's good enough for me.

CHAPTER THIRTEEN

Father Martin

December 2000

I have been thinking about miracles, on and off, since I came home from France. I have discovered that one has a tendency to do this when one's mortality is called into question. A couple of weeks ago I went into the parish bookshop and purchased Sister Briege McKenna's *Miracles Do Happen*. From the back cover I learned that the Director of the Catholic Communications Institute of Ireland had read the book and declared, 'This book is a real faith-builder.' And so it is! It is written with the simplest but strongest of faiths and with a light and easy heart. Sister Briege's ministry takes her all over the world from Europe to the USA, from Latin America to Korea and points East. She relates in her book stories of healing, from the sublime of extraordinarily miraculous happenings, to the ordinary of the Lord's practicality in commonplace material circumstances. There was one occasion, for example, when a pickpocket in Rome stole Briege's handbag and all her money. The full story is Briege's, of course, and can be read in her book but I can't resist an abbreviated re-telling. A Franciscan priest on pilgrimage to Rome, who had plenty of money with him, found that no-one would take anything from him in payment for various services. Saying Mass one morning, he sensed a strong message to leave his money for Sister Briege McKenna at her hotel. Another friend procured for Briege some additional travellers' cheques in case anything else untoward should happen. And then, quite quickly, the stolen travellers' cheques were refunded by the issuing bank. In all, Briege left Rome with considerably more money than she had when she arrived. A simple story, about a simple issue, but somehow it affected me more than her many stories about truly momentous miracles. Perhaps I find reassurance there that Jesus is constantly providing us with support of all kinds, in ordinary situations of need, of which we often remain unaware. Perhaps I find confirmation, too, of the little miracles I have experienced in my own life, events which, while wondrous to me, do not have on their surface the gloss and immediacy of magic. For what could have been more miraculous than that ineffable, grace-filled epiphany that carried me, in incognitant need, to Father John's confessional? How can I easily explain away the hiatus that preserved me in health until George Johnston could operate on me? How can I forget the sheer amazement on Bill Oreglio's face when he heard that I had survived for twenty-five years after an operation that has an eight-five per cent mortality rate? There will be people, many people, who can easily dismiss these events as natural occurrences. But I have lived through them; I have the sense of what they were. I believe! Others, even in the face of incontrovertible evidence, still cannot bring themselves to believe.

Even in small ways, people, quite devout people, have difficulty in accepting the possibility that the Lord intervenes in our lives in all sorts of different ways. Sean and I have talked a few times about petitionary prayer. We had both noted that people who genuinely pray for a desired outcome react in one of three ways if their request is granted. The first type of response, and probably the least common, is that the petitioner (usually someone who is constantly praying for one favour after another) does not even notice that the request has been granted and thus remains oblivious to God's generosity. Rather more common, but still in the minority, are those who, perceiving the Lord's grace and support, pray in gratitude and thanksgiving. By far the most common response, however, is that of the third group who, noticing that what they sought through desire, human hope and prayer has actually come about, attribute the outcome to natural causes or coincidence. 'Ah well! It would more than likely have happened whether I said that prayer or not.' Somehow the idea that God's hand is touching their lives is beyond their capacity to accept or, perhaps, it raises questions that, subconsciously, they do not want to have to deal with.

There is an incident in Sister Briege McKenna's book that illustrates this capacity for disbelief. (I do not want to infringe Sister Briege's copyright but the story is such a perfect example of what I am talking about that I am sure she will tolerate this literary theft if I confine myself to the bare bones of the episode.)

An Irish priest at a retreat being conducted by Sister Briege told her that it would be so much easier to believe in miracles if he could actually see one. Briege said to him exactly what I would have said myself, 'Father, the Lord uses you every morning to perform a miracle.'

The priest demurred, however, saying that he fully understood transubstantiation but that he would like to see a healing of somebody blind or crippled.

It happened that at the same retreat there was a French priest whose leg was so gangrenous that it was to be amputated. He had elected to attend the retreat before the operation. Inevitably Sister Briege prayed with him and next morning the French priest was running about all over the place, his trouser leg rolled up, gesticulating at his perfectly healthy limb with great excitement. Sister Briege looked at the Irish priest who seemed confused but who said, 'My God, it's awful hard to believe. Did he have gangrene at all?'

Sister Briege points out that the moral of this story is that people who have faith do not need to see – and, it seems to me, she is also saying that even when people whose faith is weak actually witness a miracle, they still cannot bring themselves to believe.

The strange thing for me is that, in spite of almost thirty years of ignoring all that is spiritual in our world, I have read Sister Briege's marvellous stories with total belief and no hint of inner cynicism. More importantly, I kneel each morning at the Consecration and all but leap from my seat to greet Jesus and thank him for his physical presence. In this, the greatest of all miracles, I have total and unwavering belief … a strangely contradictory statement because, as the host is raised, I pray to Jesus with all my heart to help my unbelief, to help me truly believe in this, the most incomprehensible dogma of the church.

My liver is on its last legs and I am probably dying. I know that but I do not seem to have any real awareness of it. I feel normal, quite fit in fact, apart from a few pains, and I am convinced that I have a long life ahead of me. It is not that I am afraid of dying. I just do not think about it; it is not on my agenda.

Something calm in me looks at the idea straight in the face and simply dismisses it. Is this a form of denial ... or is it something else? The rational part of me did not ask for a miracle at Lourdes yet the spiritual part of me seems to be clinging to a belief that a miracle is inevitable. Even as I write, I have to stop and consider what I have just said. It can be interpreted as being extraordinarily complacent. Do I really believe that God is going to intervene in some way to save me from dying ... or am I (and it is a well-known psychological response) truly, albeit unconsciously, in denial? Who knows? The straight truth of the matter is something I will probably know soon enough.

February 2001
Yesterday Father Niall gave me a brochure. It details a list of retreats for men at a new conference centre at Lismullin, a couple of miles south of Navan in Southern Ireland. He had been talking to me earlier about silent retreats and of the spiritual benefits they offer. He is now suggesting that I might be ready to spend a quiet weekend with the Lord. I prayed last night, 'Lord, if I do decide to go on one of these retreats, please let it be because you called and I answered and not because I want to please Father Niall.'

As it turned out I did not have to think very long about it. Sitting in my study, comfortable with Jesus and discussing the matter with him, I found myself very drawn to the idea. I would have time to sit and think, or just sit if I wanted to; to read some of the books I have gathered up; to listen to homilies and meditations that might offer answers to some of the questions that are always buzzing around in my head. As I hear it so often said on American television programmes, 'What's not to like?'

Today I completed the form attached to the brochure, enclosed a deposit of a few euros, and sent it off. I have applied for a three-day weekend retreat in April. Sadie suggested that I ask Sean to go with me for company since, as she pointed out, we are always talking about religion. But I rejected that idea. This is not a reflection of any kind on Sean; it stems simply from the conviction that I would want to spend a weekend like this solely in the company of Jesus.

Today I also booked plane flights to Nice for next July and reserved rooms in hotels we like in Antibes and Menton, two of our favourite towns on the French Riviera. Sadie was a little dubious but her love for France made it easy for me to persuade her that all I needed to do was to pack a few Paracetemol and I would be fine. She literally groaned!

'How many times have I heard that before?' she said, shaking her head.

I pointed out, however, that apart from a few little abdominal pains I have been living a totally normal life for nearly a year.

'Why,' I asked, 'would I suddenly keel over in July, the very month we have booked for our holidays?'

'Knowing you,' she replied, ' that is the very month it is most likely to happen.'

'Not at all,' I argued, 'that would be too much of a coincidence, particularly as it has already happened once. What are the odds against it happening again?'

So life is up and running again – retreat in April, France in July. I am looking forward to both.

April 2001

It is amazing how quickly things can happen if you simply act and do not think too much. I had a call from Sean shortly after I wrote my last entry. He had been able to work a special deal with British Airways for a three week golfing holiday in Portugal – flights, four-star accommodation in the Dom Pedro Golf Hotel, hired car and golf – in one very attractive package. I could not resist. Sadie, on the other hand, was rather less sanguine than I was. She need not have worried. Everything worked out as planned this time and it was great. We had three weeks in glorious sunshine, golfing in shirts and shorts at a time of year when we normally wear heavy trousers, a couple of layers of wool and rain-gear. I can understand now Sean's fascination with golf in Portugal. Superb weather, courses laid out to top professional standards, some of them visually stunning like the Old Course at Villamoura, Villa Sol, Quinta da Lago, and Peninna, the course made famous by the British golfing legend, Henry Cotton, and one at which we watched the Portuguese Open being played this year.

Portugal has more to offer than golf, of course. We will never forget the fabulous cuisine at Madame Pituxa's, at Chico's, and at Don Giovanni's, nor the huge market at Quarteira on Wednesdays. That was an experience, dwarfing anything we had ever seen in France. Everything under the sun was available for purchase, from beautiful linen tablecloths to multi-coloured beach towels, from shoes of all styles and types to leather goods of unimaginable variety. Handbags by Guicci and Hermes and Louis Vuitton, that retail around five-hundred pounds, were replicated to miniscule exactitude, indistinguishable from the originals, and were for sale in their hundreds at five euros each (about three pounds fifty pence). Wrist watches, stall after stall, of the most incredible designs and beauty ... yours for ten euros each.

And so it went on, aisle after aisle of commodities as eye-catching as any I have ever seen. Sadie did not leave empty-handed, of that you can be sure, while I did leave empty-pocketed. For me the most fascinating feature of the day was the group of Bolivian Indians, in their native costume – coloured ponchos, straw stetsons, jet-black hair – playing the most delightful music on wooden pan-pipes, ranging in size from small pipes that could be concealed in their hands to huge pipes that required almost the full stretch of the player's arms to contain them. But what an amazing sound – so musical, so rhythmic, so gloriously melodic! They had a young lady selling CDs of their music and these sold almost as fast as she could collect the money. Needless to say, I, too, was one of her customers.

Sean took us to visit a number of towns on the days we were not playing golf – to Lagos with its narrow, fascinating shopping streets, to the lovely seaside towns of Albufiera and Port-i-mao, and to Sagrés, too, which had been considered by the Portuguese to be the end of the world until Columbus set sail for the Americas. Here we were made to feel puny and ant-like in the face of the huge cliffs that border the ocean, cliffs that reminded me of the giant cliffs at Moher in Galway.

May 2001

The retreat was marvellous – and I have made another new friend. The centre at Lismullin is new and magnificent. Four star

accommodation – bedrooms with en suite facilities, superb cuisine, spacious manicured grounds for walking in, and a beautiful
oratory. The retreat was conducted by Father Martin and what a
delight it was to listen to his meditations. He offered us fascinating insights into the meanings of various gospel stories in clear,
calm and logical tones. Every now and then, after dealing with a
section that might have been a little complicated, he would look
down at us, raise his hands slightly and say, in that soft Irish accent of his, 'Look...!' as if to say, 'this whole thing is so logical
and self-evident that I don't know why I am even bothering to
explain it to you.' But explain it he invariably did, and with a
crystal clarity that made the logic of what he was saying inescapable. There were about twenty-six of us there that weekend but Father Martin assured us that he would find time for individual chats with each of us.

When I went to him for confession he asked me, because of
what I had said – whatever it was – if I would wait a while and
walk with him. I agreed, of course, and later, when we were
strolling in the grounds of the conference centre, he told me that
I was 'far too focused on "the Law".' 'There's something I want
you to read,' he said. 'I'll give it to you in a little while.'

We talked then about my attitude to the Lord and he begged
me not to be treading around on eggshells afraid to offend God.
'He loves you far too much for that sort of carry on,' he said.
'And anyway, you're not half as bad as you think you are. Read
this commentary on St Paul and the Law and God's love and forgiveness and you'll soon see what I mean.'

From the manner in which I have just related what happened,
one might be inclined to assume that Father Martin is a little
abrupt. Nothing could be further from the truth. When Father
Martin offers advice in the spiritual sphere, it is straightforward
and direct. His desire to help, support and encourage is so
strong that he states his perceptions with the forthrightness of
charity. There is nothing other than sincerity and friendship in
his manner.

I have been extremely fortunate in the priests that have been
entering my life during the past few years – Father John, Father
Niall, Father Andrew, the priests in the Newry parish (all relatively young men who are living witnesses to Christ and sub-

lime exemplars of the priestly calling). When I say 'fortunate', I mean 'favoured by God', not in the sense of 'lucky'. Luck has nothing to do with it. (I must digress here for a second. When I wrote 'favoured by God', I suddenly remembered, for the first time in years, that the O'Hare family crest has been hanging on the wall of our hall for the past thirty years. The motto beneath the crest reads 'Favente Deo'. I feel like saying, as I have had occasion so often before in these pages to say, 'Isn't that extraordinary?' But I'll leave it.) Luck, as I was saying, has nothing to do with it. Our dear Lord, in his generosity, has obviously ensured that I am to meet priests whose influence in my life is destined to be inspiring and far-reaching. That doubtless explains why I have seemed to develop an instant rapport with these men of such deep faith and spiritual integrity.

Father Martin has had the same impact on me as the others. He is, however, not quite as young as they are. He is, in fact, more or less my own age. Strong and decisive in the conduct of his priestly duties, he possesses an endearing unpretentiousness, even a hint of shyness, when the circumstances are purely social. By an odd coincidence, he lives in the same residence that I myself lived in during my three years of study at University College, Dublin.

His advice to me, during our first meeting, was inspiring and encouraging. I went to my room and wrote down as much as I could remember of what he said. I have these notes in front of me now and they will be kept in my daily prayer-book as a constant reminder of how I should live my life. (I did read the chapter that he gave me but, to be honest, I can't remember very much about it. Father Martin's own words made a far deeper impression on me than the book's complex discussion on St Paul's views on the law and the spirit.)

'Do not be concerned about your weakness,' he told me, 'or your perceptions of weakness. If you note these things and fight them, they will become strengths. And do not be over-rigidly focused on the Law, on your perceived inability to conform to high ideals. None of us can achieve our spiritual aspirations. Trust in God's help (I hear echoes of Father Niall here), accept your limitations – for that is the essence of Christian humility – and fall, get up, take God's hand, move on, forget about it.'

I was not so sure about 'forgetting about it'. After all, should I not remember and learn from my mistakes? But his next words, with remarkable insight, clarified this point for me.

'Prolonging guilt and remorse beyond a specific event becomes, eventually, a tool for the devil. It is one of his most insidious ploys – it challenges our hope!'

It challenges our hope! What a truly profound observation – so apparently straightforward and yet so demanding of long and earnest meditation. And then, after asking me to pray for the church in these difficult times and for the Holy Father, he took his leave, promising to speak with me again. He had scarcely taken three steps before I found myself looking forward to my next conversation with him.

May 2001

True to his word, Father Martin came to speak to me again. The retreat had been quite intense, filled with reflections, meditations, homilies, benedictions, Stations of the Cross, and other devotional practices. At night, I loved nothing more than to sit in the Oratory, alone with the Blessed Sacrament, often towards midnight. This was easy for me to do since the Oratory was only a few steps from my room. My meditations led me to realise that, despite my attempts to form a real and close relationship with Jesus, there were huge swathes of my normal day when I did not think about him or speak to him. I brought this to Father Martin and he responded immediately by giving me a structure for my day that would ensure regular and consistent contact with Jesus.

'Structure your day deliberately,' he advised me, 'around four things – God and prayer, wife, work, and recreation – and make your whole day a prayer by offering up to God all your activities in these areas.'

He then went on to suggest that I organise my day into a structure that I can cope with and adhere to without falling away from it after the initial flush of enthusiasm. Again I pulled out an envelope and wrote down his ideas as best I could. I have it in front of me.

He suggested that each day should have about nine signposts for God – four large and five small.

The five small signposts he proposed are:

  i. morning offering / prayer to my Guardian Angel;

  ii. the angelus at least once a day;

  iv. a daily visit to the Blessed Sacrament;

  v. three Hail Marys daily (for the world, for Father Martin);

  vi. a three-minute evening examination of conscience (focusing on those areas that I need to improve on; selecting two each evening for meditation; revisiting periodically the areas where I am failing.)

The four large signposts are:

  i. daily Mass;

  ii. daily rosary;

  iii. spiritual reading each day (minimum fifteen minutes – gospels / other spiritual literature);

  iv. evening meditation.

When I took out the list in my room later and looked at it, I immediately thought, 'Oh my God! I think I'll go back to being a pagan again.' But on further reflection I realised that I was more or less doing all of them. There were a couple I was not consistent about, i.e. the daily visit to the Blessed Sacrament (other than Mass), the three-minute examination of conscience, and the daily rosary. I thought, however, that with a little effort and practice I could turn those into daily habits as well. And now that is what I am working on. Hopefully, if I succeed in patterning my day around these signposts, I will not end each day guiltily realising that large chunks of it have passed by without my having once turned my thoughts towards Jesus.

I had brought some spiritual books to the retreat with me, one of which was a fascinating study on the psychology of the characters presented in the parable of the Prodigal Son, a little book of rare insights.[1] Father Martin had used this parable in one of his many meditations and, since I had already read the book, I offered it to him, telling him that I could easily replace it. Sometime after the retreat Father Martin wrote to thank me for the book that he, too, had by then read. This initiated a correspondence that I have entered into with pleasure. I like and ad-

1. Stickler, Gertrude: *Far from the Father*, Marian Press, Stockbridge, Massachusetts, 1986

mire Father Martin and I know that if the correspondence continues, I will not only benefit from a lifetime of spiritual wisdom
but also form a new and rare friendship. I have already written
to him a couple of times – long, rambling, incoherent letters that
probably baffle the poor man. But he will get to know my whims
and vagaries soon enough … I hope!

June 2001
For the people of Newry the date, 23 May 2001 may not carry
any immediate significance but thousands of them will remember the occasion. During the past couple of months the
Reliquary of St Thérèse de Lisieux, a small ornate casket carrying the mortal remains of this revered saint, has been visiting
several countries in Europe. In death she was now enabled to
carry out the missionary work she had been unable to undertake
during her lifetime. Father Andrew, who loves this saint and
was the priest who had introduced me to *Story of a Soul*, told me
last week, with a deal of enthusiasm in his voice, that the relics
were to visit Newry and were to be placed for veneration in the
cathedral for a number of hours on the afternoon of 23 May. He
invited me to be one of the stewards for two of those hours. I
told him I would be delighted, remembering my experiences in
the little chapel at Alençon.

In the days preceding the visit, there was a bustle and a sense
of anticipation among the clergy and faithful of the town. The
priests explained from the pulpit who St Thérèse was, the wonders of her life, and her fame as one of the few women Doctors of
the Church. An hour was devoted, one Sunday evening, to a
ceremony involving a theatrical piece by students from a local
school, a video of the life and times of the saint, and a talk about
her various sayings and prayers many of which had been printed
on little coloured cards for distribution as well as being projected
on to a large screen in front of the altar.

The day came. I was stationed with two or three others at the
back gate of the cathedral which was designated as an entrance
point for the disabled, aged and infirm who could not be expected
to stand in the anticipated queues. This particular duty meant
that I was continuously helping individuals and couples in
through the sacristy and out to the main altar where the

Reliquary was placed. It also meant that I was given several opportunities myself to touch the casket and talk to St Thérèse.

I was caught up in the euphoria along with everyone else but I was totally unprepared for the crowds. During a short break I went to the front of the cathedral. Queues, yards wide, were trailing down through the middle aisle, down the steps in front of the church, and back through the main street, literally as far as the eye could see. It was amazing! Thousands of people, inching slowly towards the casket, hour after hour, some having remained for up to four hours in the main queue before gaining a few precious moments before the Reliquary. As steward, with my little sash, I was empowered to walk in and out as I wished. I passed through the crowds back into the cathedral. I genuflected before the altar and, as I passed by the Reliquary, I paused and said,

'Dear St Thérèse, you know I love you, but something isn't right here. I know, I know … I always seem to be getting at you about something. None of this is your fault. It's wonderful that the presence of your dead bones can bring so many thousands into the cathedral; there are people here whom I have not seen inside a chapel for years. But what are they thinking about, my dear, dear friend? What are they doing? What are they expecting from this visit?'

I left the main chapel, shaking my head and, for some reason, feeling distressed. It was not that I thought, in some kind of arrogance, that many of these people did not know how to pray in front of the casket. It was nothing like that. I suddenly had the realisation, as I genuflected before the altar, that here present in the tabernacle was the living Body and Blood, Soul and Divinity of our dear Lord Jesus and yet the thousands were ignoring him in the venerating of what was essentially a box with a few dead bones in it. Every morning and evening in life, the Lord of heaven and earth, the creator of the universe, the Jesus who walked the shores of Galilee, the Christ who suffered and died for us, makes himself physically available to us in our chapels for a ten or fifteen minute uninterrupted audience, for a communion of extraordinary closeness. Why do we not have these massive crowds every day to greet him? Why are people not knocking down the church walls to reach him?

I went home that evening feeling low. Feeling low because I could see the delight and pleasure in the faces of the priests around the cathedral and I was not sharing in it. Feeling low because I did not experience the same joy before St Thérèse's casket as I did before St Bernadette's. Feeling low because I could not help thinking that something in my attitude was dishonouring St Thérèse.

Next morning at Mass, after I had received communion, I was praying quietly, listening to the ebb and flow of the priest's soft tones as he distributed the hosts: 'Body of Christ ... Body of Christ ... Body of Christ ...' For some reason it caught my attention and I found myself thinking, 'Background noise'. A vague thought, barely articulated, but it generated an immediate and startling response. How can it be background noise? The priest is holding the host in front of each communicant and saying, in the clearest possible terms, 'What I am presenting to you now is the Body and Blood, Soul and Divinity of Our Lord, Jesus. This is not a small wafer; it does not represent Jesus; it is Jesus.' Over and over again, the same message softly spoken to each recipient. Ah, dear God, how many of us truly hear? Father John Cunningham OP, said in a journal article the other day:

> That Christ is truly present in the Blessed Sacrament as he is in heaven should elicit the most profound reverence for the Sacrament of his Body and Blood. However, a lack of understanding of the Eucharist as the Body and Blood of Christ inevitably results in a lack of reverence.

For 'understanding' I suppose I could substitute 'faith'. The Eucharist is an immense mystery and most of us have to rely on faith to accept it. St Thomas Aquinas did try to offer some explanation of the miracle by reference to Aristotle's Theory of Hylomorphism. This is a complex foray into metaphysics. A simplistic explanation might be (and I must point out that I am 'remembering' this from a lecture I heard at university back in the late fifties) that Aristotle postulated that anything that exists can be metaphysically subdivided into 'substance' and 'accidents'. 'Accidents' is a collective noun for the physical attributes of a thing – colour, hardness, weight, shape and so on – that give a 'form', for example 'table', its characteristics and its appearance.

'Accidents' are *physically* inseparable from 'substance' but *metaphysically*, beyond the level of science, 'accidents' and 'substance' *can* be separated. St Thomas used this theory to explain transubstantiation. The substance of bread is changed at the consecration into the substance of Jesus and thus it becomes Jesus even though the 'accidents' remain unchanged. It may look like bread, feel like bread, and taste like bread. But its very 'substance' has changed. It has become the Body and Blood of Jesus. I am drawn to this interpretation because it helps me to understand, and understanding helps my faith. What Father Cunningham asks for, however, is the simple understanding that the host is the Body and Blood of Christ. We do not need to know *how* that can be; we simply need to believe that it *is*. And that is what faith helps us to do.

It is a sad fact that for many Catholics confusion has arisen about the precise nature of this wonderful sacrament. Our pope has more than once pleaded with the body of the Church, particularly some of those caught up in the struggle for ecumenism, not to allow the sacramental and, indeed the sacrificial, truth of the Eucharist to become obscured. In some areas the Eucharist has been reduced to the level of fraternal banquet, a serious breach of sound doctrine and practice. The Second Vatican Council was at pains to eliminate any ambiguity that may exist in the minds of the faithful when it stated, in the clearest of terms,

> For the most holy Eucharist contains the church's entire spiritual wealth: Christ himself ... now made living and life-giving by the Holy Spirit.

In 1968, Pope Paul VI was even more emphatic:

> Every theological explanation ... must firmly maintain that in objective reality ... the bread and wine have ceased to exist after the consecration so that the adorable body and blood of Our Lord Jesus, from that moment on, are really before us under the sacramental species of bread and wine.

Yet so many express doubt; so many come to the altar as a matter of ritual. And I find myself distressed to my very soul, may God forgive me for my judgementalism, when I see so often that gross modern example of disrespect, the chewing of gum *en route* to the altar. I have been perhaps alerted to these signs more

than I might otherwise be, after having read in Mamma
Carmella's messages,[2] of Jesus' own distress at the cold manner
in which he is received by many communicants. I have read, too,
that St Faustina was invariably compelled to pray after communion: 'I want to make up to you, at least in part, for the coldness
of so great a number of souls.'

Her prayer was a response to what Jesus himself had earlier
told her in a vision about the sadness caused to him by people
receiving his sacred Body and Blood in thoughtless, casual and
even sinful fashion. And it is so easy to be casual. All we have to
do is to watch the movement of the other communicants and our
attention is gone, our devotion is gone. I am guilty of it myself
and often I have to bury my head deep in my hands to search for
Jesus, as if in a fog, calling his name until the fog disperses, until
there is the faintest of lights that I can attach myself to.

There is something strangely contradictory about our recep-
tion of the Eucharist. If I was pressed to do it, I could probably
write a detailed analysis of exactly what happens when we receive communion. I could speak eloquently of the extraordinary
gift that the Eucharist is, the vastness of its mystery, the overwhelming fact that the creator of the entire universe, the God we
so often perceive to be distant and untouchable, literally gives
himself to each of us, individually, in a humble little wafer but a
wafer that is, nonetheless, fully and totally his real self. This
great and wonderful God gives himself to me! How mind-shat-
tering is that? Yet somehow these words, which sit so easily in
our intellect, do not penetrate into our spirit. Imagine it! I receive
the Eucharist on my tongue and I try to understand what is happening. I say to myself the very things that I have just written.
And yet, try as I might, I can apprehend with only the faintest of
comprehension. I truly believe that what occurs, each time we
receive the Eucharist, is so momentous that the Lord has to put
some sort of a curtain over our spiritual eyes. If he did not, if we
were allowed to have true and full awareness, we simply could
not cope with it. I read somewhere that if we were ever allowed
to see the full glory of God we would die immediately. I think
something similar applies here. God is, literally, hiding himself

2. Mamma Carmella, *The Messages of Merciful Love*, Divine Mercy
Publications, Dublin, 1991

from our full gaze. But the fact that full comprehension is impossible should never discourage us from seeking that comprehension. We should never allow our inability to grasp this momentous truth to permit us to become habituated to, or even unmoved by, this wondrous gift. We should strive with all our hearts to force ourselves to understand, to remind ourselves over and over about what is happening, to reach out with all our minds to Jesus present in us, to touch him, to make him happy.

These reflections, of course, emanate from my own present stage of development. They contain a certain frantic determination to touch the mystery somehow. I spoke to Joan and Briege about it once. They are contemplative nuns and Joan's response reflects that. She said, 'All we can do is sit in wonder and joy at the mystery of it.'

There is a calmness here but not the calmness of unknowing. It is the calmness of trust, of acceptance, of love. Maybe one day I, too, can aspire to that level of contemplation.

I remember once, a few years ago, listening to a radio discussion. I do not remember the exact composition of the panel but, as I recall, there was a Catholic priest, an Anglican minister, an atheist, and one or two others, no doubt including an agnostic or two. The discussion centred on belief in a real God and the Catholic priest was stoutly defending the dogma of the Real Presence. The atheist said, and I cannot forget his words:

'You Catholics talk a great talk. You maintain that the great God, the creator of the universe, is permanently present in the tabernacles of your churches, yet you saunter casually in and out of the place; you chitter and chatter with your friends in front of the altar. Let me tell you this. If I believed what you profess to believe and entered one of your churches, I would have to crawl up the aisle on my hands and knees, so conscious would I be of the greatness of the One who is present before me.'

I find it extraordinary that an atheist should utter words of such enlightenment when so many of the faithful remain in sad disregard of this sublime truth.

CHAPTER FOURTEEN

The List

July 2001

The past few weeks have been good to me. My health seems to have settled, I have played plenty of golf, and have suffered only minor and occasional pains. Sadie is highly relieved. Our holiday in France begins in two days and she is keeping her fingers crossed that no sudden illness of mine will blight our sojourn on the Riviera. Our two sons, Peter and Brian, with their families, have also rented mobile homes in Antibes where we will be spending the first nine days of our vacation. This prospect makes Sadie happy. Inevitably, as a mother, she is very family-oriented and so, too, are the boys. Oh, I'm happy about it as well! So we are looking forward to our holiday and some enjoyable family get-togethers.

August 2001

Antibes is a lovely old town on the French Riviera and, because of its age, architecture and general lay-out, it is the type of town that Sadie and I deem to be truly French. It is filled with impressive squares (or *places*, as they are called in French), surrounded by tall, imperious French buildings and rows of hundred-year-old trees growing out of the pavements and offering welcome shade to the many tourists. Add the blue sky with its bright sun, the colourful parasols and tables outside the many restaurants, the crowded streets with myriads of little shops and ateliers selling the most unusual wares, the corner areas with cool fountains, little bar-cafés, street artists, performers, balloon-sellers, and you begin to understand how the heart lifts just to be part of it.

We have been here before. One afternoon, a couple of years ago, Sadie and I were wandering around the huge *Grand Marché* that is located under a street-long roof at the upper end of the town. I say, in passing, that this market is incredible. Everything under the sun is available for purchase – vegetables; farm goods of all kinds; fruit; clothes; footware; fish; home utensils; gadgets for preparing food; books; magazines; photographs; posters; sculptures in metal, wire or stone; paintings and art – from the skilled and impressive to the most garish and lurid concoctions imaginable. And the crowds! How anything is sold is beyond me. People are milling in such huge numbers in the narrow pathways between display tables and stalls that movement seems impossible. Yet commerce thrives at January sales pace. Unforgettable!

Sadie and I left the meleé to wander, ever upwards, through the quieter streets of the 'old town', the original Antibes where streets and buildings are two and three hundred years old. The streets are extremely narrow here, the houses very high. We surmised that this might have something to do with shade from the sun. Alone now among these ancient dwellings, we felt were stepping back into history. Little open areas with water pumps lay in the convergences of tiny *rues* that led off in several different directions. To the stranger, these alleyways, all so similar, are a genuine maze. We imagined, with horror, the panic and fear a four-year-old, on holiday and living in one of these little houses, might experience were he to wander unconsciously only a few yards from his front door.

We followed a route, however, that led ever upwards towards the famous Ramparts, arriving at a little street called the *Rue de Haut Castellet*. On one side was a high wall; on the other, a row of the high but very narrow houses so prevalent here. All were not of the same design. Roofs separated and jutted in various patterns. Some houses had small balconies of black iron bars outside their windows. The usual shutters, so much a feature of continental architecture, were there in profusion but instead of the customary green, here there were greys, blues and browns. Sadie was struck by the variety of shapes and sizes of the doors. Some were very tiny, so much so that she suggested at one point that 'the seven dwarves must live here.' Modern plaster crumbled from the walls in places, exposing old mortar-joined stones of various shapes and sizes underneath. Some owners had stripped the plaster away altogether revealing the stone walls in their original state, to our eyes aesthetically much more appealing.

Something of what I have written might easily give an impression of decay and degeneration, even ugliness. Nothing could be further from the truth. Colour was everywhere! The little balconies were festooned with plants and flowerpots; blossoming hanging-baskets hid windows, hid doors, virtually hid the walls. The wall on one side and the houses on the other were enveloped in masses of greenery that bulged two and three feet into the street. A profusion of clinging plants intertwined with the greenery, filling it with a riot of blues, whites, yellows, reds, purples, oranges – Sadie, unlike myself, knows the names of a lot of these plants. I am no horticulturalist (I do not do the gardening at our house. I only mow the lawns). I do know that it was a sight beautiful to behold.

We turned a corner. The wall on our right became a high iron railing through which we could see the orange and ochre roofs of houses, packed together and clinging to the hills as they tumbled, ever downwards. On our left was a huge and impressive house, seemingly crushed into a space too small to hold it. The walls were a jigsaw of irregularly shaped stones, yet surprisingly smooth; a round tower abutted on the left, the whole surmounted by a high flat roof that slanted at a most unusual angle. Windows, eccentrically differing from each other in shape and size, adorned the walls, and a little balcony ran in front of the entrance which, as far as we could discern, was approached by a narrow set of stone steps hewn into the rock upon which the house was built. Tight against the base of the house, and to the left of an incongruously tiled modern driveway, was a mass of huge purple flowers (Don't ask; I have no idea!) partnered on its right by an extraordinary plant. It was a huge green thing with massive fronds as long and as broad as the boards the French use for *faire de la planche-à-voile* (to wind-surf). We discovered some time later that it was a species of giant cactus. The overall impression – the house, its location, its shape, the plants – was one of great originality and beauty. Sadie loved it. She photographed it from several angles and, when we got home, painted it. (My ex-boss saw the painting at a small exhibition. He bought it for the Institute where it now hangs in his office.)

At that time, however, we missed one small but significant detail. This became clear to us when we returned to Antibes last month. We had thought the house was simply someone's private home but on this, our most recent visit, we were looking at postcards outside the various Tabacs and Maisons de la Presse and noticed with surprise that the house featured on many of these cards. This led us to wonder if perhaps it was some kind of public building and we decided to go back and have another look at it. This time we met a man there who was watering the plants. He turned out to be some kind of curator. The house, he told us, had been donated to Antibes by its previous owners as a monument to a famous French poet and writer who had been born and lived close by in a little street that ran off from the right-hand side of the house. He pointed to a section of the wall that housed a plaque that we had missed seeing on our previous visit. It bore the following inscription:

Nikos Kazantzaki
Poète et Ecrivain
(1887-1957)

'Je ne crains rien
Je n'espère rien
Je suis libre'

(Nikos Kazantzaki, Poet and writer: 'I fear nothing; I hope for nothing; I am free.)

Cool, as my grandchildren would say. A wealth of philosophical thought, packed with superb restraint and economy, into three tiny lines. Definitely cool! And, truth to tell, I was assuredly impressed … initially! Not knowing the context, not pondering too deeply on the lines, I thought they looked good, sounded clever, tripped musically off the tongue … echoes of Edith Piaf's 'Je ne regrette rien!'

I wrote the verse on a piece of loose paper I found in my pocket and took it back to the hotel. As I reviewed it later, I felt that the verse was rather less admirable than I had initially assumed. I began to sense an aura of nihilism in the repetition of 'nothing'. I found myself questioning the cost of the freedom that he boasts of with such *élan* in the final line. He fears nothing. He wants nothing. Obviously without the context in which the lines appear, it is difficult to form any real assessment of them.

Nevertheless, the double 'nothing' does provide some clues. Are these 'nothings' absolute? Does he claim to have no fear of man, of authority, of sickness and disease, of loneliness, of poverty, of death, of God? What, truly, does he not fear? What 'nothing' does he hope for? Has he no longer hope for love, for peace, for comfort, for companionship, for intellectual or spiritual sustenance, for eternity? What is the nature of this 'freedom' that he prizes so highly? Can one find in these words the roots of the pseudo-philosophical tendrils that insinuated their way into the psyche of the 'swinging sixties'? Is his 'freedom' the same 'freedom' that gave us flower power, free love, a blossoming drug culture, the self-indulgence of the developing *me* generation? I fear nothing! I hope for nothing! A person without fear, to my mind, is indeed a person without hope. A line from a Kris Kristopherson song from that era puts the 'liberation' or perhaps the 'liberality' of the sixties into perspective: 'Freedom's just another word for nothing left to lose.' Bottom of the heap! Ground zero! The gutter! When you are at rock bottom, emotionally, spiritually, materially, you cannot lose any more, hurt yourself any worse. No-one scrutinises your actions, listens to or criticises your words, considers your feelings to be of any relevance. Nothing you do matters, so you are free to do anything you please, think what you like. The lines of another morbid song from that era touch my memory. I believe the song was the theme for a television programme, MASH:

> *Suicide is painless,*
> *It brings on many changes*
> *And I can take or leave it if I please …*

Horrific in its sad lostness!

Poor Kazantzaki! Without any knowledge at all of the context of his writing, I am tearing his philosophy to pieces. It may well be that he is speaking from that level of spirit, that independence from the material, sought so diligently by Buddhists, Tibetan monks, and Chinese Shaolin priests. I know nothing about their philosophy other than it seems to involve a kind of inward navel-gazing that seeks communion with the essence of things. I recall reading once about an Indian fakir on board an aeroplane who was being racially abused by three drunken louts. They criticised his beard, his robe, his sandaled feet. The fakir stared straight ahead, unflinching, unresponsive. At the end of the flight one of the stewardesses spoke to the fakir, apologising for the behaviour of the rude passengers and complimenting his imperturbability. The fakir turned his calm gaze on her. 'Am I concerned about the thoughts of the ants that scurry beneath my feet?'

His ability to move into himself had removed him from any concern about, fear of, or need for anything the world has to offer.

Yet, as a Catholic in knowledge of the nature of love, I have to wonder about this. It is still for me an empty kind of freedom, a freedom without love, without dependence on neighbour and, seemingly, without dependence on God. It is a lonely, solitary, inward-living existence that does not echo the vibrant sharing of the committed Christian.

Freedom is such a vital concept, abused in so many ways – abused by radicals who hate their government; abused by nationalists who use it to murder, maim and destroy; abused by all who do not want to obey. Freedom, in our world of unbalanced values, has become costly. Our children are given freedom to build self-esteem at the cost of discipline; freedom to govern is won through abuse of power; freedom of expression has polluted the air with profanity and the airwaves with pornography; the freedom of the 'enlightened' has cost us the values of the civilised.

When I think of the words 'free' and 'freedom' as used in the New Testament, I find in them no relationship to the 'liberation' so beloved of today's radical thinkers, to the 'liberal' views so mindlessly espoused by modern youth. The New Testament refers so often to our goal 'to live in freedom and in peace'; St James speaks of 'the perfect law of freedom'; St Paul tells the Romans that 'creation itself will be set free from its bondage to decay'. Am I free? If I fear something ... poverty, loss, death ... am I no longer free? If I live in hope and anticipation ... of a love to be fulfilled, of a new birth, of forgiveness, of happiness, of a glorious eternity ... am I no longer free? Is one free if one is able to live a life of self-indulgence, pursuing and participating in pleasures of every kind, licit and illicit, without moral constraint? Is this freedom? Or enslavement? I remember one of my professors at UCD defining free will as 'the power to say "no"!' Animals do not have that power, he said, only humans. But the power to say 'no' is the very essence of self-discipline, of restraint, of moderation, words that do not even appear in the dictionary of the 'liberal'. Nonetheless, it is this control over one's actions, this power of choice, that is the only true freedom. The person who can deny himself the urges of the flesh, the lure of ego, the betrayal of the spirit, is the person who is truly free. He is not controlled by his passions; he is in control. I long to be such a person; I strive to be such a person; it is not easy to be such a person. Basil Hume touches on this thought, warning us to

> ... *have no illusions about ourselves or about the world in which we live. We have to engage daily in the struggle against selfishness and sin within our very selves. That is a relentless warfare.*

Maybe it is but, thank God, we do not have to battle alone. If we did, we would never be free.

> *I fear nothing;*
> *I hope for nothing;*
> *I am free.*

Cool, it ain't!

August 2000

We spent about nine days in Antibes, enjoying the company of the boys and their families, occasionally enjoying, too, evening family barbeques under the tall, shady trees outside their mobile homes. Our last night at Antibes was special. As we left the cathedral after evening Mass, Sadie noticed a couple of lorries packed with chairs.

'There must be a concert tonight,' she said.

It has happened before. There is a lovely old cobbled square directly in front of the cathedral, bordered on one side by some buildings and on the other by a high wall edged with iron railings. Beside the steps which lead to this upper area is a huge tree which towers above the square and shades most of it. The square eases downwards from the cathedral to the *Grand Marché* below.

As always, we had reserved a table at the *Aubergine* for our last meal in Antibes, a small family-run restaurant that only seats about thirty people but which, despite the plethora of eating places in the town, is invariably full. It is impossible to have a meal there without a reservation, so delicately French, light and delicious is the cuisine. Maybe, as an aspiring Christian, I should enthuse less about a pleasure of the flesh but the good Lord gave some people great skills for others to appreciate and enjoy. The skills of the chef at the *Aubergine* are truly God-given; to ignore them would have been un-Christian. We actually ate there quite often and the chef's wife, who 'rules' (there is no other word for it) the front of house, now recognises us as honoured guests, greets us with handshakes and two *bises* (those French air kisses that are planted a couple of inches from each cheek) and leads us with ceremony and grace to our table.

A languid two hours after we left the cathedral we returned to the *Place de L'Eglise*. Chairs had indeed been set out in rows in front of the church and a large orchestra, some twenty-five instrumentalists, were settling themselves on seats on the church steps. I was glad of this opportunity to sit. Usually after our meal we walk for a couple of hours around the busy streets, particularly those near the marina with their many stalls, street performers, artists and artisans, mummers and mimers. Sometimes we go to the marina, at one end of which are moored the huge ocean-going yachts of millionaire Arabs and wealthy tourists, yachts like the *Ivana Trump* that look for all the world like floating hotels. Sadie and I used to speculate about what life on one of these luxurious vessels would be like but we honestly could not see how such wealth and opulence would allow the happiness of an ordinary life. Too much, accessed too easily, without the anticipation and sacrifice that makes so much of what we strive for valuable and appreciated – the bedrock of normal existence eliminated by wealth. What effect must that have on the psyche, and even more, on the spirit? Not for us! Trite, I know, but truly, we love our lives the way they are.

Anyway! I said I was glad of the seat because I had been noticing over the previous few evenings that our post-prandial strolls were becoming, for me, increasingly demanding. I seemed to grow weary very easily and, though I said nothing at the time to Sadie, I was beginning to suspect that something might be amiss.

The concert was great. The conductor, typically French in attitude and manner, unwittingly provided us with some gentle amusement. Prior to the opening piece, he strutted importantly among the members of the orchestra, adjusting, fiddling, consulting, with the utmost seriousness. He eventually walked to his podium and, before stepping up, lifted a page or two of music, studied them with pursed lips and with such exaggerated care that I began to suspect he had never seen them before in his life. He finally stepped on to the podium, bowed grandly to the audience (who were not only in the chairs before the cathedral but were lined also along the railings of the upper area) and, turning his back to us, arms widespread, raised his hands aloft, baton quivering. He held this statuesque position for about ten seconds and then, with a wonderful sweep of his arms, led the orchestra into the rousing 'Entrance of the Gladiators.'

Hung on the walls on either side of us were some arc lamps that were there to light up the cathedral at night. It is customary in these towns for important landmarks to be lit up after dusk but tonight the lamps had the additional duty of lighting up the orchestra. When we sat down in the balmy Riviera evening air, the sky was a pure blue. There was not a wisp of cloud. The lights were on but were having little impact. Twilight here, however, falls quickly. During a roistering rendition of 'España', I noticed the sky turn from royal blue to deep blue and then to navy blue. As if inspired by the music, the façade of the cathedral (relatively straight walls with a triangular area on top, surmounted by a large granite cross) lit up, preened its brightening ochres, creams, and whites, and etched itself ever more starkly, in impressive three-dimensional sharpness, against a sky that was rapidly becoming inky-black. Magnificent! And, as I said, a lovely way to spend our last evening at Antibes.

August 2000
Next morning we packed, paid our bill and moved on to Menton, probably our favourite holiday destination on the Riviera. It is situated just south of the Italian border, has a magnificent coastline that nestles tight against a mountain landscape, dotted with trees, houses, gorges and bridges. The town itself is dominated by a splendid seventeenth century church –

the Church of St Michael the Archangel – that stands in the heart of the old town and towers over it. The three steeples, rounded in shape, are superb examples of the baroque art of that century. To reach it we had to walk up many stone steps through steep narrow streets, a substantial climb but worth the effort. From between tall buildings on the heights, the views of the bay and the Mediterranean coast with their extraordinary blues and colours, are glorious.

The cathedral itself is also most impressive. It is laid out in a basilical plan with three naves and there are, perhaps, twelve minor altars, or chapels as they are referred to, consecrated with impressive and colourful statuary to such devotional objectives as Our Lady of Graces, The Sacred Heart, St Joseph, the Souls in Purgatory and a number of others.

Our twelve days in Menton were somewhat marred by the inexplicable evening malady that persisted throughout the rest of the holiday. I was fine during the day. We still enjoyed wandering through Menton in the mornings, relishing the ambience, purchasing the provisions we needed for our lunch – usually baguettes, French cheeses, tomatoes, and making the inevitable visit to one of the many local patisseries for our daily ration of those delectable French pastries which quite simply cannot be replicated in Ireland, or anywhere else in the world for that matter. I still enjoyed our afternoons on the beach, swimming, sunbathing, and reading under a large parasol. Evening Mass was never a problem nor was dining at one of the few superb small restaurants we discovered hidden away from the main concentration of tourists.

I would barely have walked two hundred yards after dinner, however, when I would be struck with sudden and complete exhaustion. I felt no pain; I was not sick in any way. My batteries would simply drain totally flat. Inevitably I reached a stage when I had to return to the hotel room each evening immediately after dinner. Sadie was forced to take her evening walks alone; I was forced to let her. I could do nothing else.

Our last night at Menton was just as memorable as our last night at Antibes but for entirely different reasons. Nights in southern France, as I have already pointed out, are balmy and warm. A light sheet on the bed is sufficient cover. That night, however, I began to feel cold. I began to shiver and Sadie dug a couple of blankets out of the wardrobe. She laid these on top of me. I continued to shiver so she also piled on top of me the two coverlets that dress our beds during the day. I burrowed into these but could not get warm. The shivering got worse; my body was shaking with terrible tremors. Suddenly I recognised what was happening. I had experienced these shakes before – back in 1972 and in 1974 when I was having serious liver problems.

'I think it's a rigor,' I said to Sadie through clenched teeth as I struggled to abate the shivering.

'Oh sweet Lord! Do you think it's the liver again?'

'Yes.'

A pause. Then Sadie said,

'OK. We'll make an appointment with Mr Diamond as soon as we get home. Thank God it has only happened on our last day.'

I shook uncontrollably long into the night, the tremors and Sadie's concern keeping both of us awake. At some point, however, I drifted into sleep.

The strange thing is, I was absolutely fine the next morning. I easily shook off the gloom of the previous evening, ate a cheerful breakfast, packed without effort and carried our cases to the *Arrêt Place d'Armes* across the road from the hotel, where the airport bus was due at 8.30 am. Even at that early hour the sky was bright blue, the sun very hot. All we needed to wear were light shirts and shorts.

The bus was one of those huge, whispering monsters often found in the south of France. We sat high, in air-conditioned comfort, anticipating as always the visual delight that is the Mediterranean coastline. Nowhere in the world, especially when the sun is its usual sparkling self, is scenery so impressive, and nowhere are the words of the Jesuit poet, Gerard Manley Hopkins, more apropos:

The world is charged with the grandeur of God.

From this coastal road, which wounds, twisting and turning, up into the very mountainside, we were offered superlative views of the cliffs that spill down almost into the sea. Huge blue-grey snow-capped mountains, far in the distance, climb tall and proud into the azure sky. Below us, on the left, we could see the sheer falls to rocky shores and, occasionally, small inlets where the little beaches were already dotted with morning bathers and multi-coloured umbrellas.

We drove past the lovely coastal resorts of *Roquebrune, Cap Martin, Beaulieu-sur-Mer,* and soon, across the bay, we were able to see Monaco rising out of the edge of the sea, with thousands of glinting windows towering into that remarkable southern sky. Sometimes on our right (the side we were driving on) the mountain, a huge rocky uneven wall, encroached to the very side of the road, a road so narrow that it seemed impossible even for a bicycle to pass on the other side of the bus. Yet the French drivers tore around the bends and past us with fearless panache. (If I had been behind the wheel myself, I might have been more inclined to describe their driving as reckless insanity.)

As we constantly turned new corners, we saw little villages, the inevitable mass of pinks, browns and ochres, packed and squeezed into the mountainside as if tossed there in random heaps by a giant hand, lying where they fell with no discernable order or pattern. Some of the grander houses were perched on the edges of huge high promontories, seeming almost ready to spill over in breathtaking defiance of gravity.

We glided through the packed streets of glitzy Monte Carlo with our usual neck-craning and pointing, unfailingly impressed by the glorious profusion of coloured flowerbeds that spill down towards the famed Casino and impressed, too, in spite of ourselves, by the huge ocean-going yachts that float haughtily in the elegant marina.

We finally arrived at the airport, just outside Nice. The plane took off more or less on time. The air-conditioning came on and, shortly after take-off, I began to feel cold. Sadie asked the stewardess for a blanket, normally not a problem. But this time, unfortunately, no blankets had been stored on board. I was still in my light shirt and shorts having foolishly neglected to dig a sweater out of my luggage. The shivering started again and soon became a full-blown rigor. It was horrendous! Sadie put her arms around me and I leaned as close to her as I could in that awkward aeroplane seat, trying to absorb some of her body's heat. The tremors were fierce, sustained, and continued unabated until we reached Heathrow. It was agony for me and it must have been equally bad for Sadie.

At Heathrow we went straight into one of the airport stores and bought a tracksuit which I pulled on over what I was already wearing. (Our baggage was being ferried straight on to Dublin so we had no access to it during this stop.) Two cups of hot tea later, the shaking began to subside. By the time we boarded the connecting plane to Dublin I was fine again and this leg of the journey proved uneventful. I was comfortable, if somewhat apprehensive, in my new tracksuit. I was also a little depressed. What did all of this portend? I could not shake off the feeling that I was running out of time, that George's miraculous achievement in holding my liver degradation in abeyance for so long had now run its course.

That night, when Sadie had gone to bed, I went into the study and had a serious conversation with Jesus about what was going on. I broached as many possible eventualities as I could conceive and tried to consider the kinds of help from him that I might need. When I spoke before with Father Niall about God's will, it tended to be from the viewpoint of analysing my life and attempting to find ways to a do his will in some form of service. As my conversations with Jesus that night progressed, I became conscious of a shift in perspective. I began to realise that the notion of acceptance of God's will was as much a part of being a Christian as searching for ways to actively execute it. At one point I touched on the subject of death but, looking back now at the neutral manner in which I raised the topic and how truly unmoved I was by the prospect, I can see that I did not consider dying a very real possibility. What interested me more at that point was the nature of any future prayers I should be saying. Should I ask for miracles or simply support? I remember saying at one point, 'Lord Jesus, dear friend. If it is your will that my liver should now be permitted to degrade, am I allowed to ask you to change your mind? I know we have talked about this before but the same questions keep buzzing around in my brain and, anyway, I can't remember what you said. You did say, "Ask and you shall receive." But I have seen enough good Christians 'storm heaven' without receiving the answer they hoped for. You yourself asked your Father at Gethsemene to change his mind but I think we both understand that you knew this was never going to happen. But the same questions recur, dear Lord. Over and over I ask, "How do I pray?' Do I say, "Dear Jesus, please heal me"? ... a raw request, and I can see nothing in my life that justifies my making such a request. Do I say, "Dear Jesus, what is your will in this? Help me to deal with it."?'

It is an odd thing, although for me it has long ceased to be odd, but sometimes when I ask Jesus a question he encourages me to poke through the pages of some of the spiritual books on my study shelves. This happens so often that it has become the most natural thing in the world. I ask the question, talk about it for a little while, and then we sit in companionable silence. After a time I feel the urge to lift a book. On this occasion I thumbed briefly through Basil Hume's *To be a Pilgrim*. Nothing jumped out at me. If I do not see it almost immediately, I know the answer is not going to be there. I picked up *On Song with God* by Vincent Travers. In less than three seconds I was reading the following:

> *We follow a crucified leader. So the question is not, 'Am I going to be crucified?' but rather, 'How am I going to deal with the daily crucifixions which are the making of a disciple of Jesus?'*

How indeed? Obviously, until the end of my prayer, I was asking the wrong questions. Much food for thought here. I can see that these lines point the way I have to go but how do I actually proceed? This is clearly a question for Father Niall.

October 2001

It was very few weeks later, sometime in early August, that Sadie and I found ourselves once more gazing at X-rays on the wall of Mr Diamond's office. This time his demeanour was rather more serious.

'The disease has progressed faster than I thought it would. Your liver is now less than two-thirds normal size and very scarred. Look here ...', he pointed to a large fuzzy vein leading into the liver. '... your blood should flow down this Portal vein through the liver and out here. But the scar tissue has become too compact. See here ... the blood has had to find little veins and tracks around the outside of the liver and make its way around and under the liver to rejoin the Portal vein ... here!'

'Not good?' I hazarded.

'Not good,' he replied, with a shake of his head.

'So what now?

'I'm going to have to contact my friend in the Edinburgh Royal Infirmary to see if I can get you into their assessment programme with a view to possible transplantation.'

'Assessment?'

'Yes! It usually takes a week. Everything is tested – heart, lungs, kidneys, pancreas, blood, muscle wastage … little biopsies are done for matching purposes. There are some other things, psychological compatibility … that kind of thing. These guys are good … and they're very thorough.'

I thought for a while.

'Assessment to me, a schoolteacher, has connotations of "pass" and "fail". I take it that progression to the transplant list isn't automatic?'

'No! Health and fitness for operation comes into it. There is also the possibility that transplantation might not be the answer in your case. And then there is the age factor.'

'Age?'

'Yes! You're sixty-four. I believe heart transplantation stops around sixty. But don't worry about that just now. *[No problem, Tom! Of course I won't!]* I'm not sure whether they have an age limit in Edinburgh on liver transplants. I'll talk to them anyway. In the meantime, I'll try to get you on to their assessment programme as soon as possible.'

And thus I arrived at the Scottish Liver Transplant Unit (in the Royal Infirmary, Edinburgh) during the second week of September, the most abiding memory of which is of lying in bed watching the television in horror as the minions of Bin Laden blew the great twin towers in New York to pieces.

I have other memories, of course. Tom Diamond was right. These 'guys' were thorough – almost to the point of obsession. There were indeed X-rays … and machines for testing respiration; ultra-sound scans; endoscopy; echocardiograms. ECG; dental assessment for signs of tooth infection or decay; nose, throat and ear testing; biopsies, as predicted; energy assessment and muscle wastage measurements (I had been losing a deal of weight since those rigors in France.) Then there were visits from physicians, psycho-therapists, as well as dieticians, social work-ers, chaplains, pharmacists, young doctors seeking my permis-sion to research, take readings, and analyse results of particular operative techniques should I be placed on the transplant list.

It was not, however, as bad as it sounds. To begin with, I had a private room, a reasonably accurate timetable of assessment events, and permission to go for walks into Edinburgh with Sadie (who had come over with me for the week) during the quiet times. We were both naturally a little anxious at this time because, since I left France, my health had definitely been deteri-orating. I had lost something in the region of twenty-five pounds – down from my normal weight of eleven and a half stones to just under ten stones. I was suffering permanently from fatigue now which meant that our walks were inevitably short and trips into town meant finding buses and taxis. Nonetheless, we were heartened to hear that my heart and lungs were sound (the advantages of being a non-smoker) and that my condition, poor though it was, was much better than normal for a person whose liver was in the chronic state mine was in.

'Chronic state' can be defined by reference to a conversation I had with one of the principal medical (as opposed to surgical) men who were involved in my case. One morning during a fairly lengthy examination by this doctor whom I was getting to know quite well, I asked,

'Just how badly is my liver diseased?'

He was writing something in my files and, almost absently, he murmured as he continued to write,

'Pretty bad! Our best guess is that if you were to go on as you are, you have about fifteen months left to live.'

'Oh! That long?' I said, somewhat facetiously. I mean, what else was there to say? He laughed. Looking back, that seems quite odd. We're discussing my imminent demise and the mood is essentially humorous. I went on, 'Looks like I might get on the list then?'

'I can't say for sure at this point and, anyway, the decision is not mine to make. But you are a good candidate for a transplant. You're still quite strong; there's no sign of any cancer or threats of other organ failure. If you get on the list and get a new liver in time, the prognosis is good.'

Of course! I didn't ask what the prognosis would be if I did not get on the list. Instead I asked,

'What is the normal waiting period?'

He shrugged. 'How long is a piece of string? Some people get a match inside a month; some people wait for over a year. I remember one time we had just sent a man home after his assessment week and had to phone him at the airport about an hour-and-a-half later. A match had turned up in the intervening period. It's really luck of the draw.'

Among the various intentions of the assessment procedure is the added purpose of providing the patient and his family with full information about the transplant process. I had many callers – medical, nursing, psychiatric, and so on – filling my head with more information than I could absorb. A Transplant Co-ordinator, Maureen, a very caring and kind lady, took me through the whole process – pre-op, operation, post-operative care – and brought me to the Transplant Unit to introduce me to the Intensive Care Room, the High Dependency Room and the main recovery wards. It was all very civil … and it scared the living daylights out of me! All that machinery, all those poor patients with wires and tubes sticking out of them everywhere, nurses with masks speaking in hushed whispers. I would have been better not to have witnessed any of it.

I was given a thick blue folder, a book really, with beautifully printed pages, well laid-out sections, sharply focused colour photographs, detailing the entire process. It was entitled: 'Liver Transplant – Your Questions Answered.' It included a section on an area we had already discussed with the Co-ordinator: 'Complications.' I was talking to a consultant the day after I had been presented with this tome.

'I have read every Stephen King novel ever written, ' I said, 'and none of them has lifted the hair on my head the way this blue book has. It's horrific!'

'Don't worry,' he smiled. 'We are obliged to inform patients of every possible complication. It's this litigious age we live in. If something happens to a patient that we haven't prepared him for, it could cost us more than we can afford to pay. But most people would experience very few, if any, of these complications.'

Still, it is not easy to sit and read about possible internal bleeding, lung problems, long-term kidney damage, acute rejection, recurring liver disease, osteoporosis, heaven knows what else, and remain unaffected.

The normal pattern at the end of the assessment week is for all involved medical and surgical personnel to have a meeting on the Friday morning about the case. Afterwards, sometime in the afternoon, the senior medical officer comes to the patient to relay the decision. Sadie and I prayed that whatever God's will for me was, we would try to accept it. Apart from that one fairly positive comment about my being a good candidate for transplant, the team had been consistently non-committal throughout the entire week and, thus, at 3.00 pm on that Friday afternoon, despite our prayers, I was on tenterhooks.

The senior medical officer arrived, pulled the curtains around my bed, and sat on it beside me. I sensed right away that the news was not going to be good. I was right ... but it wasn't all bad. The short version is that they wanted me to spend the next month monitoring and recording specific aspects of my condition – fatigue, nausea, itch, food consumption, daily activities, and a series of other measurable conditions. I was to design some sort of graphic pro-forma and record daily progress and changes in the designated areas. I was to come back at the end of the month and they would review my case.

In the list above I mentioned 'itch'. This was a huge torment to me in 1972 and again in 1974 and is now becoming equally huge in 2001. I cannot understand why I did not mention it when I was reviewing my experiences in the seventies because it is one of the symptoms that Sadie and my family remember most of my previous illnesses. And now it is back ... and it is a terrible affliction. Something in the blood causes the skin to itch fearsomely and non-stop throughout the day and the night. And, bad as that is, there are certain varieties of the itch that cannot be eased by scratching. One particular type occurs just below the skin and no amount of scratching can reach it. Worse, it moves to another area the minute the sufferer begins to scratch, thus initiating an excruciatingly frustrating game of hide and seek that never seems to end and in which the itch is invariably the winner. I have been reduced to tears at night with it, as have a number of the other patients we met at the Transplant Unit. It has been the subject of numerous articles in medical and support journals but there is no really successful medication that can ease it. We are advised to take a foul-tasting powder three times a day mixed with water, milk or some other liquid. I tried squeezing a couple of fresh oranges into it but I am hopeless at taking medicine and had to abandon the effort. In any event, it does not really work.

And so here I am again, consigned to a separate bedroom because the scratching goes on all night and it would be impossible for Sadie to sleep with that. How could I have forgotten those awful months of scratching in 1974? Perhaps it was so horrific that I simply blanked it out of my mind. I have a tendency, anyway, to dismiss things from my mind once I am finished with them. I do, however, remember an elderly lady in the Female Liver Ward at the Royal in 1974 who had to have velvet gloves tied to her hands by the nurses because she had virtually torn her skin to pieces and she was constantly covered with freshly bleeding sores. I am not at that stage at the moment but it is bad enough as it is, believe me.

How am I dealing with this 'daily crucifixion which is [or should be] the making of a disciple of Jesus'? Very badly, I am afraid. I am trying constantly to offer the distress to Jesus for sinners but, just as on that beach in France, I am experiencing that same inability to suffer with any kind of stoicism. I keep thinking that this diminishes the value of the offering and my most common prayer is not, 'Lord, I will suffer this torture for you!' but 'Lord, is there not something you can do to take this awful itch away?' There is, however, a further prayer, and all that I am capable of offering at the moment. 'Lord, I am sorry that I cannot gladly accept this suffering for your sake. Is there any chance that you can accept the suffering itself as a second-rate or, perhaps, a third-rate offering, even if I do not welcome it as the saints did?'

November 2001
In spite if everything that has happened during the past couple of years, I have somehow managed to remain detached from the reality of it. I have, I suppose, suffered a bit but psychologically I

have been tending to view events as if they were happening to another person. I am fine; this other person isn't so good. Lately, however, that defence mechanism is faltering. It is I who am ill; it is I who has the seriously diseased liver; it is I who has only fourteen months to live.

How do I feel about it now? I am not sure! Obviously I have to hope that I will be put on the transplant list and then I will have grounds for optimism again, even if I have to endure for a while the physical disintegration of a body that is, literally, dying. I am recording daily the measurements I was asked for. I have designed a quite-fetching grid with the days of the month across the top and the various symptoms down the left-hand side. Each square is divided into top, middle and bottom sections, into one of which I place a black dot each day (probably the same 'black dot' that Blind Pew handled in Robert Louis Stevenson's *Treasure Island*). The black dots indicate how I am doing with each of the symptoms – well, moderately, or poorly – on each specific day. The great majority of the black dots, sadly, are in the bottom sections.

My sisters, Briege and Joan, who currently live in a small convent house in Monasterevin, near Kildare, were recently in Newry on business of some kind. They came to visit and, despite their best efforts to remain poker-faced, I could see they were shocked by my appearance. I have lost yet more weight, my cheeks are sunken, my eyes are dark hollows, my hands and wrists are claw-like, and my overall skin colour is a greeny-yellow. Norman Bowden, with rather more candour than diplomacy, told me he would not like curtains that colour in his house. Hardly prepossessing then, and my sisters' initial reaction neither surprised nor disturbed me.

I have had a couple of phone calls from them since, especially from Joan since Briege is yet again lecturing in Europe … Rome, I think. Joan tells me that 'this is a period of great grace.' She says, 'You are so loved. God has laid his hand on you.' I made suitable agreeing noises into the phone but I am not altogether sure that I perceive my situation in quite the same light as Joan. Ah, that's a bit facetious! I am not altogether dismissing the idea. I will definitely talk to Jesus about it and try to see my circumstances in that light.

Joan had one piece of interesting news for me. I had told her during a previous call that I was experiencing constant and severe abdominal pain. In her call tonight she told me that they had been in touch with Sister Briege McKenna who was not only praying for me but would also be calling into the Newry convent for an overnight stay *en route* from Derry to Dublin Airport. They have arranged for me to have a special visit with her tomorrow which will be easy for me since the convent is barely a three minute walk from my doorstep. Obviously I am very excited at the prospect of meeting her, especially when I have been talking about her in these pages only a few … Goodness! Is it really a year ago? I do not know what to expect but I cannot help feeling it will be a significant.

November 2001

Sister Briege was nothing like what I had expected. Given her reputation and fame, I anticipated a meeting with a serious ascetic, a person of almost ethereal reserve … kind and gentle, of course, but a being into whose presence I would enter quietly and tread lightly. Instead, I found a fresh-faced, jolly, down-to-earth, good-humoured nun who put me instantly at my ease and with whom I found myself in deep and earnest conversation within five minutes of meeting her. There was even a lightness and laughter in the conversation and early on I was given a clue to the touch of impish humour that lies just below the surface. In order to avoid anything rushed later on, I produced her book *Miracles Do Happen* shortly after my arrival and asked her if she would sign it for me. 'Of course! No bother.' And she wrote:

> *With my best wishes to you, Brian, and may God's blessings be upon you always.*
>
> Sr Briege (OSC)

Nothing very humorous in that you might think, but when I looked at it later I discovered that the O of OSC (Order of Saint Clare) was written like this: ☺

Joan had earlier explained to me that visits like these tended to follow, more or less, a specific pattern. There would be pleasant introductory conversation, tending eventually to issues spiritual and, at some point, Sr Briege would rise and prepare to pray over the visitor. These prayers, Joan told me, would invariably lead to visions which Sr Briege would recount exactly as she saw them, with no attempt to explain or interpret them. Sr Briege and I did chat about spiritual things, about the rosary, about prayer, about a relationship with Jesus, and I was prepared when she rose from her seat and said, matter-of-factly, 'I am going to pray over you now.'

I made to rise but Sr Briege motioned me to remain in my chair. She stood behind me and, resting her hands on my head, began to pray. I do not remember all of what she said but one part of the prayer remains clear in my mind:

And, Lord Jesus, if it is your will, and we pray that it is, please heal Brian of this serious illness, whether by your own deliberate intervention, or natural healing, or by the skills of a surgeon. Bring him back to full health so that he may live in strength to love and serve you.

She paused a little while and then she said, 'I am beginning to see a vision, Brian.'

Another short pause and then,

'I am in a huge building ... a mansion, I think or ... maybe a museum. I see a long corridor. I am walking down this corridor. I see a large picture nearby on a wall. I am going to look at it. It is a picture of a stormy sea ... the waves are huge ... there is a small boat being tossed about on the waves. There are people in the boat ... they might be apostles or saints, I don't know ... you are among them ... terrified ... Jesus is in a corner of the picture ... very small. I am walking on further down the corridor. I see another picture ... it is the boat again ... but this time it is very small ... the picture is full of Jesus.'

She paused again and then said, 'You are to read Romans 8 and John 14.'

Yet another pause. 'St Joseph is very interested in your life ... has been for a long time ...' Then, 'Drink a small sip of Lourdes' water every day and pray.'

Sister Briege made one final observation that I can scarcely bring myself to report, partly because it is so incomprehensible to me and partly because I am now beginning to wonder if I actually heard her say it. I'll write it anyway!

'Jesus has something special in mind for you beyond any-thing you can possibly imagine.'

There! I have said it. I am just going to leave it hanging in the air. I could not possibly even begin to interpret it. I will write my diary with all the truth I can muster. If anything in my life is re-flective of this prediction, it may well appear in these pages, even if I myself do not recognise it.

The other statements, I believe, require little explanation. Thirty years of stormy seas followed by a life full of Jesus. I am so moved and pleased by this vision. I read Romans 8, and the opening lines appear to echo the second picture and confirm the forgiveness I have received:

Therefore, there is now no condemnation for those who are in Christ Jesus ...

and, seemingly significant as well, is Verse 18:

I consider that our present sufferings are not worth comparing with the glory that will be revealed in us.

I have meditated a little on these words and I am finding great consolation in them despite the fact that since my visit with Breige, my pains have increased in intensity to such an extent that I am virtually bent double with them. I told Joan on the phone yesterday – I hope she knew I was not serious – that I did not want her organising any more visits with Sr Briege, that I didn't think I would be able to cope with the additional suffer-ing. No immediate miracles, then. But I am not surprised or dis-appointed. I have the sense that whatever way God intends to work with me, it will not involve a simple and immediate wave of a magic wand. I rather figure that I am in this for the long haul, wherever it may lead. Right now I am simply trying to deal with the pain one day at a time. Verse 28 of Romans also gives me great comfort ... and much to think about:

And we know that in all things God works for the good of those who love him, who have been called according to his purpose.

John 14, opening verse, echoes this: 'Do not let you hearts be troubled. Trust in God; trust also in me.'

But this time I experience no discomfort or puzzlement. This time I savour the words and hold them in my heart.

My mother loved St Joseph. She died in 1960. I am certain

that she has co-opted the dear man into the difficult task of chan-
nelling my life back to Jesus. I have spoken at length to St
Joseph. He will be my guide and support from now on and I will
love him as my mother did … does!

I left Sr Briege some forty-five minutes after I arrived and I
knew, on leaving, that I had made another life-long friend, irrespective of contact. Just this morning I received a small package
from Italy (Sr Briege gets about!). It contained some books, a
rosary, and a small but beautifully designed broach of Padre
Pio, containing within it a significant relic. It came also with the
message that Sr Briege 'got this specially' for me. It has joined
Sadie's medal on my neck and there it will remain. As I said, I
have made another wonderful friend.

November 2001

This morning a man came to me after Mass and handed me an
envelope containing five hundred pounds. I had absolutely no
legal claim on it although an argument might objectively be
made that I had some entitlement to it. I demurred, however,
and tried to hand it back. But the man, Michael McAllister, tour
guide and owner of Marian Tours, insisted that I take it.

Last June, Sadie and I had reserved two places on a return
pilgrimage to the Marian Shrines in France in September of this
year. Having what the insurance companies refer to as 'a pre-ex-
isting condition', I was able to insure us only for eventualities
that had no relationship to my liver problems. The condition
that sent me to Edinburgh in September, and thus required cancellation of our French pilgrimage, was clearly liver-related. So
we lost our money. Fortunately Michael, honest man that he is,
pares his profits to the minimum for these tours. He sees his job
as a vocation rather than as an opportunity to make money. A
little over five hundred pounds per person buys flight, bus-tour,
en suite accommodation (with breakfast and evening meal) for
ten days, and little additional explorations tossed in *gratis*. That
meant we lost only a little over a thousand pounds. It could have
been much more. And I was happy to accept the loss. We had
made the booking knowing that cancellation was always a real
possibility. Michael came to me a few times since September explaining that he was in the process of trying to negotiate return of

our money from the air-company and the hotels but was having little success. It was a surprise, therefore, when he handed me that envelope this morning. I asked him how he got it but he refused to tell me. All he said was that he was sorry that he was only able to return half of what I had lost. I was very grateful. How often do disappointed holidaymakers find themselves pressed to accept refunds to which they have no real entitlement?

January 2002
Last month we went back to Edinburgh, armed with my 'grid'. I accompanied it with explanatory notes, indicating in some detail how the fluctuations in the graph lines translated into pain, nausea, itch, fatigue, insomnia and so on. The young woman doctor who first accepted the documents admired the inventiveness of their layout and told me that she was currently engaged in post-graduate research and was puzzling over how best to present her numerical data. 'I'll bring my stuff round to you while you are in bed and you can do it for me,' she joked.

I had to stay overnight for a few more tests and examination by various specialists. On the afternoon of the following day we were told that transplant was necessary, that I was a suitable case, and that I would now be placed on 'the list'. I had not realised how tense I had been or, indeed, how much getting on to the list meant to me. Instead of responding with a beaming smile, I felt the prickle of tears behind my eyes. I covered my face with my hands and thanked God, and Sr Briege McKenna who had offered God three optional ways to work his 'miracle', one of which was 'a surgeon's skill.'

I weigh less than nine stones now. I am yellow, hollow-cheeked, nauseous, and plagued with a terrible itch but we flew home to Belfast that afternoon in buoyant mood indeed. Sadie said it was the miracle she had been praying for. Both of us are assuming that after a short waiting period, I will have a new liver and be back to full health in no time. We shall see.

CHAPTER FIFTEEN

A Period of Grace

March 2002

I have little energy. I spend most of my time imprisoned in an armchair. The same lethargy has captured my mind. I find that I do not even have the mental energy to pray very much now. I touch crucifixes around the house when I am passing and utter little aspirations. From time to time during the day I might say, 'Hello, Jesus! Just touching base ... I'm sorry, but I just don't have the energy to focus on a lengthy prayer.' Joan is constantly on the phone. She says that this kind of feeling is normal for sick people. I hate being called a sick person but I suppose that is what I am.

The first couple of months of waiting have been very difficult. I have been given a pager from the Transplant Unit that I have to carry with me at all times. It never buzzes! The phone rings but it is never a call from Edinburgh. The anticipation / deflation element that churns me up when the phone rings is too painful to bear. I am trying to find ways to accept my life as it is and, if one day a phone call does come from Edinburgh, then great! Otherwise, this is my life!

As lives go, it is not all that exciting. The itch is growing steadily worse, unbearable when I am warm under blankets at night (for a short while only because I have become more or less a total insomniac). Nausea is preventing me from eating; I seem unable to tolerate food. Fatigue keeps me pinned to the armchair in the lounge. I have had to stop going to Mass but, thankfully, Father Andrew, who visits regularly, has lent me a Citizens' Band radio-receiver which allows me to hear Mass said each day at the local Dominican chapel while Sadie, a Eucharistic minister, brings me communion every morning after she comes home from Mass.

Joan talks for hours on the phone – I'd hate to see her bill –

and is slowly bringing me to the realisation that this is a period when I can be with God, and in God, constantly, even if I have lost the energy to pray. Every now and then I find the energy to read, sometimes a chapter from a novel, sometimes something spiritual. I came across something by Michael Winstanley SDB, that is making me think. Thank God! Thinking about something abstract is better than wallowing in self-pity. Winstanley says,

> 'God calls me at the centre of my being ... The journey entails risk; it can be lonely at times and confused, giving rise to much self-questioning and the struggle with uncertainty, anxiety and fear. Sometimes it may create painful misunderstanding, conflict even. Sill ... it invites me to trusting surrender to God's immense love and faithfulness, and the experience that God is with me in my coming and in my going.'

Am I, in fact, surrendering to God's love? I am aware that I need to; if I don't, I am not going to get through this. But so far I am meeting with little success. The dualism that I experience between my intent to accept suffering for God and my innate rejection of it remains a constant struggle. One of the severest tests is the problem I have at night. In bed my brain buzzes and hisses. I am so filled with tension that my head is actually suspended about a half an inch above the pillow and not resting on it at all. My cheek appears to be lying on the pillow but it is not even touching it. The relaxation needed for sleep is not something I can even remotely attempt to access. My body, exhausted though it is, is repeatedly pulled out of my bed, five minutes after I return to it, to escape the awful inner restless and manic agitation that I can neither describe nor control. I pace the hall, the darkness, the spare bedrooms, in the blackness of the night, squeezing my fingers into my skull and crying aloud, 'Lord! Lord! Please take this away. I cannot suffer this for you. It is too much! Give me pain, give me sickness, but take away this terrible mental condition, whatever it is.' Not much trust in God's love there.

But something has come out of it, however. When I reflect (rarely these days, sadly) on the first sorrowful mystery of the rosary, I feel that I have rather more empathy with Jesus' mental torment than I had heretofore. What I am going through, of

course, is the palest of pale shadows in comparison with the sufferings of Our Blessed Lord but I can visualise him in
Gethsemene now, holding his head in his agony, seeking some
kind of ease, staggering into trees and, at one point, so distressed by the enormity of his vision that he rushes back to his
friends for momentary support and comfort. Can they even
begin to comprehend the distress in his voice when, finding
them asleep, he asks in disappointment, 'Could you not watch
for one hour with me?'

His return to prayer brings to his humanity a renewal of the
psychological and spiritual torture that builds to such a horrifying crescendo that his very body recoils and begins to sweat
blood. No wonder the Father had to send one of his angels to
soothe his suffering Son. Thinking about such excess of inner
pain makes me realise how insignificant my own discomfort is
but I can extrapolate something from it of how Jesus must have
suffered.

And yet, despite my inability to welcome my state for God's
sake, I have lately become conscious of little glimmers of understanding, momentary flashes that for the briefest of seconds take
me out of myself. I am reminded of Wordsworth's lines from his
'Ode on Intimations of Immortality':

... and I have felt
a presence that disturbs me with the joy
of elevated thoughts, a sense sublime
of something far more deeply interfused ...

Sometimes for a moment I have an idea that my discomfort is
not entirely wasted. (I say 'discomfort' because I notice now on
the phone that I recoil when Joan says something like 'your sufferings'. I have to tell her immediately that while I am not too
delighted by what is going on, I cannot accept that I am suffering
– that word is too close to what Jesus had to do. I feel happier referring to my situation as being one of 'extreme discomfort'.) But
just today – and this is why I need to write – I had a sense (It's
gone now! As Wordsworth says, 'Whither is fled that visionary
gleam?') that if I can just 'want' to offer my pain to God that will
be good enough and I can thereafter moan and groan as much as
I like. Acceptance is such an easy thing to talk about in the ab-

stract. In the middle of the night, when you cannot lie in bed for five minutes without having to leap out of it again, filled with tension and distress, the idea of 'acceptance' becomes an impossible ideal. I 'want' to accept. God knows I do so want to accept! But all I can pray is, 'Take it away, please God, take it away.'

Part of my 'visionary gleam' was prompted by lines from a little morning prayer that I still manage to say. It was written by St Thérèse of Lisieux, and the last lines are:

Oh my God, I ask of you for myself and those dear to me, the grace to fulfill perfectly your holy will, to accept for love of you the joys and the sorrows of this passing life, so that we may be united together one day in heaven.

It was when I prayed this prayer this morning, feeling depressed, deflated, knowing that my prayer to 'fulfill perfectly your holy will' was little more than words, I suddenly (and it takes considerably longer to write this down than it took to occur) felt lighter, elevated. I heard, no, I sensed, a fully formed thought in a split second. It was something like,

Remember what I told you about trying? I told you that I did not care if you never succeed so long as you keep trying. Well, this suffering business is the same. You say you cannot endure it for my sake. That's OK! I know that! But you 'want' to. That's good enough for me.

April 2002

Sadie says very little about herself in all of this. I have been so preoccupied with myself (most wives, I am sure, will express minimal surprise at that) that I do not give a great deal of thought to how all of this might be affecting her. It is very difficult for her. From my point of view I only have to turn, she's there. I only have to ask for something, she brings it or does it. I want to complain and explain in graphic detail the pains and discomforts I am enduring, she listens patiently. This has been going on for a few months now. She no longer goes out to golf; she seldom leaves me, apart from going to Mass or to do some shopping. The demands on her must be horrendous. Yet I seldom thank her; I seldom even consider what she must be going through. How Christian is that? But I do know I appreciate it and I often wonder how I could survive without her. We spoke briefly about it on the plane the other day and she told me it is tough to deal with, that her life is no longer her own, but that I am not to worry about that because she doesn't mind. Sickness or in health ... Sadie takes her vows seriously.

The other night was a case in point. Joan had called and lent me a book that is based on a combination of spiritual and yoga exercises. She explained that the purpose of the exercises is to relax the brain and enable people to find rest, even sleep. She suggested that it might be worth a try. My first attempt was un-successful. I held the book in my hand and tried to read and relax – something about blue skies and running water. It was hopeless! I told Joan about it and she suggested that perhaps Sadie should do the reading. A couple of nights ago I was in ter-rible straits. I was virtually running through the house in the dark, hands to my head, bumping into walls and doors, and just a step away from howling in desperation. At 3.30 am I could en-dure it no longer. I woke Sadie and pleaded with her to try the experiment with the book. She rose, uncomplaining, wrapped a blanket about herself because it was cold, and we went to the lounge. There I lay on the floor while Sadie sat on the sofa and read aloud from the book. I tried to give myself over to the soothing words but to me they were inane, contrived and self-satisfied. I did try not to move as I lay there but the tension built up in me until, after five or six minutes, I leapt in frustration from the floor, virtually into the air, and cried, 'This is pointless!'

Sadie held me in her arms until I settled and then I urged her to go back to bed, assuring her that I could handle the rest of the night alone. I couldn't really; indeed, I handled it very badly. But at least I was able to refrain from disturbing Sadie again.

The daytimes I do not have to handle alone, however. I have plenty of visitors. Sean invariably calls a couple of times a week after golf, regaling me with details of shots and scores and some-how filling me with the hope that one day I'll be back out there again. Willie has started to call one evening a week as well. Like myself, Willie has his share of medical problems so we have lit-tle discussions comparing and contrasting our health condi-tions, arguing a little over which of us has the greater share of ailments. An ex-colleague and friend, Pat Raftis, is another regular visitor. Our conversations range far and wide turning a promised half-hour visit into something over two hours. And there are, as well, the visits from Father Niall and Father Andrew, which I very much enjoy. All of these friends, despite my weakness and, sometimes, initial reluctance to shake off my lethargy enough to talk to them, help me to pass days of quite interminable boredom.

I have to go to Edinburgh every month for check-ups. These visits are becoming marathons, making immense demands on my already depleted physical resources. I am just over eight stones now, and if I sit on any kind of hard seat there is nothing of flesh to cushion the pressure on the nerve-ends in my buttocks. This results in pain, a kind of sciatica, in my back and legs, pain that demands that I constantly stand up, walk, loosen up, and massage my back and hips. That is fine at home but when Sadie drives me to the airport, we have to stop several times en route while I walk up and down the road outside the car trying to pick up the will to get back in and move on. Sadie's patience must be stretched to the limit but there is never a murmur of complaint. When we reach the airport she immediately leads me to a seat and goes off to find a porter who will push me around the concourse in a wheelchair and on out over the tarmac to the plane. (Being pushed around an airport in a wheelchair sounds something of a luxury. Believe me, I hate it; I hate to be stared at; I hate to be helpless … I must remember to try to offer that up as well.)

Sitting in the plane presents much the same problems as sitting in the car. Thankfully, Sadie is quite an organiser. She always arranges with the stewardesses to have me put on the plane first so that we can get seats at the front of the plane where we have room to stretch our legs and, indeed, where I can stand up and move around a little bit. The flight, however, lasts little more than forty-five minutes, so it is bearable, apart from the fact that being strapped in makes it very difficult to access the many itching areas, a struggle that never ceases. (It is also a struggle that causes Sadie no end of embarrassment; but I suppose that, when one has a husband who is constantly behaving like a flea-ridden monkey in the zoo, a little embarrassment is excusable.)

I had to stay overnight the last time. There is some concern about this nightly problem with my head. I am told there is a 'chemical imbalance in the brain'. Sadie could have told them that already but this 'imbalance' is caused by my dysfunctional liver. They brought a psychiatrist to see me. He had me taking in deep breaths – 'hold … and release; hold … and release.' It was innate good breeding, nothing more, that enabled me, having been holding and releasing until I was dizzy and exhausted, to refrain from telling the psychiatrist what I thought about his 'hold … and release'. He also advised me to sit quietly every now and again and write the first thing that came into my mind. I asked what that would serve and he suggested that it is frequently cathartic. I have reservations about that but I will give it a try.

Whatever about the writing, the breathing idea certainly did not work. Trying to get it right caused me far more stress than any benefits that might have accrued. Sometime in the middle of that night I gave up on it and asked the nurse for a sleeping tablet. She came back half-an-hour later and told me that, since any medication would have a detrimental effect upon my liver, I was not to be allowed any.

I had a miserable night, walking for hours up and down the corridors outside the wards. Despite my fatigue my brain kept driving me to movement. Another liver patient in the bed beside me expressed astonishment at the amount of walking I was doing, given my obvious deterioration. He said that it was as much as he could do to walk to the toilet. The nurses inevitably noticed me and brought me into their office about 4.00 am, offering me tea, toast and some cheerful conversation – a welcome respite.

One of the most unpleasant aspects of these nightly meanderings is the intolerable boredom. I would read if I could, I love reading, but my brain will not let me relax. I do not know what I am going to do. I try to offer it up but that brings no comfort, particularly as I seem to be only going through the motions rather than actually meaning it.

One thing is interesting, though. Someone asked me a while back if I ever rail at God, if I ever ask 'Why me?' I can honestly say that the thought never crossed my mind. I have no animosity towards God at all. I still love him. I would love to be able to talk to Jesus the way I used to but that seems to require a level of mental energy and concentration that I simply no longer possess. It has nothing to do with not wanting to. I know God is not doing this to me. This is one of those natural inevitabilities of this broken world in which we live. Joan says, however, that God is using this illness, that it is all fitted somewhere into his divine plan. I love hearing that though, I have to say, the comfort it brings is ephemeral indeed.

April 2002
I tried the psychiatrist's idea of writing things down. I gained no relief from it whatever. Its very pointlessness made me resent the time and energy it demanded. The following is a verbatim transcript of my brief and only attempts:

20 April 2000, 11 30 am

The nights are driving me mad. Apart from the fact that I can't sleep, a heavy burden in itself, I can't find any respite from the turmoil in my mind – panic attacks, sleep anxiety attacks, press upon me constantly. I jump in and out of bed and wander around the house in a state of unbearable mental distress. And I thought I was strong! I have been given advice from various sources about breathing exercises to deal with this, but focusing on the breathing seem to emphasise and enlarge the problem. I feel completely helpless.

What is happening now is that the dread of the endless nights starts coming over me in the mornings as soon as I start my day. Here I am at 11.30 am already in a panic about tonight. The night before last I thought I had discovered the answer – just accept that I can't sleep and pass the night reading or doing things, make a cup of tea around 3.00 am, tidy the study, deal with correspondence, read. I did get through that night OK, but last night I was so exhausted that I couldn't read, I couldn't do anything.

I wish the breathing exercises would work. According to the leaflet that I was given in Edinburgh, the panic attacks should fade when I become practised at breathing slowly through my nose. I am trying … but so far, no success whatever.

Later: 1.05 pm

Dozed off! Any sleep during the day means that a bad night is definitely coming up. How am I going to deal with it? Sadie advises me to adopt my usual positive stance and treat it as a challenge. Don't I wish? All my experiences with this thing have been negative and being positive is not an option. It's altogether too horrific. I read somewhere that Albert Einstein suffered terribly with similar panic attacks all of his life. How on earth did he endure it? It's enough to drive me crazy. But maybe I focus too directly on what is going on. The key – but how to find it – is to focus outside myself, away from my anxieties and sleep concerns. The other night, by some strange quirk, I was able to read for hours; I have to hope that I will have the mental energy for that again tonight. Last night I hadn't ... I was just too exhausted from the utter sleeplessness of the night before (no sleep between 11.30 pm and 7.15 am). You'd think tiredness would be a bonus, that it would induce some kind of physical collapse if not sleep. Sadly, not this crazy head of mine! It's a dynamo! As soon as I lie down, my mind is in turmoil. Sleep becomes impossible and, with utter suddenness, clothes are tossed violently from the bed and I am back pacing the darkness of the house again. Ah God! I hope I can read tonight ... that helps. But I can only read if I am enjoying the book, not because I need a crutch.

Afternoon: 3.30 p

Small waves of anxiety, at different intervals of the day, continue to sweep over me. I think the breathing exercises don't work because what I am afraid of is real – the long, sleepless nights. These are a genuine fear. The panic attacks are different; they are formless, stemming from an unknown dread. Fast, almost frenetic, breathing results from these (I think it is called hyper-ventilating) and some kind of breathing control is necessary if I am not to go mad. What I find works, when these attacks are severe, is to rush to where Sadie is and cling on to her for dear life until the attack passes. It is probably some form of being 'grounded', I suppose. But the anxiety I experience does not respond to this treatment. Anxiety attacks are longer-lasting, more invasive of the peace (what peace? The peace I would have if I wasn't so irritatingly ill, that peace!) that we all experience without either realising or appreciating it. I think I am also anxious for the phone to ring, for the 'call' that is going to get me out of this insanity and, indeed, into the blessed oblivion of total unconsciousness for a few continuous days. There has to be a strong undertow in my psyche, stemming from this unfulfilled yearning that never leaves my subconscious. That has got to be distressing even if I am not consciously aware of it.

My sisters, Sadie, Sean, all tell me that they feel the 'call' is due anytime, that they have 'experienced good feelings'. I appreciate their desire to buoy me up, to help calm me. But the problem is that such encouragement breeds an anticipation that in turn feeds the anxiety and impatience that the wait brings with it. I am not calm; I am up the walls. I keep hoping that the phone will ring.

I wrote no more notes after that. This form of writing is cathartic in the sense that it brings out into the light all that I am thinking and feeling. But it does not alleviate it. Indeed, it makes me far more aware of the trouble I am in. I would be better not thinking about it at all.

April 2002

Yesterday brought amazing news. Briege and Joan, along with three colleagues, have come to live in Newry. Joan had not prepared me for this remarkable, and very welcome, event although she had mentioned once or twice that Briege and herself, along with the three colleagues who had been living at Monasterevin with them, had been in constant supplication to the Holy Spirit over a matter that was to have a significant impact upon their spiritual and vocational lives. Although my sisters have visited me from time to time over the years, it is only lately that we really talk. And I am wondering now about the selfishness of this; most of that talk has been about me. I realise now that my knowledge of my sisters' lives is slight. I do have some acquaintance with the highlights, especially Briege's widespread recognition as an expert on Franciscan spirituality, and her growing recognition also as a composer and writer of spiritual and meditative music. I do possess copies of her CDs that are now selling all over the world, CDs which contain the contemplative and melodic hymns she composes. These hymns are beautifully sung by a Sister of Mercy, Marie Cox, and are largely based on the spiritual writings of St Francis and St Clare. I have, in fact, constantly been playing of late her latest CD, 'The Company of Angels', and I find for the first time in my life that I am beginning to develop a close and real relationship with my own dear guardian angel. For a long time, even after my epiphany, I could not look him in the eye; I tended to talk to him out of the side of my mouth, so hard a time have I given him over the years. But now I can face him directly; and I can feel his loving hand gently rest on my shoulder several times during the day, especially when he accompanies me in adoration of the Eucharist at the consecration.

Joan's life, lived earnestly in God's will was, as far as I know, untroubled and serene and was to be spent in the relatively small confines of the British Isles and Ireland. Briege's journey, however, was to bring her from a small convent in a small town in Ireland to traverse the world – UK, Europe, USA, Australia. Hers was to become a life of extraordinary highs and lows – from the lows of humble, sometimes humiliating, service to the highs of authority, leadership and influence; from the highs of artistic and spiritual creativity to the lows of physical and mental exhaustion. It is a story of unwavering faith and spiritual tenacity and one which Briege herself must one day tell.

Their travels have taken them, accompanied now by their three friends in Clare, full circle to Newry, and their lives, quite accidentally, have begun to impinge on mine with an impact that is much greater than familial. The circumstances that have brought them to a rented house near where I live have been described by them as a 'step of faith'; to me, it is 'a monumental leap into the dark', the wonder and the mystery of which has seized my imagination and intensified my faith.

Briege, as I said, must tell her own story but the influence that she and Joan, each in her distinct way, are having on my spiritual life, and the miracle of total trust and dependence on the Holy Spirit that is taking place right under my nose, makes it impossible for me not to recount, from however limited a perspective, something of the succession of events that have led to this unprecedented circumstance. Jesus said once (Matthew 6):

> *Therefore I tell you, do not worry about your life, what you will eat or drink; or about your body, what you shall wear ... Look at the birds of the air; they do not sow or reap or store away in barns and*

yet your heavenly Father feeds them. Are you not much more valu-
able than they?

I never could quite believe that these loving words had anything
of a truly literal import. Now I witness my sisters testing the lit-
eralness of this demand on trust beyond the limits of anything I
could possibly have imagined. Only a couple of hours ago
Briege and Joan told me, with a great deal of laughter but with
the utmost determination that, in spite of the fact that the entire
material wealth of themselves and their three colleagues consists of two small pensions, a rented house, a few small cases
containing their clothes and some books, and the sum of 105
euros in the bank, they have just instructed a firm of architects to
design for them a monastery which is estimated to cost in excess
of one million euros. At this point (and they are laughing?) they
have no idea where the money is going to come from. What has
brought these five nuns, late in their lives, some past retirement
age, to this extraordinary pass?

April 2002
I have been thinking about the nuns' story. It seems to me that it
begins with Vatican II. A call was issued from this great Council
to all religious orders to look again at their origins and the
inspirations of their founders, and to consider earnestly how
this research might lead to a renewal, perhaps even a restate-
ment, of their religious aims and of their religious life. The Order
of Saint Clare holds a number of Regional Assemblies each year
during which individual sisters lecture on renewal, study
groups meet and write papers, and large plenary sessions are
held to summarise, examine and make sense out of the proceedings. As a result of the Council's call, many members of the
Order have had access to the original writings of St Francis and
St Clare. As well as finding inspiration in these writings for her
music, Briege developed a passion for the spirituality she found
there and lectured on these antecedents many times at the
Assemblies.

Briege's background is, of course, academic. She has under-
taken teacher-training, as well as spending three years at the
Royal College of Music in Manchester. Here she specialised in

Voice and Composition, a study which ultimately led to the production of the series of successful CDs I have already referred to. Among her life's responsibilities she served as a teacher in Wales, spent some time as a Principal in Nottinghamshire, engaged in practical catechetical work in Dublin. But the more she studied the true essence of the word 'poor' in the spirituality of St Francis and St Clare, the more she felt drawn to other ways of living her vocation. Her pursuit of this spirituality led her to the inner city of Liverpool, an area called Kirkby, where she lived for twelve years in solidarity with the poor. Despite earning many plaudits throughout her vocational life for her lecturing prowess across America, Europe, Australia and her growing fame as a composer, Briege considers these twelve years the high point of her life. But they took a severe physical and mental toll.

Exhausted at the end of this period, she left Britain to spend a couple of years recuperating in Australia. Reflecting on her life while she recovered, Briege realised that her practical, hands-on attempts to assist and support the poor were no longer the way she felt that her vocation should be lived. In her time in Kirkby, she learned the key lesson that only prayer can change anything. The more she contemplated this realisation, the more she felt herself drawn to an eremitical existence where she could seek God, and a spiritual solidarity with the poor, in solitude and prayer.

Briege spoke of her reflections and convictions at Regional Assemblies and found that she was not alone in this thinking. She discovered that Sister Rose McSherry, coincidentally also from Newry, had been thinking along similar lines, as had Sister Margaret McGill, a Scottish nun who had recently stepped down from the role of Abbess General.

Many of the sisters at these Assemblies listened to, and approved, what Briege was saying. Briege's clear exposition of the thirteenth-century papers of Clare and Francis, and the extent to which they supported the logic of her current position, won a lot of support at the assemblies. The agreement that seemed to prevail among many of those who attended the assemblies, gave Briege, Joan, Margaret and Rose the impetus they needed to urge their respective communities to move forward in a different direction to reclaim the original thrust of St Clare's vision.

It was the pattern of the Regional Assemblies to compile reports and documentation, detailing the proceedings of their consultations. These reports were written up and the information disseminated across the world, back and forth, between Britain and America. It was in America that Sister May Mahon, originally from Wicklow, had spent most of her vocational life. She had, for some time, become conscious that the Rule in America lacked some aspect of the Franciscan spirituality that she felt she needed. In her reading of some of the reports that emanated from Britain, she found herself strongly drawn to the new vision outlined by Briege, i.e. living an eremitical life in solitude and contemplation, and living that life in a poverty that was dependant upon the care of Providence. May then spent a couple of years in Australia where she met Margaret who had arrived there for a six-month sabbatical. Much of their conversation inevitably centred on this new vision.

St Paul once said something about '… the Charity of Christ compels you.' It was this kind of compulsion that led these nuns to consider seeking permission from the main Order to withdraw into the eremitical life. A Passionist priest, Father Gerry Arbuckle, after years of research into spirituality in institutions and organisations, was forced to the conclusion that '… the new is elsewhere' (i.e. not in the institutions).' Briege and her friends were deeply influenced by this finding and confirmed in their decision to live a more contemplative existence. As an element of the permission they sought, the Chapter (i.e. the voice of the entire Order) suggested that Briege and a couple of her colleagues experiment with this pattern of life that they had chosen and report back to the assemblies after a certain period. Initially Rose, Briege and Joan were given this commission but they were later joined by Margaret and later yet by May.

The five nuns finally settled, in 1993, in a small convent (a two-storey house, really) at Monasterevin in County Kildare. There they prayed constantly to the Holy Spirit, poring over the writings of Clare and Francis, and seeking enlightenment in the gospels for affirmation that the path they were following was, indeed, led by the Spirit.

It is clear to me that Briege and the others are innovators, people who, faced with the convincing possibility of a need to do things differently, are prepared to change, and more, to endure psychological discomfort to achieve the perceived need. I have had occasion in my life to study the psychology of change. I have learned that adults are characterised by stability and that anything which threatens that stability is resisted unless clear reasons to accommodate the disequilibrating influences present themselves. For these nuns, an inner crisis in their vocational lives, coupled with a new vision, was enough to trigger the desire for change. Strangely, they often received unanimous support at the assemblies but (and it is psychologically predictable) when the other sisters returned to their stable existences, away from the influence of the 'animateurs', their instinct for stability reasserted itself and their support for the new vision faltered and waned. This is perfectly normal and understandable. Radical innovation invariably generates resistance. There is no blame attached to this. Inspirational leaders can engender and promote change but they themselves must be convinced of its value. I would surmise that the other members of the Order, including those in authority, were generally content with the *status quo* and were unable to perceive the eremitical approach in quite the same light as the five innovators. And thus, also predictable, because they were moving away from the established pattern of the Order, however sincere their reasoning, the five became increasingly marginalised.

How little we truly know about other people's lives! For ten years Joan and the others have been agonising, praying, analysing, discussing over and over again the validity of their choice, and I wrote only days ago that Joan's life was untroubled and serene. How wrong I was! The ten years of questioning, the effort to be true to the founder's vision, the risking of the friendships and the security they had known all their lives in the Order, all had to take their psychological toll. Heartache and hurt were never far from their lives, despite their conviction that the path they had chosen was the path laid out for them by the Spirit. Eventually the five, as Joan told me, had to 'step out in trust and faith and love of God, in total dependence on the Holy Spirit, to the new.' Breige, reflecting sadly on the anguish the decision cost them, pointed out that all of them were in their sixties, or close to, and had lived their entire vocational lives in total obedience to the Rule. 'Can you imagine how traumatic to the psyche it must have been,' she asked me, 'to seek to plough new furrows with only faith to support us and with no guarantee whatever that what we were doing was right?'

Briege, as I have already mentioned, had spent two years in Australia, during which time she discovered that the same seeds for renewal were already there. The five decided to become part of the Australian Order, a canonical necessity since they could not simply sever links with their existing Order and strike out on their own. The two groups developed their approach to the new vision in tandem and the five Irish nuns moved forward in obedience with the Australians. As Joan said, 'We joined them in their poverty, in faith, and prepared ourselves for a new approach to the Franciscan and Poor Clare life in Ireland.'

Joan also pointed out that while initially they stepped out in faith alone, reflection on the logic of certain factors did provide them with additional intellectual conviction that their decision was solidly founded. There were a number of specific facts that brought them a degree of comfort. They knew

i. that they were answering the call of the church to find a renewed vision;

ii that, after intensive study, they were being true to the teaching of the founders

iii. that they were still being true to the mandates of the Chapter (seen in the unanimous affirmation of their ideals at the assemblies);

iv. that they were all convinced in their hearts that they were being led by the Spirit (all had found affirmation of this in many ways once they had decided to follow the new vision);

v. that their colleagues in Australia were being led by the same inspiration as themselves.

After some consultation with Rome and others, a Procedure of Transfer according to the Code of Canon Law allowed them to become members of the Order of Poor Clare, Waverley, Sydney.

In April 2002, no longer members of their original Order, they were naturally obliged to leave the convent at Monasterevin. With nothing but hope in the Holy Spirit, they came to Newry where a member of the family, luckily,(?) was able to provide them with temporary accommodation until, quite simply, the Spirit was ready to make his move. That is not quite accurate. The Spirit had already initiated some movement, a story in itself that has me almost shaking my head in disbelief.

During January of this year, distressed at having to leave Monasterevin and desperate to find some positive way forward, Briege and the others besieged the Holy Spirit. Over and over Briege received a memory of a Franciscan nun she had met only briefly several years earlier. She told the others that she felt she was being compelled to contact Betty Cotter. 'I have no idea why,' she said. 'I don't really know her and I can't imagine what she can possibly do for us. She is as poor as we are.'

Eventually the others persuaded her to contact this nun. What happened was interesting. Briege had totally lost contact with Betty and had no idea where to start looking for her. She had the vague impression that she was somewhere in the African Missions. One of the others reminded her that there was a Franciscan convent, Mount Oliver, near Dundalk. 'Why don't you phone them to see if they know anything about her?'

Briege agreed to do so and asked the person who answered if she could tell her the whereabouts of Betty Cotter.

'Well, isn't that fortunate' said the nun who answered the phone. 'Betty has just arrived here for a conference and she is standing right here beside me.'

Briege was startled and, when Sister Betty came to the phone, began to explain who she was.

'Good heavens! I have just been praying about you.'

'About me? But we've barely spoken two words in our lives …'

'I have been on my knees for the past forty years before the Blessed Sacrament, and at St Brigid's Shrine when I could, begging the Lord to bring a group of contemplative nuns to Faughart, to St Brigid [who has a well and a shrine there] and I have just about given up. I told the Lord that there was a group of nuns in Kildare who would be perfect but that sadly they seem to be very settled at Monasterevin. Then I was pleading again with him to do something – and when the phone rang … I knew … I knew it was something …'

Briege was amazed. They chatted, but nothing about their

move was resolved other than that Briege promised, at Betty's pleading insistence, that she and her group would come to Faughart and pray at the shrine to St Brigid.

Briege brought this strange request back to the others and, although it was a seventy or eighty mile journey to the shrine, they all agreed that they would make time to get there during the course of the next few days. They cleared any outstanding appointments they had and eventually made the little pilgrimage.

Next day a friend from their days in the novitiate rang. She said that she had been in chapel trying to pray but that Jesus would not give her any peace until she would phone her friends in Monasterevin. What's up? I think it was Joan who took that call. She explained the situation and said they were in dire need of help. The nun said 'Wait!' and hung up. She phoned back an hour later with the instruction that they were to visit a farmer, at Faughart of all places, who would allow them to pick, at no cost, two acres of land for their new monastery. So, at least they have land. (How blasé is that? The Holy Spirit is demonstrating his approval and support in the most tangible way and I write, with unruffled complacency, 'At least they have land'. I think I am getting too accustomed to miracles!)

In February the five nuns flew to Australia for the transfer procedure. In April Sr Louise, the Abbess there, accompanied them back to Ireland to stay with them for a while in Newry and also, because she was the Order's Superior, to negotiate with Archbishop Sean Brady their acceptance into the Archdiocese of Armagh of which Faughart is a part.

Almost immediately (It seems inevitable!) an anonymous donation of two hundred thousand dollars was pledged from America, followed by a substantial, and very welcome, donation from the Order they had just left. Help is now pouring in from many sources and, while they still have substantial need, they are filled with happiness, excitement and a glorious lightness of heart and soul that has come from these miraculous affirmations that they have, indeed, been truly led by the Spirit.

April 2002
I have not mentioned Father Martin for a while. I still have regu-

lar contact with him and, indeed, he has called on the phone a couple of times. He is naturally disappointed that I am still waiting for a liver but, like Joan, he tends to view this period positively, to see it as an opportunity to gain grace and to build my relationship with Jesus rather than as a situation to be decried. In a letter a couple of weeks ago, he wrote:

'You can be sure that the good Lord is using the period of waiting, and the uncertainty, to sort you out in many ways. He is helping you to build patience and to love his will. And he is testing and developing other virtues … faithfulness, humility (that is always the most difficult one [How well Father Martin knows me!]) as well as trust and hope (which people need so badly) and so many other good qualities which, as you say, will make us better men, better Christians, better children of his.'

Obviously, in my letters to him, I must have been bending his ear with the same problems that I have been discussing in these pages. But it is nice to receive his letters and this kind of response. It is very encouraging and affirming, and helps me to become that little bit more positive about things when my psyche starts to wilt.

I write about him today because this morning I received another letter from him which contains a little paragraph that has switched a light on somewhere in my head. Constantly in this diary and, I would surmise, in my letters to Father Martin, I have been trying to explain things to myself, trying to puzzle out, intellectually, the kinds of demands that my situation is placing on me and how I should respond. I seem to want to be able to spell out in black and white exactly what is being asked of me, exactly what I should do, and exactly how I should do it. I have not considered my thought processes in this way before but Father Martin's letter has made me realise that I am trying to find answers where answers may not be available, that I am trying to understand things that may not be susceptible to comprehension. He says:

Do not be surprised that you find it difficult and that sometimes you do not seem to understand. What matters is that you have faith and trust that he knows best and is, in fact, using these things, es-

*pecially the ones we do not understand, to free us from our tendency
to self-sufficiency and to lead us to place our trust in him.'*

I see now that I still do not understand what it means to hand
myself over to Jesus, to place my trust in him. I say the words, of
course, frequently, but in the final analysis I, me, am still the one
trying to make things happen, to shape myself, to shape my
thinking, to shape the manner and nature of my responses to my
situation. I am not handing over to Jesus and I am not really
trusting despite the fact that I say I am. That 'tendency to self-
sufficiency' remains as strong as ever. I am still trying to understand, to know the precise elements of everything that is going
on in my physical life and in my spiritual life and that, of course,
is probably a reach too far.

There is much here for me to think about. I am excited by
what Father Martin has said. It is another one of those 'gleams'. I
know it makes perfect sense. I know there are answers here for
me but I still have not quite figured out how I am going to
spread my arms in surrender and say, 'OK Lord, I quit! I'll leave
it to you.' I will think about it.

I should mention that there is a little post-script to Father
Martin's letter. It says,

*P.S. I probably have already explained that I always try to type my
letters for reasons of charity towards the reader.*

I am casting no aspersions whatever on Father Martin's handwriting; I wouldn't dream of doing that. I just think his post-
script is interesting, that's all!

May 2002
Six months and still no sign of a liver! I was back in Edinburgh
again a couple of days ago – the usual shattering experience. I
am assured by the co-ordinators that there is concern now that I
am still waiting, so I have been placed on top of the list. There is
something of a problem in my case. While the blood match will
not be too difficult to find, there is rather more difficulty with
tissue match and even more, surprising in its ordinariness, a difficulty with size. I have become so small and wasted now that an
ordinary man's liver will not fit into my abdominal cavity. I
need a liver from a woman, or even an adolescent. Apart from

the usual platitudes – 'one is bound to turn up soon', and, 'you'll be getting the phone call when you least expect it', and so on – no-one is able to give me any real assurance that I will actually survive the wait.

Nonetheless, some good things, very good things, are happening. I managed to have a discussion this time with the senior doctor who had refused me the sleeping pill because of possible damage to my liver. I blame it on my weakened condition but, I have to confess, I was rather aggressive and cross.

'What the heck are you trying to protect?' I snapped. 'My liver is banjaxed. You know that! I know that! I need some kind of medication to get me through the night. If it kills me, so be it! I can't endure this torment any longer.'

Once I got that off my chest, I calmed down. He is a nice man and does not deserve this kind of acrimony. (On top of that, he plays golf off a seven handicap – virtually a brother!) A lengthy discussion followed which resulted in my being allowed to take one specific tablet every night. It is a painkiller but it also has something in it that helps ease the turmoil in the brain. I have already started taking it and the nights are so much easier to bear. Sadly, it does nothing for the abominable itch which is everywhere now. Can you believe that I itch behind my eyes? I keep digging the heels of my hands into the sockets to find some relief and I think I have pushed my eyes so far back into them that soon I am not going to be able to see out of them. Still, anything is better than the horrendous mental torture.

I still cannot sleep but, thank God and thanks to the new tablet, I can sit in reasonable quietude at the kitchen table (there is some sort of heating under the floor that keeps me warm all night) where I can read or write as I wish. Even with the itch, even with the nausea, even with the abdominal pains, all I can think about is that the brain is at rest. What a blessed relief!

The impact reaches further. Since this episode of illness began some months ago, I have sat in an armchair all day, every day, trying to doze the day away. When I would hear the introductory jingle for the six-o-clock news on television, I would immediately sweat and panic. This music represents for me the start of the night again … awful night! But now, that dreadful fear is gone. I know now that I can face the night, despite my other less-than-pleasant symptoms, with a level of equanimity. And now, instead of watching the walls of the lounge closing in on me as I try to doze the day away, I have begun to pull myself together – no doubt with God's help, for I have used what little energy I have, torturing him for some kind of respite – and when Sadie comes home from Mass, I muster enough energy to accompany her down town to go shopping, just for groceries, newspapers and the like. So mundane, yet such a joy for me to be out and walking … well, shuffling … around the town. I meet friends whose reactions remind me of my appearance, but to be out of the house after a winter of dire imprisonment is a boon indeed. The sun shines now in May and on good afternoons Sadie drives me to a small seaside resort not far from the golf club where we enjoy short and slow but pleasant walks along the promenade beside Carlingford Lough, 'where the mountains of Mourne sweep down to the sea'.

Each day I also try to walk a few hundred yards from my house. Sadie urges me to do it to keep my heart and lungs strong for the operation (more her optimism now than mine, I confess). It is a slow, painful process but I have come to the conclusion that I am in powerful good condition considering the state that I am in. I have made a new friend on these walks. I mentioned earlier that my house is only a few minutes from the St Clare Convent. Attached to the convent are two schools, St Ronan's Primary School and the Sacred Heart Girls' Grammar School. The Principal of this school is a pleasant, good-humoured nun, early forties, I would guess (I hope that doesn't get me into trouble; she might be younger than that!) who passes me frequently in her car while I am out shuffling. Sister Julie (McGoldrick), a sister of Poor Clare, is a friend of Breige and Joan and never fails to stop for a chat when she sees me, complimenting me (on my energy, not my good looks) and assuring me that I am always in her prayers.

I am still dying but I am enjoying a real revival of spirit and strength. Where has this revival come from? I do not know. I can offer some speculation but I think, bottom line, that God in his mercy and love is simply giving me a break. I have been praying a little better lately and for some time now I have accepted the very real possibility that I will not survive the wait. I have a cousin who died a while back with the same disease I have (obviously genetic, then). A liver had become available for him but, sadly, the call came to his family the day after he died. How traumatic must that have been?

It is quite extraordinary, but I can now contemplate my own death with little fear or concern. I am trying to suffer for God's will (still very poorly) and I am trying also to talk Jesus into going easy on me when we met face-to-face. I told Joan recently that I was very apprehensive about that first meeting with him. 'Why?' she asked. 'Isn't the person you are going to meet that same Jesus you talk so comfortably with in your study every night? Why would meeting him be a problem?'

She is right, of course and, despite the shivers of trepidation that I might feel, I am looking forward to hearing him answer all my questions. In the meantime, unless a liver comes (and I truly believe I have reached a point where I am no longer distressed by the possibility that it might not) I have just a few months left to live. It is almost summertime. I will walk a little bit in the sun when I can, chatting with Jesus and my guardian angel as I walk, or just enjoying the sun on my face with my mind empty and quiet.

I have had a look at myself these past few months. I have seen things I do not want to see, things that puzzle me, and things I need to think about. I told Father Niall during one of his recent visits that I have tried so hard to develop my spiritual life but when I look at my foibles, I see that I still have a huge mountain to climb. Father Niall shook his head, smiled and, pointing to the floor, asked me to look away down to the very bottom of the mountain. He told me that that was where I had been a while back and asked me to look at the part of the mountain where I am now. It was a comforting image. He was implying, I think, I hope, that I am somewhere halfway up the mountain. He went on to tell me not to worry, that most of people are nowhere near the top, that my spirituality will grow as my relationship with Jesus grows.

That letter I received from Father Martin the other day has started a train of thought that has helped me tremendously. I remember reading about 'personality', in psychology studies years ago. Some people, I learned, have an 'internal locus of control' and others have an 'external locus of control'. The latter are controlled by factors external to themselves; they tend to be submissive, unassertive and accepting. I have always had an 'internal locus', always seeking to be in control, always seeking to influence events rather than be influenced by them, seeking to make things happen rather than wait for outcomes I did not want. When I was struck down a few months ago, the fact that I could no longer control events was a torture. Father Martin's reference to self-sufficiency has led me to realise that, because of this inner compulsion to be in control over the events of my life, it is no wonder that I find such great difficulty in handing my life over to God and letting him deal with it. This realisation was a milestone for me. It was at that point that I began to acknowledge that my thinking and my attitudes would have to change if I were to learn how to 'surrender to God's love'. I realised that I would have to relax, to take the tension out of my mind and spirit, to leave God something a little more malleable to work with. I realised, too, that I would have to live in the present. Trying to live in the future was disturbing my peace. With this awareness came the usual messages. I accept these now with total *sang-froid*; they are part of my life. In a short space of time I came across three different writers, two of them as far apart in their lives in terms of vocation, status and education as it is possible to be, and yet who shared the common fact that they were both in prison when they wrote messages that contain identical advice. The third is a priest whose prayer seems to incorporate everything that I have been puzzling about in this diary.

The first message came from the pen of a prisoner on Death Row, by name Gary Miller, who was executed on 5 December 2000. He had been befriended by a visiting nun, found his faith and, just before he died, left her this beautiful short poem:

I am
I was regretting the past and fearing the future.
Suddenly my Lord was speaking:

'My name is I Am.'

He paused.
I waited. He continued.
*   'When you live in the past*

With its mistakes and regrets
It is hard. I am not there.
My name is not I Was.

When you live in the future
With its problems and fears
It is hard. I am not there.
My name is not I Will Be.

When you live in this moment
It is not hard. I am here.
My name is I Am.

The second message came from a book Father Niall had lent me during one of his visits. It was written by a Vietnamese Cardinal, F. X. N. van Thuan, who had been imprisoned for a number of years for practising his faith against government orders. In gaol he wrote a little book of 'thoughts', little paragraphs of spiritual guidance. One read:

> *The present moment alone is important. Do not remember yester-day in order to weep over it; it is now in the past. Do not worry about tomorrow; it is still in the future. Entrust the past to God's mercy and the future to his Providence. As to the present, strive to live it in his love.*

I remember, sometime last year, listening to the panegyric at the funeral Mass of a well-known local man. The priest related a history of a life spent in service, holiness and prayer, a life of charity and good works, a life lived in love and in the Spirit. I listened with a growing distress and guilt, realising that no priest would ever be able to speak of me in these terms. My distress did not stem from reasons of ego but from a sad regret that my life has cast no reflection of service or sustained Christian love. I was in tears as I left the church. When I got home I did reflect a little upon the early lives of St Paul and St Augustine but it did not help much. These two messages, however, are compelling counsel not to succumb to that guilt and distress but, rather, to live in the Spirit now and make the very most of it.

How to live in the 'now' has become my quest, my goal. I think to myself, 'Enjoy this moment. Am I able to cope with what is happening to me at this precise moment? Of course I

can. Am I suffering? Not a whole awful lot. Right then – live
now and make the most of now. Love Sadie. Go to Warrenpoint
with her. Enjoy her company, her love, the walks with her. Enjoy
the shopping in town each morning. Enjoy the books I read
when I can't sleep. Use this 'now' to improve my relationship
with Jesus, to become what he would want me to be, to be
"dressed for action" as Luke says.'

Something positive has come out of this and while, in all sincerity and with my best will and hope, I have handed over my
life to God, I still have some control of how I live the 'now'. And
I can live in it in *his* will while making the most of it with *my* will.
(I do not quite understand that, but it seems to work.)

The third message is a prayer I found in a spiritual journal. It
was written by Father Thomas Merton:

My Lord God,
I have no idea where I am going,
I do not see the road ahead of me.
I cannot know for certain where it will end.
Nor do I really know myself.
And the fact that I find I am following
Your will does not mean that I am actually doing so.
But I believe the desire to please you
Does in fact please you,
And I hope I have that desire in all that I am doing.
I hope I will never do anything apart from that desire,
And I know if I do this
You will lead me by the right road
Though I may know nothing about it.
Therefore I will trust you always.
Though I may seem lost and in the shadow of death
I will not fear, for you are ever with me,
And you will never leave me
To face my perils alone.

There are more than echoes here of 'If you try to pray, you are
praying', of 'If you want to offer up your suffering, you are offering it up'. And now, to desire to please God is to please him.
But there is much else of relevance in the prayer – not being certain where the road ahead will end, groping to follow God's will

without actually knowing how to do it or even if I am doing it. And the mention of the 'shadow of death' may have been figurative for Father Merton but the message for me, I am sure, is truly literal – not that I am necessarily going to die but that I truly am 'in the shadow of death'. Not that this is to be feared. The last few lines of the Canticle of Zachariah offer comfort to people like me:

He will give light to those in darkness
Those who dwell in the shadow of death
And guide us into the way of peace.

May 2000

When I mentioned earlier in these pages that my reformation seemed to have had such minimal impact on my outward behaviours that few people seemed aware of any change, I might, perhaps, have added that my children noticed some differences. Joanne, my daughter, all arched eyebrows and mystification, tends to sidle towards the nearest exit when I begin to pontificate. Brian Junior, the quiet one, watches, observes, says nothing, sees everything. (Reminds me a bit of Brian Senior.) And then there is Peter, our eldest, open and extrovert, who tends to use me as a sounding board in matters spiritual.

I recall one evening, just after a barbeque outside Peter's mobile home at Antibes, when twilight was setting and another balmy French evening was in prospect, Peter brought me a second cup of coffee and sat down beside me. Sadie was chatting across the way with Peter's wife, Sandra. Peter turned to me, pointed his elbows towards the ground, forearms straight, and made an arch with the fingertips of both hands.

'This,' he said, 'is the portal to eternity. You know with absolute certainty that in ten minutes time you will have to walk through it. How do you feel?'

I should point out that at that time neither Peter nor myself remotely envisioned my present circumstances. The question came from Peter's own concerns, not mine. I laughed and said,

'How one feels depends entirely on how one believes one has spent the life that has led up to these ten minutes. If you are asking me how I feel, then I would like to think that I would be reasonably comfortable with the prospect.'

This led to a long and speculative conversation involving Catholic teaching, modern myths about the afterlife, lifestyle, and notions of eternity.

Given my current status 'in the shadow of death', it will come as little surprise that I have been reflecting again on this question. What lies behind Peter's 'portal'? What is that 'undiscovered country from whose bourne no traveller returns' – a thought that gave Hamlet pause when he was contemplating suicide. John Keats, in his twenties and dying of consumption, did not perhaps consider suicide but once, listening to the song of a nightingale, he longed to

... fade far away, dissolve and quite forget ...
the weariness, the fever and the fret ...
where youth grows pale and spectre-thin and dies.

I can easily empathise with his wish to escape the torment of his illness in which

... but to think is to be full of sorrow and leaden-eyed despairs.

But escape to where? Keats would follow the nightingale's song into oblivion:

Now more than ever seems it rich to die,
To cease upon the midnight with no pain
While thou art pouring forth thy soul abroad
In such an ecstasy.

Poetic, a strange but compelling mix of lyricism and melancholy. But not for me this empty substitute. I will find my solace in meeting with my God. But the questions remain. What is eternity? What is the nature of the three states that I have, however vaguely, contemplated throughout my entire life – heaven, purgatory and hell?

May 2002

I have been doing a little reading about 'last things', about the issues prompted by my recent reflections on Peter's question. One book I found on my shelves, *Afterlife* by Michael H. Brown, deals with heaven, hell and purgatory in extraordinary detail, using not only theological explanation but also accounts of mystics' visions and, even more improbably, reports from a variety of people who had 'near-death' experiences. I read it first a few years ago and came away impressed. Now, reading it again from the perspective of vested interest, I am not so sure. I also looked at the *Catechism of the Catholic Church* for something definitive, as well as elsewhere. During my search, I came across a meditation in a spiritual journal by Edward Norman, Chancellor of Yorkminster, who urges us to recognise the stark truth that

> 'Christians need to die with realism and always be conscious that beyond the grave lies a fate which for so many will prove truly terrible. When Jesus spoke of the coming judgement, he was not speaking in images or using the vocabulary of symbolism. Christians know that they are called to account and that life ... is a preparation for an eternal existence.'

All of the texts I examined are agreed, of course, that death is not an end; it is a transition. 'Consciousness,' M. Brown says, 'survives.' The *Catechism* defines the three states quite matter-of-factly, affirming their existence and explaining that hell is self-exclusion for eternity from the Divine Presence, that purgatory is a period of purification to ensure the complete holiness necessary for a soul to enter heaven, and that heaven, itself, is a state of supreme definitive happiness. No attempt is made to describe or explain the nature of these states although it is made clear that God predestines no one to hell. This is something a sinner brings upon himself by his own wilful disregard for love, by his attachment to mortal sin and his persistence in it, and by his refusal to come to repentance.

Some famous mystics have made it clear that hell is a horrifying place. I am somewhat of the belief, given the casualness of many Christians (my former self included) towards our faith and its obligations, that a return to the old 'hellfire and brimstone' sermons might not be amiss in our churches. St Thomas Aquinas once said that Jesus often spoke about the fires of hell because to the sinner such consideration is often more compelling than thoughts of heaven. In my own schooldays we were strongly focused on the concept of 'attrition', being sorry for our sins because of fear of the consequences, rather than 'contrition', which stemmed from a genuine sorrow and a love of God, something most us felt was beyond us. But attrition at least kept us on the reasonably 'straight and narrow'.

Sr Lucia of Fatima once described a fearful vision of hell given to the three children by Our Lady. They were shown hell as:

> A great sea of fire ... [filled with] ... demons and souls in human form ... blackened ... falling back on every side ... amid shrieks and groans of pain and despair.

St Teresa's view of hell is frighteningly similar:

> Hell is ... an oppression, a suffocation and an affliction deeply felt and accompanied by ... hopeless and depressing misery.

Father Sean Fagan, theologian, is uneasy about such descriptions, that is, in the sense that they are not truly definitive and could be allegorical or figurative (my words, not his, but I sense this is what he means). He does say that all the church definitively states is that

> hell exists as a consequence of final personal separation from God, that it begins immediately after death and that it lasts forever. Anything beyond that is guesswork and theological opinion.[1]

Betz and Von Balthazar, two theologians of a strongly philosophical bent, analyse the 'time' element in God's gift to us of eternal happiness, an eternity which includes a form of progression. Betz concludes that this gift is denied to those souls who deliberately chose to separate themselves from God, that they '... are trapped in an unchangeable rigidity that no longer desires conversion and no longer seeks forgiveness.'

Von Balthazar, in his book *Dare We Hope (That all Men may be Saved?)* argues that we cannot, in human terms, begin to understand the extent to which God's judgement may be tempered by his infinite mercy and that hell, as a final destination, is not necessarily certain. Nonetheless, he admits that hell needs to exist and describes it in terms similar to those of Betz:

> [Hell is...] characterised by a total withdrawal of any temporal dimension by being tightly bound into the most constricted, airless and exitless now, and this in the vilest of all locations.

These analytical descriptions may lack the drama of the horrific visions of Sr Lucia and St Teresa, but one only has to reflect

---

1. Fagan, Seán SM, *Has Sin Changed?* (Gill & Macmillan, Dublin, 1978)

briefly on them to recognise, and mentally recoil from, the utter horror of a static, unchanging state in which nothing can be hoped for and nothing more can be done.

Is it any wonder that my most constant prayer for my children, for my extended family and, indeed, for all who have to die each day, is that God will give them his greatest and most necessary grace, the grace to repent their sins just before they die so that they can die into the Divine Mercy and into an eternity of love?

There is much scope here for a reflection on sin and, indeed, I may well write something about that later. Certainly Fagan makes it clear that he believes it is a mistake to assume that hell (or heaven or purgatory) starts at the end of life. Hell begins on earth; it is simply the logical consequence of a selfish pattern of life. Purgatory, too, I should imagine, has its beginnings here on earth. The experience of repentance and conversion, and the subsequent slow process that involves the struggle to reorient our lives back to God, is virtually the church's definition of purgatory.

Brown has a much more dramatic view of purgatory as a place of fire with various levels, each more ghastly than the previous one. The level to which a soul is assigned depends upon its level of faith and redemption. He quotes mystics who say that purgatory is '… hotter than any earthly fire' and tells stories of souls who appear to the living, crying in agony and pleading for prayers and Masses. I don't think that this is quite what I meant when I suggested a return to the old fire and brimstone sermons. I find myself annoyed by these stories. I cannot accept them as truth. I see them as fearsome myths that do not reflect in any way the loving and tender Jesus I have come to know. Father Fagan, too, is more than sceptical of such accounts and he, too, is clearly irritated by them when he says, 'Our faith in purgatory is not helped by … [such] … stories.'

His own view of purgatory is at an enormous distance from Brown's but there is a certain theological shift here that I am not comfortable with either. It is a view, however, that might appeal to Christians of little faith, and even less self-discipline, who might want to hear 'easy' news about what lies beyond the 'portal to eternity'. He says:

> *To come into the blinding light of God's infinite love ... with the*
> *awareness that our spirit of sonship has not penetrated to all levels*
> *of our heart, is to suffer intense pain. To look into the eyes of love in*
> *this state can be a searing agony ... but it is a purifying, transform-*
> *ing one ...*

My first thought, if this were the case, would be to wonder why
there is need to pray for the dead. Fagan says that people under-
going this painful experience '... can be helped by our prayers in
the sense that they are supported by the solidarity of the communion of saints.'

I am not convinced and I cannot help but feel that the average Catholic, prone to a secular and a material existence, might
find a degree of spurious comfort in Fagan's purgatory. A few
minutes of psychological pain, no matter how 'searing', is something I believe most people would feel they could cope with.

I remember some words of Basil Hume's on 'judgement' that
seem to me to represent a balanced statement on purgatory. He
simply speaks of the Father meeting the Prodigal child in an embrace of extraordinary love and forgiveness. The sinner, con-
trite, '... whispers his story into his Father's ear' and it is then
that the process we call purgatory begins. But whereas for Fagan
purgatory seems to last little more than a couple of searing minutes, Hume sees the soul leaving the Father and, knowing that it
is not in a sufficiently fit state to enter heaven, it goes voluntarily
to purgatory '... certain that it is for a time only.'

It seems to me that there is more than enough uncertainty in
these views to confirm that the *Catechism*'s simple affirmation of
the existence of these states is as far as speculation can legitimately go. The obvious lesson, and it is a powerful and compelling lesson, is that we should live our lives in God's grace and
service, trusting to his love and mercy, to ensure that our eternity
will be spent in his everlasting tenderness, compassion and love.
As Father Fagan says, 'Preoccupation with future states could
distract us from the business of everyday living and cause us to
forget that the realities of heaven and hell begin here on earth.'

There is also in the literature a tendency to agree that few but
the most saintly of mortals will die directly into heaven. That,
however, does not stop us wondering what heaven is like.

Brown initiates discussion on heaven by saying that it is beyond knowledge and comprehension and, in the next breath, proceeds to regale us with stories galore about visions of 'brilliant light', 'beyond happy', 'angelic music', 'beauty', 'delightful meadows', 'sweet-smelling flowers' – page after page in this vein until, frankly, I began to find the whole exercise faintly ludicrous. Indeed, his views led me to wonder whether an eternity in the heaven he envisions might even be quite boring. I was almost afraid to articulate this seemingly blasphemous thought to Father Niall, but I did, and he lent me a book by Peter Kreeft that actually has a chapter entitled: 'Is Heaven Boring?'

Kreeft offers several reasons why heaven will be endlessly fascinating. He engages initially, however, in a long and philosophically convoluted explanation of the transcendence of eternity, quoting Boethius en route: 'Eternity is … the whole, perfect and simultaneous possession of endless life.' He speaks of the fascination of striving for a future that is 'a drama to be lived' but it is not an insecure, missable future because '… it is inviolable, already there in God's plan.' He refers to the dynamism and speed with which the spirit can move and think, making time seem frozen, although the soul's movements are energetic and real. Heaven is like 'play' – it has no goal beyond its own activity and, since the objective is infinite, unlike the objectives of earthly play, boredom can never set in.

He offers further argument, like the fascination of angels and prophets, like the fact that in heaven we are always beginning. Some fascinating stuff here, but while everything he says is intellectually stimulating and philosophically valid, it does not touch that deep atavistic yearning in us that seeks real specificity. Brown offers drama with no substance; Kreeft offers substance with no drama. Not very satisfying.

I spoke to Joan about it and her response will be my last word on the subject. She attempted to explain nothing, to describe nothing, but hers was a reply that most satisfies my intellect, and most fills me with hope and anticipation. Hers is a simple view, full of love and the certainty of true faith:

I have no idea what heaven will be like. But I know the beauty of this imperfect earth, the wonders and the amazing variety it offers, its endless opportunities for joy, interest, love, exploration, creativity,

play, happiness. And the God who created all of these marvels, in
what we recognise as a 'vale of tears', is the same God who created
that perfect happiness which is 'heaven'. Coming from that vast
and creative mind, what wonders and joys must await us there?'

Need I say more?

So out of all of this, what lessons are to be learned by Peter,
by other seekers after truth, by myself? It seems to me that,
whether we operate from genuine contrition, or are persuaded
by these speculations into some form of attrition, this very moment should be the first moment of our attempt to win heaven.
No matter what our lives have been before, now is the time to
start anew, to make a new beginning, to renew and refocus our
relationship with Jesus, with God, to restore friendship with him
that may have been lost or disregarded – now, rather than wait
for some unspecified future moment when we hope vaguely to
prepare for our transition into eternity. I love a line in my morning prayer, a line, indeed, that I turn to again and again during
each day, especially at times when I have found myself failing to
live the commandment of love or after some other failure to
maintain my spiritual life:

Thank you, Lord, for this chance to make a new beginning.

Every single moment of every single day is an opportunity to
make a new beginning! How wonderful is that? Brown says in
one of his more sensible pages:

… no matter how imperfect you have been … you have the opportu-
nity right now [my emphasis] *to change everything in the direc-*
tion of Paradise.

June 2002

Seven months, and the wait goes on. Although I am on top of the
list, I am told that several people (and God bless and save them)
have passed me by because those livers that have become available have not been suitable for me. Different medical personnel
give me different reasons for the long wait but, in general, there
seem to be fewer donors – and not just of livers. There seems to
be a more than normal shortage of kidneys and hearts as well. I
accept, with what grace I can muster, the continued encourage-
ments, the 'should-be-soons', from those who attend me during

my monthly check-ups in Edinburgh, but inside I am little affected by them. Their words are no different nor of any more substance than the hopeful 'has-to-bes' and 'chin-ups' of friends and relatives at home. To be honest, I am quite weary of the whole business and would happily be rid of this affliction either way. 'Dear Jesus, loving friend. If I am to be cured, that's great! If I am to meet you face-to-face soon, that's great too! But Lord, whichever it is to be, let it be soon. In the meantime, help me through his period and accept my discomforts and wee pains as if I were gladly enduring them for your sake. I know that doesn't fool you, Lord. I do not gladly accept the ill health and its attendant debilitation. I hate it! I wish it would all go away. But if I could, Lord, if I could at all, I would try to suffer gladly for your sake. I am truly sorry that I can't. Dear Lord, I hope that doesn't invalidate my offering because I do so want what is happening to me to do some good for a poor sinner or for a lonely soul in purgatory.'

June 2002
The other day we had our usual monthly torture – the check-up visit to Edinburgh. Although we accept the necessity for these visits and simply get on with them, one or two members of my family are beginning to express some concern about them. I can see why. The day of the review appointment demands that we rise at 4.30 am – a signal for a weary struggle with ablutions, dressing and breakfast. At 5.30 am we head for the airport, stopping frequently because of the distress my sciatica causes me. We arrive at check-in at 7.00 am and I have to endure an hour-long wait, pinned to a small wheelchair, before finally boarding the plane at 8.05 am. During this time I am plagued by itch and generally try to keep the scratching to a minimum lest the other passengers notice and begin to fear that I have some kind of infectious disease. I certainly look as if I have. Forty-five minutes in the claustrophobic confines of the plane takes us to Edinburgh for nine-o-clock approximately. A slow coffee and scone at Edinburgh airport passes some of the time, after which a taxi takes us to the Royal Infirmary where we face a further delay in the surgery waiting area of up to another hour.

My check-up consists of three parts. Firstly, a brief run

through a short series of questions read by the doctor from a standard form, the same questions and the same answers every month. Then the doctor tests my blood pressure, lungs and heart – a two-minute process. Finally, and the most important element of my visit, a few phials of blood are extracted from my arm (with great and painful difficulty because my veins are now thinner than thread) for later analysis of my liver functions. A brief but friendly chat with the physician, often someone I have not met before, ends the check-up and I am politely ushered out of the surgery. All-in-all, a total of ten minutes!

There follows a three-hour sojourn in Edinburgh. Sadie loves shopping in Princes Street, especially in Jenners' big store. While we are there, I find a chair somewhere and just sit. General fatigue makes it impossible for me to do anything else. About 4.00 pm we taxi back to the airport, more embarrassment as I am wheeled about the concourse ('the Cynosure of neighbouring eyes', to quote John Milton), flight at 6.15 pm, another stop-go car journey, home around 8.30 pm – haggard, weary, exhausted, wiped out, but still scratching. And all of this for ten-minutes during which the only event of any moment is the taking of blood.

We did ask if the 'bloods' could be done in Belfast at the Mater but there was resistance to this idea. I believe that this reluctance stems from a sincere concern for my welfare, from a need to see, to examine, to monitor for themselves, from a need to ensure that the tests continue to be conducted to their own exacting standards. Truth to tell, I have no problem with this. For me there is no safer place to 'go for check-up'. And anyway, everyone is always kind, welcoming and considerate. One or other of the co-ordinators is always there to ensure I meet a friendly face. And there is even the occasional hug from Donna! What, me complain?

June 2002
Even into the saddest lives a little joy must fall. Yesterday morning, during shopping, I managed to get into the cathedral for a visit to the Blessed Sacrament. While I was kneeling before the altar, I was approached by an old colleague of mine, Micheál O'Hagan, who had served with me on the management team at

the Newry and Mourne Institute. Micheál has been sending me
Mass-cards on a regular basis since my illness began, the most
recent one of which was a bouquet of Masses which I received
last week. I was glad of the opportunity to thank him and when I
brought up the subject he said,

'Did you notice the name of the priest who signed that last
card?'

I had to confess that I had not.

'Father Oliver Treanor?'

'No! Doesn't ring a bell.'

'He knows you, ' he said. 'When I told him who the card was
for, he said that you had taught him Religious Knowledge at
school. Something you said in class had a tremendous effect on
him and encouraged him to consider studying for the priesthood. He now lectures on theology at Maynooth.'

I felt an immediate tear in my eye and a sparkle of sunlight in
my heart. At least once during my teaching career I had said or
done something right, and what an extraordinary spin-off must
that single act be having through the life of this priest. All that
evening I felt as Baron Von Trapp must have felt when he discovered that his love for Maria was reciprocated. As did he, I,
too, sang in my heart: 'Somewhere in my youth or childhood, I
must have done something good.'

When I spoke to Jesus about it that night, I told him that
while I was sorry that my life in general had not measured up to
any half-decent standards, I was beginning to think that maybe
it had not been all bad. 'You will remember, Lord, that lovely
quotation of Wordsworth's: "... those little unremembered acts
of kindness and of love." There has to have been a few of those
in my life too, Lord. Don't forget to count them in when the day
of reckoning comes.'

I suppose I was inordinately pleased with myself but it was
such a great story to hear.

June 2002

Briege was on the phone earlier this evening. She tells me that
the meetings with the architects are now resulting in a firm concept of what the new monastery is to look like. She related another of those odd incidents that occur so frequently within this

little group. There had been a period of somewhat fruitless discussion and vague but non-specific ideas being tossed around in
the architect's office for the past few weeks without any real
progress. At one point, one of the nuns (I do not remember
which one) suggested that all five of them withdraw to a quiet
space of their own and each separately draw, without any consultation with the others, a crude version of how they imagined
the proposed building should look like. Imagine the moments of
stupefaction when, some time later, all five returned with virtually identical diagrams. All of them are aware that St Brigid,
near whose shrine the new monastery is to be built, had espoused a form of life that was 'Celtic monastic' – a tradition
which meant that a monastery was not a single large building
but a series a small buildings, each one of which had its own
purpose. Influenced by the fact that their own origins are Celtic
and that they desired to interpret their Poor Clare life in the context of their ancient Celtic, spiritual and monastic culture, each
came up with a design that featured three main circular buildings, largely timber in construction, inter-connected by enclosed
corridors, and surrounded outside by five much smaller constructions – individual wooden cells, or 'hermitages'. These are
five little hermitages they already owned in Monasterevin and
they could not envisage any new monastery that did not include
them. Briege explained to me that arrangements are already
made to have them transported from Monasterevin to Faughart
in the very near future. When the architect was presented with
this basic design – a *fait accompli* as far as the nuns were concerned – he was shocked.

'A circular timber construction? We can't do that! Nothing
like it has been done before.'

The nuns are adamant, however, and I cannot see any firm of
architects flouting the wishes of this doughty five once they
have made their minds up.

Briege went on to explain to me something of the significance
of the new design. The three circle-shaped buildings not only
denote the Celtic symbol of the inter-twining circles, but each of
the three principal buildings represents a member of the Holy
Trinity and, indeed, the function of each building will be relevant to the Person it represents. The permanent presence and

love of the Son is in the main building that houses the circular Oratory which, in turn, is surrounded by the spiritual guidance rooms where the Word is explained and disseminated. The gifts from the Father of shelter, of nourishment, and of each other are in the living and relaxation quarters. And the wisdom of the Spirit is in the section that houses the small library of spiritual books and the sleeping quarters where each night the Spirit will refresh their bodies, their minds and their souls. When built, it will be the first living monastery operating within a Celtic tradition for over a thousand years. As I write this, I believe the architects are still shaking their heads in bewilderment. It will be interesting to see how it transpires.

June 2002

There is now one small note of concern in Joan's story, hopefully not serious. She has been limping lately and thinks she might have sciatica, a bit like the same annoying pain in the butt I have. Doctors, however, and she has been to a couple, are puzzled by the symptoms and have been so ineffective in treating the pain that Joan, whose nights are disturbed by it, has been trying acupuncture and other holistic treatments.

Nonetheless, despite her aches, she still remains concerned about my situation. I find that I can now tell her not to be worrying, that I am not too distressed by my situation any more. I think that I am beginning to come to terms with what is happening. I have to be careful here; like all human thinking, mine remains multi-layered. I am not leaping about in joy. At night I scratch. I bemoan my inability to lie in bed for any length of time. I could do with a bit more energy. But something is happening to my psyche, something ... comfortable. I chat with Jesus about things other than my illness ... that has become almost a side-issue now. I find I do not have to agonise so much about whether or not I am offering up my 'sufferings' properly. The phone no longer affects me when it rings. I am enjoying my days, my shopping and walking with Sadie. The books I am reading absorb me. Life is ... strangely content.

I do not talk to Sadie about dying but I think about it an odd time without the slightest frisson of concern. I am experiencing a peace, a calmness that I cannot explain. I said something of this

to Joan who immediately interpreted it as acceptance, as a handing of my life over to God. But those terms are just a little too
grand for me. I do not think I have yet reached those dizzy
spiritual heights. Maybe I have just worn myself out trying to
figure things out, trying to be better than I am. Maybe I have, indeed, reached a form of 'acceptance', but it might be the acceptance of the exhausted, a surrendering to a knowledge of who
and what I am, a realisation that God loves me as I am and that
there is not much more that I can do about it anyway. When I
think about it, I suppose there might well be an element of trust
in it. I can hear myself thinking occasionally, 'OK Jesus. I'm leaving it all to you. I am just going to enjoy my books, my days, my
'now'. Whatever it is you're planning, I'll just wait quietly for it.
I'm sure it will be great, whatever it is.'

July 2002
Some years ago, 1981 in fact, I was studying at Magee University
College in Derry. A few of my classmates, like myself, were not
particularly keen on discussing football, sport or general gossip.
Our preference was for conversation that tended towards matters philosophical or academic. We became friends and congreg-
ated regularly in the Breakfast Bar of the college during our various breaks. On the surface we seemed an ill-matched group – a
cigar-smoking Anglican canon, large in personality and size,
who professed not to believe in an afterlife; an attractive
German lady who made no secret of her active past on the continent during the university unrest of the late 60s; one of our lecturers, a lady whose doctorate was in psychology and who was
possessed of a strong feminist bent; and myself, conservative
and traditional in background and attitudes.

One morning we were discussing religion and I noticed that I
was suddenly the recipient of rather strange looks because of
some comments I was making. None of my friends suffered any
reticence when they felt that they had something to say, even if it
was a direct challenge to one of the others, indeed, especially if it
was a direct challenge to one of the others. The psychologist said
to me,

'Brian, I can't believe what I am hearing. You think sex is a
sin?'

It is easy to be nonplussed when one of your lecturers attacks you from under raised eyebrows and with a smile of sympathy for the weird and wonderful beliefs that life has saddled you with. I stuck to my guns, however, and stated what I believed.

'Not if it occurs in a legitimate marriage. But I believe sex outside of marriage is a sin.'

The others smiled. My clerical friend's beam was immense. The unspoken message was clear. Brian has said some strange things in the past but this time he really is off-the-wall. I loved these people, still do, but sometimes their views simply did not coalesce with mine. They are sophisticated people and I, perhaps, am not – certainly not in the wisdom of the world. But as George Santayana pointed out, 'The spirit's foe in man is not simplicity but sophistication.'

I mention this incident because, a couple of weeks ago, I was listening to the tail-end of a radio programme on which my psychologist friend was a member of the panel. I recognised her voice immediately and, more than that, I recognised the exact tones that I had fallen victim to more than twenty years before.

'The logic of sin? The logic of sin? Pray tell me, what on earth does that mean?'

I had never heard the phrase before but I immediately thought it made perfect sense. I have often stated to Father Niall, and to my sisters, my conviction that the Catholic faith and its theology is based on the most complete and circular logic imaginable. The logic of sin is, in fact, quite inescapable. Sin itself may be an illogical act *per se* but the logic of sin emanates perfectly from its original base in the commandments, any infraction of which is directly hurtful to God, to our neighbour, or to ourselves. We were given this blueprint for living which, if sincerely observed, would lead to harmony, peace and happiness on earth. Any act that has been deemed sinful since Jesus' time, and any human behaviours or interactions that cause grief or hurt, can all be logically traced back to infractions of these ten key commands.

I have been thinking about sin since I began to reflect on Peter's 'portal to eternity'. An article in a newspaper I read yesterday, written by a non-Catholic, deplored the loss of 'moral responsibility' in this present generation. It strikes me that there is a certain inevitability about such loss. Sin is a much underused and infrequently discussed word, even, I truly believe, in our churches. The 'Good News' of the Lord's love, mercy and forgiveness is wonderful news; I have experienced it too deeply not to know that. But since the Second Vatican Council, this positiveness has been emphasised almost to the exclusion of reference to the sin element that demands the forgiveness in the first place. I know I am treading on complex and carefully laid pathways here but I am not alone. Father Sean Fagan talked to a psychiatrist who stated that a lack of moral responsibility can do great psychological harm. He called for

'... clergy to reassert their moral leadership, to study sin, identify it, define it, warn people about it, and promote measures to combat and rectify it.'

'And what is confession for?' someone may ask. It seems to me that confession is for the converted, for those who already understand and know their sinfulness and who have the grace to seek the wonderful forgiveness that Jesus offers through this peace-giving sacrament. But what of those who, like my university friends, think sin is an outmoded concept? What about those, myself probably included, who may be over-scrupulous about sin and its nature and who need guidance?

The Catechism of the Catholic Church carries two full columns, not on sin, but page references to sin, in its Index, so clearly sin is something that has not gone away. Here sin is defined as:

... an offence against reason, truth and right conscience, a failure in genuine love for God ... it wounds the nature of man and injures human solidarity.

Details about sin, its nature, types, varying levels of gravity, are discussed at length and the conclusion is specifically drawn that the root of all sin lies in human hearts.

Jose Maria Escriva said once that 'pride is the root of all sin ...', that fearful belief in our own all-embracing importance that causes us to put ourselves before others, often at the expense of others.

To think of sin as a specific negative act within a whole series of neutral acts, or even blessed acts, is to misunderstand its nature. How many of us go to confession with our list of 'wrong' deeds as if they were independent of the rest of our lives? Sinfulness is a general tendency of one's life away from God, away from the values of truth, honour, and love. It is a following of one's baser instincts even though we know these to be wrong. Ruth Burrows came to an understanding early in her life that '... sin is an orientation, a more of less continual series of choices against what one knows in one's deepest heart to be right. It is an evasion of life, a refusal to stand in the truth of one's being.'[1]

The gospels continuously urge us to turn away from sin to the love and forgiveness of the Father but, as Sean Fagan says, 'we cannot repent and be converted unless we take sin seriously'. Joan once said something similar to me: 'We cannot be freed from our chains until we know we have them.'

Today's generation of Catholic parents are themselves victims (I truly believe) of a liberal and increasingly fuzzy understanding of sin. Their understanding is blunted even further by the godless attitudes and values that are transmitted perpetually and with ever-increasing lack of subtlety by the media. As a result, they are unable to pass on Christian ideals and practices to their children. The children grow up subject to the same media barrage, to the influences of a society that reflects in its condition the mores of the media rather than the reverse. They grow up lacking the bedrock of true values by which they would be enabled to form moral consciences. Some might argue that many films and television programmes promote the values of honour, integrity, loyalty and the importance of good over evil. I have used this argument for years to defend myself against Sadie's constant ridicule of my predilection for 'Star Trek', a programme that is underpinned with truly moral values. But these are the values of a civilised society and promoted as such. Good pagans espouse them. As portrayed in these dramas they are not rooted in Christianity; they are not rooted in any understanding of the intricate nature of sin. Hence, I come back again to a point I made earlier in my reflection on Afterlife, that there is a need for a return of 'sin' to the pulpit, to a re-education of our children in the complexities of right and wrong.

I am myself, of course, groping for answers here. In his last

1. Burrows, Ruth, *Before the Living God*, Sheed and Ward, London, 1975

letter to me Father Martin joked, with some underlying serious intent I would imagine, that '… you're an awful puritan.' I took no offence whatever at this. Father Martin has absolutely no idea how to give offence. But I did wonder what I had said in my previous letter to spark this response. It tends to sit side-by-side with Father Niall's constant injunction that I am too hard on myself.

It may be that I am over-focused on sin, on behavioural weaknesses, on limited love for Jesus, but so many people of saintly reputation have expressed similar concerns over and over in spiritual literature. William Barclay, a Church of Scotland minister and a Professor of Divinity at Glasgow University, states categorically that,

> *Christianity begins with a sense of sin. It begins with the sudden realisation that life as we are living it will not do. We awake to ourselves and we awake to our need of God.*

I am conscious, too, of the argument that preaching on sin might alienate the faithful who still go to church. But I cannot accept that the 'faithful' can be driven away. The 'errant' can. I have long sensed in those who attack the Pope and his 'conservatism', who dismiss as 'old-fashioned' his repeated calls for Catholics to return to and embrace the moral life, an undercurrent of conscience that they are trying to deny. If they can rationalise as 'out-of-touch-with-modern-living' the specific rules of faith that might inhibit how they wish to live their lives, then they can persuade themselves that what they seek to do is morally legitimate. (Echoes of 'Lest having you, I might have naught beside'!) There are grave dangers in this kind of rationalisation. We can, by and large, avoid the huge sins. They cannot easily be rationalised away. Ruth Burrows says that these capital vices, the seven deadly sins, in their gross form offend human dignity and they are thus actually less harmful than we might imagine. But she goes on to say:

> *It is their subtle ramifications which are deadly. More harmful than any single, even grave fault, are the attitudes we have adopted, stands we have taken, without realising their sinfulness.*[2]

---

2. Burrows, Ruth, *Guidelines for Mystical Prayer*, Sheed and Ward, London, 1976

Something of this can be seen in the elder brother of the Prodigal Son. He, dutiful though his life may have been, is as lost as his wayward brother but in more subtle ways, and ways that probably make it more difficult for him to come to reconciliation with the Father. We see this in the sudden flare of resentment, anger and selfishness that this 'loyal' son experiences at the sight of the Father's unconditional forgiveness. To be over-preoccupied with the 'law' of living life dutifully is to run the risk of a moralistic intensity that puts the 'law' above forgiveness, that substitutes rectitude for a loving heart. I rather imagine, given my tendency to seek always the minutiae of things, that this is why Father Martin asked me to read that chapter on The Law. But in this brother, who scorns the sinfulness of his younger brother, we see more than traces of at least three of the seven deadly sins – pride, envy and wrath.

Henri Neuwen, writing about the prodigal's elder brother, extrapolated from the parable that he, himself, was victim to the same 'lostness'. He felt distress at what he saw in himself and was moved to write:

> There is so much judgement, condemnation and prejudice among the 'just' and the 'righteous' … so much frozen anger among the people who are concerned about avoiding sin.

Do I hear echoes here of my own question to Father Niall, 'Where is the love?'

The problem with such puritanical attitudes is the impact they have on others. When people are harangued for their sinful behaviour in what are generally simple and natural activities, e.g. sport on Sunday, listening to rock music and other such sanctions or, more frequently, drinking and gambling, they will tend to become impatient with any talk on sin and, perhaps, reject the notion of sin altogether.

How then are we to recognise sin? We are told that an 'informed conscience' will provide us with the moral compass we need but that is a particular mentality that is not easily acquired. To begin with, there are often too many grey areas in situations where it seems that morality may be compromised. There are circumstances specific to the individual that make objective judgement of a particular act extremely difficult. Secondly, mere knowledge of sin is not sufficient to generate a moral response. Nor, indeed, will intellectual desire and the determination of human will, no matter how focused, bring about spiritual growth and the capacity to avoid sin. It is really quite simple: we must first be led by grace. I do not write as a theologian; I write (desperately striving for humility in the truth of it) as someone who has experienced this grace. Thomas Merton said something about this. I do not have the reference to hand but if I remember correctly it was something like:

> A saint is not someone who is good; a saint is someone who has experienced God's goodness.

That reminds me of a Country and Western song I heard on the radio the other day. I do not know who the singer was. I do not know the title of the song. But the refrain, constantly repeated, caught hold of my ear and stuck there. At first I thought it was theologically askew but when I had time to think about it, I realised it was remarkably astute in its simplicity:

> The only diff'rence 'tween a sinner and a saint
> Is one is forgiven … the other one ain't.

I was initially disturbed by 'the other one ain't'. We are all forgiven. Jesus died on the cross to ensure that. But then I thought it was rather like winning the lottery. In God's love we are all winners. We have the ticket; the prize is guaranteed. But unless we present the ticket (repentance), we cannot claim the prize (forgiveness). Perhaps those who 'ain't forgiven' have yet to present their claim tickets.

So where am I going with all of this? I know that I have already gone a lot further than I intended to; but having gone this far, I'll play it out.

Sin is clearly real. Are we then to live our lives guilt-ridden, with long sorrowful faces? Of course not! That would be the very antithesis of Christ's message of love and forgiveness and joy, a message that Vatican II was so determined to emphasise – the good news of God's love. But the problem with any message is that it can be just words. Jesus himself told us that even his words often fall on stony or infertile ground. If we are to hear, there are some things that we must acknowledge. We are all sinners; we are incapable from our own resources of changing that.

To change, to find a way to the truth and to a life of some holiness, we must rely on God's grace.

God's grace works in the most mysterious ways (witness my own experience) and he probably works in different ways for each individual. All I know is that we feel its impulse, constantly, in our lives. We have to stop ignoring it; then we will begin to change. Nonetheless, somewhere along the line, there is our own contribution to the healing, a willingness to be converted. As Father Niall once told me, God opens the door, but we have to walk through it ourselves. Ultimately it is about balance, about perceptions of justice and fair-mindedness. (Remember Jesus simple dictum: Do unto others …) When we possess these characteristics, we begin to know ourselves; we recognise our weaknesses, our selfishness, our disregard for the needs of others. As Christians we cannot be unaware that the whole of Jesus' preaching sought to convince us of the limitless love of the Father and to plead with us to let that love guide every part of our daily lives. If we are guided by love, we will recognise sin but we will not be overwhelmed by its darkness. If we fall we can turn to the Father, confident still in the unconditional nature of his love. No sin we commit will make him love us less. Shakespeare said in one of his sonnets:

Love is not love which alters when it alteration finds.

Love, true love, is unaffected by the loved one's behaviour. The Father's love is like this; nothing we do can alter it. And if somehow we can come to 'experience' that love, because 'knowing' is not enough, then we will be filled with the urge to repent and beg forgiveness when we sin. Love can do nothing else.

How do we experience that love? It starts with prayer – often the simplest of prayers. God will take his time, ease us along gently, but eventually, if our prayer persists, he will give us the great gift of 'experiencing' his love. The path, as I experienced it, is generally slow, a gradual, easeful unfolding and opening to the light. Even after four years, I realise how little I understood about my experience, how little I was able to comprehend and identify what was happening. Only now, as I am left for long hours, long months indeed, in my sick chair, with endless time to do little but think, am I beginning to see some chinks of light in my musings.

There is a contradictory, almost paradoxical, relationship between sin and love. Julian of Norwich had the courage to express it in the surprising but somehow comprehensible statement:

We need to fall and we need to realise this. If we never fell, we should never know how weak and wretched we are in ourselves; nor should we ever be able to appreciate the astounding love of our maker.

Sin, in other words, is not the most significant concern of our God. Our seeking forgiveness is. We find it difficult to do this when our sin fills us with self-loathing. Jesus once told the Italian mystic, Mamma Carmella,

Pick yourself up after each fall, asking my pardon and my help, for it is not so much the fall that afflicts me but the discouragement.

And now, too, I am beginning to understand what Henri Neuwen meant when he said, 'The greatest challenge to our spirituality is to accept God's forgiveness,' i.e. to set aside that pride in ourselves that becomes so distressed at the sight of our imperfections that we cannot let go of the guilt they engender. Only when we begin to experience God's love, to see humbly how weak we are, can we begin to appreciate what Torkington refers to as 'the fundamental principal of spiritual life', namely, that we cannot go a single step forward without God's love.

There is a kind of inevitable circularity about all of this. Grace leads to prayer ... which leads to the experience of love ... which leads to prayer ... which encourages within us the growth of love ... which leads us to pray. It is not something we do ourselves. When we accept the truth, the truth that on our own we can do nothing, that we depend totally upon God's love for all that we are and can be, then we can begin to grow. We will learn that it is love and not fear of hell that leads us away from sin. And that is the Good News and why Vatican II focused so strongly on the importance of love. The first stanza of a hymn from the Divine Office encapsulates this:

The Father's glory, Christ our light
With love and mercy comes to span
The vast abyss of sin between
The God of holiness and man.

That is the totality of the message. If only we could hear.

August 2002

Still no news from Edinburgh but amazingly, I seem to be growing stronger. I am back to walking around the block every day – it takes half-an-hour to do the ten-minute walk but at least I am doing it. Even more amazing, Sadie bought raspberries today for dessert but forgot to buy the ice-cream. Rather than have her go back downtown again, I volunteered to go myself. She was dubious about it but I prevailed. It is the first time I have been behind the wheel of the car in months. This may not sound significant but, believe me, when one has been exhausted and listless for months, when just moving from one room to another requires enormous application of will and concentration, being suddenly independent enough to drive solo in the car is heady stuff indeed.

Sadie is mystified; I am too. It almost seems as if I am getting better. Yet according to the prognosis I was given, eleven of the fifteen months that I was given to live have passed. Given my present energy, zest even, I cannot believe that only four months of life remain to me. Even the nausea has passed. There is a little story attached to that, by the way. On our last visit to Edinburgh, Sadie and I went into one of the large bookshops on Princes Street that was running a summer sale. Sadie found a set of three huge cookery books, reduced from fifty pounds to ten pounds, a bargain which she snapped up. (She really needs them; she only has about a hundred or so cookery books!) But these books began to fascinate me. They contain hundreds of recipes – everything from Italian to Mexican, from farmhouse to Chinese, from traditional to *nouvelle cuisine*. I still cannot sleep at night – a couple of hours in bed most nights is the best I can hope for – so I have recently taken to browsing through these books looking for new and appetising dishes that might tempt my poor appetite. Each night I pick out three or four options which I leave for Sadie to review the next morning. She then selects one and cooks it for dinner. (She likes cooking and is good at it.) The result is that I have suddenly started eating again and with an unusually healthy appetite.

Some little clues remain, however, to indicate that whatever is going on is not some kind of miraculous recovery. I am barely eight stones in weight and no matter how much I eat I do not put on so much as an ounce of extra weight. We spoke to Tom Diamond about that on our last visit. He said that my liver is so far gone that the food is not being processed in the normal way. It is going in but it is not having any effect.

Nevertheless, I can sit and read for hours most nights or write if I want to. My concentration has improved beyond all recognition. On the down side, however, the itch remains, worse than ever, with no sign of abatement. There are also plenty of abdominal pains and aches to keep me occupied. Coming into dusk, I am still occasionally assailed by anxiety and panic attacks which make it virtually impossible for me to remain in my chair. When watching television with Sadie in these states, I tend to pace restlessly up and down behind the sofa, a behaviour which, I believe, is not one that Sadie is particularly enamoured with. Truth to tell, I think it drives her up the walls but she doesn't complain.

August 2002
I spoke too soon, last entry. I have had rather a bad time this past couple of weeks. My weight suddenly started to balloon; my abdomen became huge, massive. My knees, ankles, hands and fingers swelled up in a most frightening fashion. In little time, I reached twelve stones and the swelling in my tummy was so constricting that I had great trouble breathing when lying down and sometimes even while sitting. The other night, in the dead middle of the night, I had gone to bed for an hour or so to try to rest. After a short time, I found myself struggling to breathe, literally gasping for oxygen. I suffered a terrifying panic attack and began to hyperventilate, exacerbating the problem. I tried to remember what the psychiatrist had advised me to do, to rationalise what was happening, to understand that panic and fear were the cause of my breathlessness, but I was totally unable to control my breathing and became sure that I was going to suffocate. Sadie wasted no time in panic or useless wringing of hands. She dressed quickly, urging me to do the same, and drove me immediately to the local hospital's Casualty Department. Her history with the hospital smoothed the way for

us and soon I was lying in a bed in a private ward with two
junior doctors in attendance. They quickly diagnosed fluid retention, a common symptom with failing livers, and immediately
prepared to drain some off. They said something about a possible shock to my system if too much was taken off at one time,
but they nevertheless filled two quart jars. I was still obese when
they finished; my ankles and hands were still hugely swollen.
But I now could breathe easily and that was a blessed relief.

They left me for a couple of hours, having cleaned and ban-
daged the small hole they had made in my side to access the
fluid. The assured me that this entry wound would automatically
close within a couple of hours. I actually dozed off. Relief, coupled with the aftermath of panic and exhaustion, probably triggered sleep. I would have been happier about this, however,
had I not woken up about an hour or so later to find the bed absolutely soaking. The wound would not heal! After two or three
experiments with different kinds of bandages, none of which
was successful, a nurse finally attached a rubber bag, with a little
protuberance on it, to the wound, allowing fluid to drain into it.
The doctors told me that this continuous draining was not supposed to be happening but I am glad it is. A couple of weeks
later the wound appears to be making no effort at all to heal. I
am still wearing the rubber bag. It has been filling up almost
three times each day and, if that is supposed to be some sort of
aberration, I am delighted about it because the constant draining
has left me now almost back to normal, that is, my normal eight-
stone, skeletal self. Bad as that is, it is hugely preferable to that
awful swelling. Thank God, however, I am now barely filling
one bag a day, so I hope soon to be rid of it altogether. Sadie
does, too. It has been her job to change and dispose of it after
each filling, not a chore she particularly enjoys. I am due back in
Edinburgh in a couple of days. It will be interesting to hear what
they have to say about this.

August 2002
Joan was on the phone this evening. All the usual bother one has
when building – architects' meetings, site clearance, meetings
with contractors – is practically taking over their lives. There remains, however, that undercurrent of joy and security in know-

ing that the Spirit has led them this far and that what had seemed an impossible dream is now heading for realisation.

She mentioned her limp again and has no good news to report. Nights are now difficult for her and she often has to get out of bed and find something to lean across in order to ease her lower back pains which, she says, are becoming more pronounced. Joan tends to minimise her suffering, to compare it with what she imagines mine to be, erroneously making her own seem little. I am concerned, however. Suffering is relative and there is a constant debilitation in Joan's condition that is disturbing. Perhaps her problem is something other than sciatica. All I can do is to continue praying that she will get better soon. Her condition and her disturbed nights are beginning to limit her involvement in the monastery project. A pity, after all these years of waiting.

September 2002
I do not possess quite the energy I thought I did. The visit to Edinburgh a few days ago was quite exhausting, about as bad as usual, in fact. And worse than that, they want me to come back again next week (next week!) for a bone-density scan. They have an appointment arranged for me in a hospital at the other side of Edinburgh. My will fails! I can just about cope with monthly visits. To have to go back again in a few days … it drains me of all my energy just to think about it.

They were unconcerned about the fluid retention problem. Well, perhaps that is not fair, they were not surprised by it and it did not worry them. In fact, they said I was extremely lucky that the little wound did not heal, allowing the fluid to drain off slowly – the ideal way to get rid of it. The wards are full of patients with the same problem but who, unlike myself, are unable to do anything about. As I have said so often before, 'Somebody up there likes me …'

Briege phoned today. The architects have bowed to the inevitable, she said, (and, I presume although she did not say this, to the combined irresistible will of five nuns whose faith in what the Holy Spirit wants is unassailable). They are currently visiting places that deal in timber constructions and talking to experts about how such buildings are designed and built in

Sweden and Canada. She talked enthusiastically about under-ground heating, solar panels, and much other technical detail that I was not able to assimilate. There is excitement among them now. They believe it will not be long until the contractors begin bulldozing and preparing the site for the foundations of the new monastery. More contributions are being pledged; their sister-in-Clare who chooses to remain nameless continues to cajole wealthy connections into offering support. Briege sounds very upbeat and cheerful. I am happy for them.

9 September 2003, 5.15 pm
I have only half an hour to write this entry. Donna, one of the Transplant Co-ordinators, phoned a little while ago to tell me that I no longer have to go for the bone-density scan. The con-versation went like this:
   'Hello?'
   'Brian? It's Donna.'
   'Oh, hi!'
   'Remember that bone-density scan we arranged for you?'
   'Oh aye, indeed I do!'
   'Well, we're going to let you off. You don't have to go.'
   'Ah gee, that's great! I was not looking forward to it. What changed your minds? Something in my bloods?'
   'Noooo… not that exactly! It's just that we have found a per-fect liver for you. It is on its way here. A driver has been contacted to call for you and your wife in an hour's time. He will drive you both to Belfast airport where a small chartered plane is waiting to bring you to Edinburgh immediately.'
   And then she laughed.
   I couldn't believe it. I was stunned. I backed into the wall, dropped the phone, bumped into doors as I ran looking for Sadie to tell her the news. The excitement was incredible. Sadie noticed the phone lying on the table. She picked it up, listened, and found that Donna was still there. Donna had been able to hear all that was going on. She chatted for a minute or so and hung up. I phoned each of our three children. All are delighted. I was particularly moved by their expressions of love and sup-port. Our family, in the main, tends to be restrained in the man-ner in which we express our feelings. At a time like this, however,

there is no room for reticence. They are a little bit apprehensive, of course. There are no guarantees that the operation will be successful but they are thrilled that I am being given the chance.

Somewhere in the midst of the mental chaos I give a moment's thought to the donor. I experience some unease and manage to whisper a prayer for the person who had to die that I might live. But I cannot think about this now. What is happening is monumental. I am stunned. I can't believe it. Ten months of anxious waiting come to an end! Ah, dear God! Is this to be the miracle of 'a surgeon's skill' that Sr Briege McKenna prayed for?

Joanne is on her way to see us off. She will be here shortly. I have asked Sadie to get in touch with Father Niall, Father Martin and Father Andrew as soon as possible after we get to Edinburgh. I was thinking just now that I asked Father Niall to be my spiritual counsellor for just a 'little while'. The 'little while' has expanded to four years and there is still no end in sight. God help the dear man!

PART FOUR

New Life

CHAPTER SIXTEEN

A Surgeon's Skill

January 2003

In the great old post-Victorian novels, there was always a chapter that began, 'It was a dark and stormy night ...' And, in truth, the evening when Sadie and I arrived at the City Airport was dark, rain clouds were gathering and the wind was freshening. When we saw the tiny plane that was to transport us to Edinburgh, Sadie's heart dropped. Her misgivings were in no way allayed when she discovered that we had to climb along the wing to get into the tiny passenger area – two seats for pilot and co-pilot, and two seats for passengers. Sadie's apprehension mounted even further when two others, who looked like adolescents in uniform, joined us.

'My heavens!' she said. 'These two can't even have done their GCSEs yet.'

One overheard her and laughed.

'It's OK, ma'am. We're both over twenty.'

Take-off was a little daunting. The wind caught and tossed the tiny plane around but the pilots seemed unconcerned. Sadie clung to me. I could hear her whispered prayers, even above the noise of the plane.

'Don't be so worried,' I said. 'God wouldn't have taken us this far to drop us in the middle of the Irish Sea, would he now?'

She remained unconvinced and continued to cling.

My own mood was entirely different. I had no interest in the plane or in the nature of its flight. Oddly, I was also unmoved by the prospect of the forthcoming operation. I remained in a strange, surreal calm, reflecting absently on the previous ten months and wrestling with some most peculiar feelings. Did I really want to live – or was there something in me that, prepared for death, was now creating a psychological confusion? I did not resolve the matter.

In little more than ninety minutes we were in a side ward of the Scottish Liver Transplant Unit at the Royal Infirmary in Edinburgh. A pleasant nurse helped me to settle in, left, and returned shortly with a hypodermic syringe.

'This will put you to sleep,' she smiled. 'When you wake up, you will have a new liver.'

For the first time since I had heard the news, I experienced a frisson of concern and whispered a quick prayer to Jesus to protect me. In no time I was asleep. Sadie told me later that all during the time she was waiting for them to take me to theatre, about an hour, I continued to scratch and scratch, even in that deep sleep.

January 2003

In the past few years Jesus has taken me on two strange converging journeys, one spiritual, one physical. One was a journey into growth and awareness, seeming to culminate in that extraordinary epiphany in 1998, a climax, yet oddly, only a beginning, that left me deeply moved. It was a signal event, but only part of a story that cried out to be told, a story that, despite my limited ability to relate it, demanded the fullest expression of my heart. The second journey culminated in that most extraordinary of physical events, a liver transplant. It is a truly amazing episode in physical terms but, in writing terms, it is strangely anti-climactic. I am seriously tempted to simply write: 'I have now received my new liver and I am doing great.' Nothing in me strains to tell the story. It is not that I am ungrateful. Totally the contrary; I am overwhelmed with gratitude. But the story itself appears already to have been told. The ten months of waiting were for me the real centre of this story. Something of this thinking can be seen, I think, in a comment I made to one of the nurses a week of so after my operation. A man, drugged, bristling with wires, tubes and bandages, was wheeled into the bed beside me. The nurse told me that he, too, had just had a liver transplant but that he had only been on the waiting list for one week before receiving 'the call'. I looked at him for a moment. Then I turned to the nurse and said, 'Poor fella! What could he have learned about himself in a week?'

Her look said it all. She had no idea what I was talking about.

But I did. I knew exactly what I was talking about. In that moment, I realised that the wonderful gift of a new liver is no more of a gift than those ten months when Jesus gave me the privilege of sharing my life and my heart and my hopes and my fears with him in a closeness that many will never know. Poor fellow indeed! He will never know what he has missed; and I know that I will never want to forget those ten months or ever to lose anything of their special magic.

Nonetheless, I would be a poor diarist indeed if I did not write a few words at least about the operation and its aftermath. And, in truth, the couple of weeks in hospital were not without their moments of interest. The operation was performed by a team of surgeons, led by the dedicated Stephen Wigmore. I say 'dedicated' because Stephen had just completed a complex double-organ transplant (pancreas and kidney), a session of some seven hours and then, without pause, came straight to me for a further eight-and-a-half hours. He must have been exhausted at the end. His skill, however, is immense. I am, as I intimated earlier, 'doing great'. Stephen called to see me in the ward sometime during my second week. He is a very handsome man, wavy blond hair, and in his forties, I would guess. He was pleasant and solicitous but also surprisingly diffident, considering the nature of his vocation, and during our meeting it was I who did most the talking. Or perhaps, he was not really diffident. My friends tell me that most people in conversation with me are barely permitted to contribute more than monosyllabic responses. But to be fair to myself, I was conscious of how much I owed this kind, unassuming man in front of me, and I used the time to let him know exactly how grateful I was. At that point, about ten days after the operation, I had literally sailed through the whole process in the most trouble-free manner imaginable. My memories are all of smiling nurses, jokes, suffering-free recovery, eating everything that was placed in front of me and being, for the most part, in a state of suppressed glee at my incredible recovery, luck, and joy.

It was a strange and remarkable two weeks in many ways. My first memory was one of waking up from some weird and incomprehensible dreams. My eyes were still closed and I could feel a heaviness in my stomach, something I immediately assumed to be a very uncomfortable constipation. I considered pressing my self-administering morphine button but something in me argued that morphine would be useless for constipation, so I refrained. I should mention that patients in the high-dependency unit, where I had now arrived after three (unconscious) days in Intensive Care, are given little hand-held cylinders with a button on them and, prior to the operation, are well schooled in their use. This little cylinder is attached to a wire leading into the patient's system and the button can be pressed when the patient is experiencing post-operative pain. Each press releases a small amount of morphine that enables the patient to deal with his own pain as it occurs. Apparently the average patient presses his button every fifteen or twenty minutes (although the morphine is measured and therefore no-one can exceed established limits). Pressing times are monitored and thus doctors can assess how much a patient is suffering and whether to increase dosages.

It was during that moment of first awaking that I opened my eyes to find a doctor and a nurse fiddling with, and unwinding, some of the innumerable wires and tubes that I could now see were sticking out of me everywhere.

'What's going on? I asked, sleepily.

'We're taking away your self-administering morphine button.'

I was disturbed.

'What am I going to do about pain?'

'We're going to put you on a course of strong pain-killing tablets. You have only been pressing your button every seven hours. We cannot leave you lying there suffering like that.'

I was mystified.

'Suffering? I'm not suffering! I've just got a bit of constipation; morphine's no good for that!'

The doctor looked bemused.

'How can that be?' he asked. 'You have not eaten anything for several days. And you're bound to be in pain. You've got a huge cut a mile long running all around your tummy and on up into your sternum.'

And I thought, 'Dear God! Father Niall has mobilised the half-tenners (those who go to half-ten Mass every morning at home) and I bet Briege and Joan have launched their troops into the fray as well.' I chuckled inwardly. 'With all that prayer, is it any wonder I don't feel pain?'

Five days after my operation I was wheeled into a small open ward to join four or five other recovering patients. I felt stiff and weak but I felt surprisingly good as well. My spirits were great! I enjoyed laughing and joking with the nurses and medical staff and, with God's enormous grace, I had no complaints to offer. Every 'How are you?' was responded to with 'Great! Couldn't be better.' Indeed, I could not avoid realising how fortunate I was. At nights I could hear terrible moans of pain and distress, sometimes even continuous loud crying, emitting from several of the wards along the corridor. At such times I thanked God with all my heart for my amazingly trouble-free recuperation and tried not to wonder too much why I should have been so blessed while those others had to suffer, in case he noticed and realised that he had forgotten to allocate me my share of pain as well. I did pray each night for the poor sufferers. Their cries in the middle of the night were truly heart-rending.

Sadie, of course, was a tower of strength. She stayed in the Nurses' Home during the entire two weeks that I was in hospital and spent long hours every day with me. I think her presence contributed substantially to my recovery. I was delighted to have her there. I noticed that the other patients who, like myself had come from a distance, had few visitors. Because of this I appreciated Sadie's constant company all the more. In fact, as the days went by, I think the other men in the ward began to look forward to her visits as much as I did. Some of her old caring skills from her days as a radiographer had begun to reassert themselves and she made friends with all of my fellow patients, chatting with them as much as she did with me.

There was one little hiccup, I suppose. The operating table had been hard and, as luck would have it, I had lain for the entire eight-and-a- half hours on the sciatic nerve that had given me so much bother during the 'waiting' period. When I regained awareness a few days later, I discovered that I was totally unable to move any part of my right foot, not a toe, not even a tremor. It was completely paralysed. The doctor to whom I first mentioned the problem said it was a 'dropped foot' and, with physiotherapy and exercise, it should be back to normal in a few weeks. That did complicate things a little bit. It meant that walking was out of the question. Fortunately, in the corner of the ward there was a zimmerframe which had been used by a patient, now discharged. I asked Sadie to bring it to the side of my bed and found that with its help, and dragging my dead foot after me, I did have a degree of independence. This was necessary for me because on my fifth evening I had been told that a nurse would be taking me to help me have a shower the following morning at seven o'clock. I set my alarm for six and, with the help of the walking-frame, dragged myself down the corridor to the shower. With a great deal of grunting and effort, I managed to get myself on to a plastic chair under the shower, remove my bandages, wash my hair and, again with a great deal of difficulty, dried myself, pulled on my pyjamas, and made it back to the ward just as the nurse came looking for me.

'Time for your shower,' she all but yodelled.

'Oh, I've just had it.' This with great nonchalance.

'What?' She looked amazed.

'Oh, I just decided to save you the bother. I will need my wound dressed, though.'

Another sideways look, and she lifted my chart from the rail on the bottom of the bed and wrote something on it. I checked to see what it was after she left. It read: 'Independent.' I discovered, through observation and the experiences of the rest of the week, that this word was a shortened version of: 'This guy does not need to be helped; he does not have to be dragged out of bed at all sorts of awkward times to sit on the chair beside the bed; he does not have to be taken for a shower; he does not have to be forced to walk around the ward when it suits any of the staff to make him do so. This guy can look after himself.' It was great! When I saw other patients being pressured into effort of all kinds and realised that that one simple word on my chart had rendered me exempt from this kind of 'tough-love bullying', I was delighted. I had been driven to efforts that I would normally have been incapable of, by uneasiness about a procedure, valid and perfectly normal though it may have been, that I could not help but consider to be an assault on my modesty.

I did have to have the dressing on the wound changed every

day, however, and a fascinating sight the wound was (and still is!). There were no stitches this time. Instead the surgeon used some very large staples to hold the edges of the wound together, staples that were bigger and much thicker than the regular office type. There were somewhere between thirty and forty of them, beginning low on my left side, running around the rib-cage and all the way up to my sternum, then upward for three or four inches, then back down around the right-hand rib-cage to low on my right side. One of the doctors told me that this is called 'the Mercedes Y'. Coupled with the untidy mess of scars that are already there, this latest addition has rendered my abdomen a spectacle indeed. (I have been toying briefly with the idea of a second career in the circus!)

Then there were the tablets! The quantity and frequency of dosages was daunting. The nurses came to me, what seemed like every five minutes, with tablets for nausea, immuno-suppressants to help prevent rejection of the new liver, steroids to help stimulate growth of new pathways or something (wild guess that!), painkillers, tablets to help me sleep, and tablets to protect my stomach from the effects of the other tablets. It was truly amazing. I counted that I was taking a little fewer than thirty tablets every day. Then I had to learn how to administer them to myself. My supplies were in a locked safe beside my bed, to which I had a key, and I was given timetables, names and purposes of tablets, dosages, frequencies, and told to get on with it because there would be no one to administer them to me when I got home. I was not left entirely to my own devices, however. Each evening a nurse would come, count all of the tablets that still remained in the safe, subtract that total from her previous tally and thus, she was able to monitor whether or not I was following the regimen exactly. The tablets came in little boxes, in each one of which were several little 'blisters' containing about twenty tablets each. A male nurse told me one evening that if I wanted to drive to distraction the nurse in charge of my tablets, I should start new blisters every so often before finishing the previous ones, thus making the counting process a veritable torture. I told him that I would consider it but that so far the nurse had given me no reason to submit her to that kind of torment.

Two physiotherapists visited me regularly, worked on the

foot, and gave me a series of exercises that I was to perform constantly. They also put what looked like a large white boot (with the toe cut out of it) on my leg for two hours at a time. Apparently its function was to hold my foot in an 'undropped position' to help restore its proper angle. While walking remained difficult, even with the walking-frame, movement gradually returned to the foot and now, a little over three months later, I am slowly returning to normal. Good job, too, because I am hoping to get out to golf within the next few weeks. Sean has been pleading with me to wait until the wound has been fully healed. He says he does not want to have to watch a repeat of my manic performances of the last time.

January 2003
I have been on the phone to Joan frequently this past few weeks. She does not seem to be well at all. Her nights are torture with the pain in her back and side. Her doctor has only been able to recommend strong painkillers but these, without some diagnosis or hope of a cure, are not very satisfying. She has had to resort to walking with a stick and, as well as that, she has been experiencing all sorts of distressing bladder and bowel problems. These have resulted in her being brought to our local hospital where they have been working on her for over a week now. Sadie and I were in to see her this evening. She told us that her doctor had examined a swelling in her foot that has become permanent and has said that it was not at all consistent with sciatica. During her time in hospital she has had an ultra-sound scan. The doctors have not told her anything about the result but Joan imagines that this silence is ominous. She looks tired and physically drained. If it was not facetious, I would be tempted to say that I am having reservations about her mental faculties as well. She told me tonight that she was using me as a model in helping her to deal with her sufferings. Me! When I think of how poorly I dealt with my own illness, I cannot for the life of me understand what there was in that performance worthy of admiration or imitation.

Joan had told us that after the ultra-sound investigation, the doctors did tell her that they were setting up appointments for her to have a CT (Cat) scan and an MRI scan. Sadie, with her lifetime of experience in the medical profession, did not like this news at all. On our way home after the visit she said to me that she believed there might be something seriously wrong with Joan. It will be a while before anything will be known. Because of the New Year holidays and busy aftermath, it will be a couple of weeks before anything will happen. However, a very pleasant and concerned consultant, I think Joan said his name was Mr Hull, has promised her that he would ensure that everything would move forward with all speed.

January 2003
I try to do a little spiritual reading most nights before I go to bed (in accordance with Father Martin's injunction). Last night I was reading Barclay's commentary on St John's Gospel and came across a reference to something St Paul said that has started me reflecting on matters spiritual again or, to be more accurate, reflecting on my reflections. I am wondering now if, in my attempts to understand what was going on in my spiritual life, I have been trying too much to intellectualise, to reduce to pure logic, what has been happening, to explain the spiritual events of my life so that they can be understood in human terms. St Paul writes that he never tried to infuse his preaching with pure logic, with what he called 'persuasive words of wisdom', in case the faith of those to whom he spoke should become 'founded on human wisdom'. His concern is that all of us should be influenced only by faith in God.

I came across an interesting perspective on this in a little book by Ramiero Cantalamessa, *The Mystery of God's Love* (one of the books Sr Briege McKenna sent me). He tells us that 'Kierkegaard effectively denounced the presumptuousness of much modern thought in trying to go beyond faith – as if there were anything beyond faith.' This is causing me something of a problem. I have begun to wonder about the nature of my own thinking and I have set about trying to understand it by seeking clarification on this notion of logic in yet other books. Barclay has something very specific to say about it:

> *The danger is that religion can so very easily come to be regarded as a matter for argument and debate and discussion, a series of fascinating questions about which it is possible to talk for a lifetime – and do nothing!*

This is very scary. It makes me want to review every reflection I have written in order to analyse the extent to which I have simply been fascinated with debate as opposed to genuinely searching for truth. Barclay goes on:

> There is all the difference in the world between being ... argumentative ... and [being] a truly religious person who has passed from talking about Christ to knowing him.

There is much to learn from this, and it concerns me. I have frequently claimed to Sadie, my sisters, my brother, that all I want to do is to get back to a simple, uncluttered faith in which the love of God and good action is paramount and in which all philosophical search is rendered moot. Yet a simple phrase, a word even, can often launch me into a series of complex questioning that is as far from the simple approach as it is possible to be. Cantalamessa makes another stinging point:

> Why are modern people afraid of certainty? Why instead of truth do they hold the search for truth as the supreme good? Simply because as long as the search lasts, the human individual and thinker is the protagonist who determines values and morality, whereas faced with the truth recognised as such, we have no way out left and have to obey.

This phrase in Cantalamessa – 'faced with the truth' – is the key. It is extraordinary how this simple concept explains the posturings, the intellectual machinations, the cynicism, the attacks on innate truth, found in the vast bulk of today's media. Faced with the truth ... we have to obey! Faced with the truth! Is it not clear that this same simple concept explains why Pope John Paul, a saintly and holy man, has been the victim of so much criticism and condemnation? Faced with the truth! John Paul, it is so often said, is the arch-conservative ... impossible to deal with ... so out of touch with modern life. Yet all he does is to repeat, again and again, fundamental truths that have survived the centuries. Is there not, in the antagonism to our Pope's teaching, an echo of Francis Thompson's line, 'Lest having you I must have naught beside'? Faced with the truth, the commandments! The commandments – a noun from the verb 'command' – I command, you obey, a tenet that is anathema to the modern liberal thinker. And yet, the commandments, despite their starkness, formulate a design for living that, if followed in love and with a pure heart, would guarantee that our lives would be filled with happiness and peace.

My concern has been whether I, too, in my musings have been afraid of the 'certainty of faith.' Why do I seek so frequently theological discussions with Father Niall? Why are my letters to Father Martin so filled with questions and analysis? I have spent a long time thinking about this. I realise now that there are different ways of thinking about religion. One is to question its legitimacy, its exactitude, its justification in terms of 'modern' thought. The other is to examine it in connection with one's own values and behaviours, to discover whether one can 'measure up', to find answers that will lead to a way of living that is in line with moral thought rather than questioning it. I hope and pray that my own questionings reflect the latter of these two approaches. I have come to the conclusion that my own innate, perhaps ultimately naïve, questioning is not part of the prevailing rationalism of the West which, according to Cantalamessa, '… is a massive relapse into the letter and the flesh', i.e. a relapse into the extreme legalism of the Pharisees and a purely human and intellectual explanation of God. For me God is a certainty; I do not have to think about that. For me Jesus is a friend; I do not have to think about that. For me, the commandments are not only sacrosanct, they are a blueprint for life and for living; I do not have to think about that.

What then is the purpose of my questioning? I think the same very simple, very human, and probably totally inappropriate, analogy that I have used once before will explain it. When a boy meets a girl he needs to know everything he can about her. He plies her with endless questions about who she is, what she thinks, how she feels, what she wants from him. It is a pattern as old as life. I am wondering that if, having only recently truly met Jesus (despite my entire life spent as a Catholic – of sorts) I need now to know everything there is to know about him, what he thinks, what he feels, what he wants me to be. Can it be that once I have filled my heart and soul with knowledge of him, once I have established who he is and what he wants from me, I can then settle down to simple faith and love, uncluttered by questions and intellectual demands, and live out the rest of my life in his peace?

I don't think so ... because I will never reach that impossible position. God is infinite. How can I know everything there is to know about him? How can I even scratch the surface of this knowing? St Augustine says that it is far better to love God than to know him but Basil Hume argues that 'a knowledge of God and love of God feed each other. If you try to love him, you get to know him. As you get to know him, you love him more.' Barclay goes much further. He says that 'to have stopped thinking is to be spiritually dead.' And he is not alone in this thinking. E. F. Scott is adamant that '... a very great part of religious failure is due to nothing other than intellectual sloth.' We need to think about our religion, our faith. We need to understand what we believe and why we believe it. We are intelligent, thinking creatures. Blind obedience comes from fear, or laziness, or habit; it does not come from conviction or love. As Barclay says, 'Religion is hope, but it is hope with reason behind it.' And this is why I will go on thinking, and reflecting, and trying to understand.

January 2003
When I was recovering at the Royal Infirmary in Edinburgh, all of my children, with their families, came to visit. They piled into their cars, booked a ferry to Scotland and accommodation for a couple of nights, and arrived in the ward one afternoon. It was lovely to see them. Peter said that he broke all speed limits getting to see me and then he walks in to find me lolling like an emperor on the bed with a huge beam on my face.

'Good heavens!' he said (or some expression that is its rough equivalent). 'What was I doing all that worrying for? Look at you.'

One by one they all arrived – my three children, their spouses, and about seven grandchildren. In that small ward there was plenty of conversation and excitement yet no one disturbed or cautioned us. We were left happily and entirely to ourselves. That was kind. Young Adam, going on four, was staring at me intensely. His mother, Joanne, might have been talking about me at home.

'Granda, were you really cut open?'

'Yep.'

'Was it sore?'

'A wee bit. Would you like to see it?'

Eyes rounded. 'Yeaaah!'

At that time, the wound was left unbandaged to let the air get at it and to let it heal and dry. I opened my pyjama jacket and there, in all their glory, glinting in the ward lights, were the thirty-odd staples. I did not think it was possible for a child's eyes to open so wide.

'Wow! Cooool!'

'Yeah man!' I closed the jacket again and soon I was chatting with some of the others. I noticed, with a great deal of amusement, that Adam's eyes kept straying to my abdomen. I hoped I hadn't given him nightmares.

During my illness and my time in hospital, Sadie and I made two very good friends. Meeting one of them was inevitable. She is a young lady, in her mid-thirties. Her name is Bernadette O'Hare, Co Down (Banbridge). My name, on official hospital documents, is Bernard O'Hare, Co Down (Newry). Bernadette and I met occasionally during our pre-transplant days at the clinic sessions and, indeed, on one occasion she was wheeled into the X-ray department for one of my appointments, resulting in much head-scratching and perplexity on the part of the radiographers who were expecting a male patient. Sadie was moved to warn the doctors to make sure that I got a liver that was meant for me and not one meant for Bernadette. I think she was joking … maybe! Bernadette got her liver about three months before I got mine and visited me in the ward on the day of one of her check-ups. She brought me a lovely glass-beaded rosary and a teddy bear! We have already crossed paths again a couple of times on post-operative visits and, I am sorry to say, Bernadette is still looking fragile and insecure. My own rude health is a startling contrast to hers. I hope she will be all right.

The other friend we made, Ian Cross, is truly larger than life. He is a businessman from Edinburgh, late fifties, fine build, loud and extremely confident, with a very commanding presence. Sometimes he tends to disagree with the medical staff and, despite the fact that his bed is surrounded by a curtain on those occasions when he feels obliged to give vent to his feelings, patients in our ward, and probably in several of the other wards along the corridor, are made fully aware of them. But I love him. He is a great raconteur and has a marvellous personality. He never fails to meet Sadie and myself when we go to Edinburgh for my regular check-ups (which were every week for a while, currently every fortnight, and soon to be every month.) He drives us around Edinburgh and takes us for meals in interesting hotels in little villages around the Edinburgh area.

Ian did his National Service in the Navy and, during an illness on board ship at one time, needed a transfusion. He was given tainted blood and this has resulted in his developing some form of hepatitis. Now he has a large, malignant tumour in his liver. He wants the whole lot removed and replaced with a healthy liver ... naturally! When I was recuperating, he was going through his Assessment Week. He was interested in my experiences, my transplant, my current status, and we had many long conversations. Eventually a friendship developed. Indeed, he is now often on the phone and just tonight he called, a bit tearful, to tell us that he had to give away his beloved Labrador. As was I, he too is suffering from the symptoms of fatigue and nausea, and can no longer walk and exercise his dog. The friends who have it will give it a great home but Ian, who lives by himself, is miserable without her. I feel a great sympathy for him that he has to endure his wait alone.

I got my news on the morning of 23 September that I was to be allowed home the following day, exactly two weeks to the day after I had arrived. No real surprise ... I knew that my condition was great and that nothing would get in the way of my release. The answer to a question that had been burning in me was also soon to be revealed. How were they going to remove these giant staples? It was an answer that I was not particularly looking forward to.

That evening a young male nurse, built like a rugby player, came to me in the ward. He explained that he was going to take out half of my staples, each alternate one, and that a day-nurse would take out the rest the following morning before I left.

'How do you get them out?' I asked tentatively.

'I clip them with this,' he replied, holding up an instrument that looked like small, silver secateurs. When I saw the huge hand that was holding the instrument, my heart froze. I rolled my eyes heavenwards and groaned inwardly, 'Oh my God! I'm dead!'

I was wrong. The man was surprisingly dexterous and gentle. He cut each staple carefully and with delicate caution eased it from my flesh. There were the occasional and inevitable little tugs and some minor smarting but, on the whole, the process was relatively painless.

I was not too worried, therefore, when one of the young female nurses, with whom I had joked a few times, came to finish the extractions next morning. 'Won't hurt a bit,' she carolled.

Wrong! She seemed determined to break the Olympic 'extract-the-staples' record. She pulled and tugged or, to be more accurate, ripped and tore. I moaned, gasped, grunted through clenched teeth, pleaded aloud for mercy, and she laughed merrily all the while, assuming that I had gone into one of my routines.

'Will you quit carrying on! You're distracting me. You don't want me to hurt you, do you?'

I was distracting her? Did I not want her to hurt me? My wound was on fire! When she finally placed little squares of gauze, soaked in some kind of liquid salve, upon it, I fully expected them to sizzle. They didn't; they felt wonderfully cool and soothing.

'There y'are now. All done. No problem at all.'

I gave her a fake smile (the best I could muster under the circumstances), lay back on the pillow, closed my eyes, and thanked God for small mercies.

February 2003
This is the second time I have had cause to rue my earlier judgement that Joan's life was untroubled and serene. Joan had told us that she was to have two scans, one a CT scan. This is a Computerised Tomography which scans the body in layers and, through the use of radiation, is able to provide the radiologist with a computerised image of the inner sections of the problem area. The other scan was an MRI – Magnetic Resonance Imaging – which uses sonar to achieve a similar image. My sister Kathleen phoned this evening to tell me the result of the scans. She was distressed.

'Joan has a fast-growing, aggressive cancerous lymphoma,

the size of a turnip, at the base of her spine. It is cracking the hip and has already caused wear around the edges of it, as well as damaging the sciatic nerve.'

I was shocked. I did not know exactly what all of that meant but it sounded terrible. Echoing my thought and my wordless gasp, Kathleen went on,

'Fast-growing and aggressive sounds terrible ... but the surgeon says that, if you have to have a lymphoma, that is the best kind to have. They are the easiest to destroy.'

'Is she going to be all right?'

'I don't know. They have taken her to the cancer ward at Craigavon and she has to have at least six sessions of chemotherapy. They'll see how she is after that. She may need another two sessions.'

'There's some hope then?'

'It's hard to get them to say anything but I think there's hope.'

After Kathleen rang off, I sat by the phone unable to move, unable to think. 'Serene and untroubled ... serene and untroubled!' How could I ever have thought that? She's heading into a period far worse than anything I had to suffer. I felt totally helpless and kept saying to myself 'I must pray! I must pray!' but somewhere in the depths of my mind was a failing of faith. I was thinking that it was a good job Briege and the others would be 'storming heaven' because I felt that any prayers of mine would have little effect. And I realised that all during my own illness I had never truly prayed for a cure or a return to health, except, of course, those pleading little ejaculations for an immediate removal of all pain. I had left the real praying to others. Now Joan was depending on my prayers. I'll talk to Jesus about it. I'll talk to him, too, about the sudden fragility of my faith. He has given me too much to deserve that from me. Hopefully that moment of doubt was little more than human panic, something that will resolve itself when I have come to terms with this awful news.

CHAPTER SEVENTEEN

Aftermath

February 2003

Exactly two weeks after I received my new liver, I was discharged from hospital. I had been safe and comfortable there but I was keen to get home. Or thought I was! When the moment for departure arrived, I was assailed by sudden concern, by sudden insecurity. The doctors and nurses at the Royal Infirmary knew me well. They knew my every muscle and sinew, my blood-pressures and temperatures, the whims and vagaries of my condition. Now I was about to remove myself a plane flight and a long car journey from their attentive care. If something suddenly went wrong, as it had with other patients in the ward, what was I going to do? I had to steel myself with the thought that I would cross that bridge if I came to it, murmured to Jesus that we had come too far for him to let go of me now, and said goodbye to my friends on the staff and in the ward. It was a strangely emotional departure; but then, it had been a strangely significant operation.

Apart from an unscheduled delay of one hour at the airport, the journey home was trouble-free. We arrived home about 4.30 pm. Sadie insisted that I go to bed immediately, telling me that I was bound to be tired. I reappeared, fully dressed, at 5.00 pm, saying that I was not tired and that I was too restless to sleep. We had bought a couple of CDs of Celtic and Scottish melodies, traditional, haunting and gloriously tuneful. I spent the afternoon selecting the best of them and recorded them on to a blank cassette for Briege and Joan. I watched a couple of my favourite television programmes and went to bed at the much-more-civilised hour of midnight. That was my first night home ... so normal, so incredibly normal!

My recovery has been amazing. And the absence of itch and of pain is a blessed delight. I am walking further and faster with every day, meeting Sr Julie enough times to start arguing with her, as I hang in through the passenger window of her car, about religion, specifically about prayer. She has a couple of books she wants to lend me so I am going to visit her one night next week to get them and continue our roadside discussions. A neighbour, who met Sadie in the grocer's the other morning, has told her that he used to watch me shuffle past his window, bent, determined but slow, oh so slow. Now, he says, if he blinks, he misses sight of me.

A couple of little problems do exist. Only recently the panic attacks have returned, some of them extraordinarily violent. I am also experiencing periods of depression, particularly upon wakening in the morning. The depression I handle by going immediately to my study and, through rationalising my state and praying fervently to Jesus for help, I can generally shake myself out of it. The panic attacks are a different story. They do not last long, no more than a few minutes, but they can occur at any time and are very frightening. I am not able to deal with them at all. All I can do is hang on to Sadie until the worst is past. I told Briege about them on the phone. Her own history has included experience of this condition and she was able to give me the phone number of a lady, a psychotherapist who, Breige reckoned, would be able to help. I wasted no time setting up an appointment. She lives in Holywood, about an hour's drive away, and I arranged to visit her once a week until we got to the root of the problem.

My discussions with this lady ranged far and wide, from significant and psychologically demanding moments in my career to the death of my mother, from my relationship with Sadie and my family to my spiritual history and growth. Eventually she was able to tell me that the problem will be only temporary. Her diagnosis is that the brain had been prevented by the anaesthetic from learning anything about what had happened to my body during that extraordinarily invasive eight-and-a-half hours of surgery. The physical trauma had been immense and now, belatedly, the brain is gleaning from the body something of this trauma. The panic attacks are the brain's response to this new awareness. They will go away soon and, indeed, they are already few and far between. This understanding of what has been happening, and why, is in itself almost enough to cure the problem.

I have been trying to push myself into returning to daily Mass. I told Father Niall on one of his recent visits that it would be any day soon. I was a bit afraid of the simple physical kneeling and movement involved, and of the possibility of a sudden panic attack in the middle of Mass. And I still had Father Andrew's little Citizens'-Band radio-receiver which allowed me to attend the Dominican Mass in spirit each morning at 11.00 am. Matters came to a head, however, the other day. For some reason a government edict has been issued, warning all churches who broadcast their Masses on Citizens'-Band radio that they are breaking the law. There is quite a furore in the newspapers about it, politicians making the usual promises to fight the embargo and have permission restored as soon as possible. In the meantime, my little radio is sadly silent now. That was the catalyst that has sent me back to my front pew in the cathedral every morning.

Occasionally, when we talk to friends after Mass, I get asked how I feel about having another person's liver in my body. Do I feel any guilt that the donor had to die so that I might live? I do not feel any guilt at all. I know quite simply, and not with any hardness of heart, that the donor would have died whether I had been given the liver or not. I am, however, deeply grateful for my new life. I pray daily, more than once, for the soul of my donor and for its eternal happiness. I had been a little upset that I could not envisage, even vaguely, the kind of person whose organ is now mine but whose life, in a sense, is now coursing through my veins. I pleaded with Maureen, one of the transplant co-ordinators, to tell me some little thing about the donor so that my prayers might be more focused. She went off somewhere to speak to someone and came back a little while later. 'All that I am allowed to tell you is that the donor was a Scottish woman, a little over forty years old.'

I thanked her. This was something much more than I had before and has allowed me to try to develop a relationship with my donor. What an extraordinary generous gift she has made to me, a gift for which she knew she could expect no repayment. I have come to understand how truly Christian organ donation is, how this act of pure selflessness symbolises nothing less than the 'laying down of one's life' for one's neighbour. How I wish the whole Christian community could come to this awareness, especially now when fewer and fewer organs are being donated. I am told that to a degree the success of modern medicine, ironically, is partly responsible for the lack of donors. But there is, too, the hard selfishness of the modern world that demonstrates less and less the Christian charity of the Good Samaritan, that is becoming less and less aware that others have needs, that is focused only on self. It is sad. I truly believe that for many people all that is needed to encourage them to become donors is a little thought, a little information, and a little chat with someone like me.

My donor has received some repayment for her gift, however. I will harry Jesus daily, several times a day, for the rest of my life to bring my donor to his loving mercy and to eternal happiness. I talk to her and let her know that she is never far from my thoughts. I tell her that I am deeply grateful for this opportunity to live again and that I will use the life-force of her liver to make my own new life worthwhile. Somehow I will try to be an example to others, to be a true witness to Jesus while I live. Something of a tall order but I know that that is what my new friend would want and I have assured her that I will try my best.

March 2003
Joan has had two sessions of chemotherapy. The plan is that she will have one every three weeks. The first experience was horrendous. She was left feeling dreadfully sick and nauseous, dizzy, wrung out, no energy, and with terrible mood-swings mostly into a tear-filled depression. Briege is guarding the ward-door like Cerberus at the gates of the Underworld. No one but herself, Kathleen and my other sister, Sadie, are allowed to visit with any frequency. My sisters have developed a close relationship over the years and, while this little coterie provides Joan with comfort and much-needed support (she sees 'God's loving hand in the support and presence of her sisters'), other visitors generally fatigue her. I do not therefore visit very often but Briege keeps me informed about Joan's spirits and I phone her at times when it is easy for her to talk.

Joan does, of course, receive visits from the other nuns in her small community and also a number of visits from the community they had just left. This was inevitable. Lifelong friendship, coupled with the natural charity of the truly spiritual and a genuine compassion for Joan's illness, brought them to her bedside. These visits from her erstwhile colleagues produced an attitudinal shift that I find fascinating even if I do not fully understand it. The success achieved by the Monasterevin group in acquiring land and funds, this strong and tangible affirmation from the Holy Spirit, registered less with the nuns of the main order than did Joan's suffering. Briege explained to me that the other nuns saw in Joan's condition the 'Sign of the Cross'. Joan's privilege of being permitted to carry the cross, to endure *vicarious suffering* to help further God's plan in the world, convinced these nuns, as nothing else might have done, that the group now had the blessing of the Lord. More than that, given their theological perspective on the situation, they had no doubt that Joan would make a full recovery. Strangely, I found something of an echo of this in a little section of Job that I had been reading earlier. Quite what the echo is, I do not know, but I sense that it is there: 'If we take happiness from God's hand, must we not take sorrow too?'

Part of the problem with Joan's first session of 'chemo' lay in the omission of a new and special drug that is designed to help the sufferer combat the terrible nausea. Someone simply forgot to administer it. The consultant was very annoyed. He is a good man and has also insisted that Joan be administered another, very expensive, drug which is not normally available, one which allows the chemotherapy to target the lymphoma with considerably more precision than would otherwise be the case. Joan has had to remain in hospital throughout this debilitating period but there are hopes that once she has rested for a few days after the third session, she will be allowed home and will be able to have the last three sessions as an out-patient.

March 2003
I visited Sr Julie yesterday evening to collect the two books she spoke of and to finish our conversation on prayer. I said we argued but that was an exaggeration. It was just that Julie was keen for me to try contemplative prayer while I was adamant

that I couldn't do it. She said that she was not intimating that the way I pray is in any way inferior, rather that I should add contemplation to my prayers in order to experience, again and again, in silence and without words, the tremendous love of the Father. That viewpoint obviously piqued my interest and I decided to do some reading to try to find an approach to contemplative prayer that would work for me.

I was surprised early in my search, and probably a bit embarrassed, to discover that I have probably done grave wrong to Nikos Kazantzaki,('I am free'), the French writer whose philosophy I rubbished earlier in these pages with little or no evidence to support my attack. I have come across a little parable that he wrote, one that clearly indicates that he was a humble and devout Christian. To someone in his story who wanted to see God, Kazanzaki's Jesus smiled and said,

'Listen old man, God became a piece of bread, a cup of cool water, a warm tunic, a cave and, in front of the cave, a woman nursing an infant.'

And the old man said,

'Thank you, Lord. You humbled yourself for my sake ... and I did see you. I bow down and worship your beloved many-faced face.'

This is pure Christian spirituality. What then am I now to make of my arrogant dismissal of:

I fear nothing;
I hope for nothing;
I am free?

I can only assume now that Kazantzaki must have been referring, in the context of his writing, to what the material world has to offer and was, in fact, claiming to be free because his spirit was free of that world. St Thérèse will be happy about my getting this so wrong. She knows that I need constant exposure to a diet of crow if I am to acquire the virtue of humility.

I was not able to find a great deal that was helpful in my search for advice on how to contemplate but I did find some interesting perspectives in Torkington. He talks about changes that come in sincere prayer after time. We pass from talking to listening, he says, sometimes without realising it. But how do we listen? Julie suggested that I try a simple mantra such as, 'Be still and know that I am Lord' and repeat it again and again while trying to sense the presence of God. There is something here of Travers' admonition that we need to become aware of 'God's transcendence' in order 'to restore a sense of reverence, wonder, awe, and adoration'. Torkington suggests that to read small passages of the scripture slowly and reflectively (and, I presume, to sit quietly while the Word of God penetrates into our hearts) might be the way to contemplative prayer. Cantalamessa tells us that prayer has four stages – reading, prayer, meditation and, then, contemplation – which takes me back to Julie's notion that contemplation is separate from other forms of prayer … sitting silent in God's presence.

I decided to give it a try. For some reason I wrote a few brief notes after some sessions. I offer them verbatim:

March 19

I tried for the five minutes Julie advised. I think I managed to drift into fourteen different topics that had nothing to do with God or spirituality. That was a bad start.

March 21

Last night I worked with the mantra and after a time I tried to say the words in my brain without uttering them with my mouth. I had a little more success with this. The distractions still come but so also did small bursts of God's presence. That, at least, is something.

March 23

I am returning to the idea of uttering the words of the mantra aloud until they resound in my head and in my heart. A stronger focus on the words enables me to fight the distractions that steal surreptitiously into my head before I am even aware that my thoughts have drifted elsewhere. I think, although I need to work at it, that I can use the words of the mantra to make contact and then, contact having been achieved, I can stop vocalising them and let them echo in my head. I still value vocal prayer, however. Blaise Pascal asks why God instituted prayer and offers the thought-provoking answer: 'To give his creatures the dignity of causality' – an answer that suggests the primacy of vocal prayer, particularly 'petitionary' prayer (which St Thomas Aquinas deems to be the 'primary form of prayer.'). This concept of 'causality', the idea that through prayer we can actually influence events, makes me wonder if our 'vocal' prayer (given the nature of love and selflessness) should be focused on the good of others while 'contemplative' prayer is a prerequisite for our own spiritual growth.

March 25
Several nights of trying and very little improvement! Tonight I tried for ten minutes (listening to a spiritual music CD). I am beginning to wonder what exactly it is that I am trying to do ... to achieve. I am beginning to wonder if I am trying too hard ... trying to make something happen in my heart and in my soul ... that old internal locus of control thing. Should I not be simply sitting back and letting God's presence wash into me? Tomorrow I will be more easeful, more relaxed, and try to let God do the work.

March 26
What am I to do about these distractions? The brain cannot 'be still'! But the ten minutes passed in a flash, listening to Breige's new CD – 'Woman's Song of God' (songs inspired by the writings of women mystics). I don't know what I am supposed to see ... to think ... to feel. What I do feel is ... helpless ... hopeless ... yet God is definitely lurking somewhere on the fringes of my consciousness. When I was thinking how hopeless I was at this contemplation business, I decided to simply go back to my little book of formal prayers. But I found that I couldn't ... I didn't want to. I just wanted to sit and let God wash over me while I listened vaguely to Breige's music. Maybe that means something!

I am still working at this new form of prayer. There is a sense in which for some it might bring the peace they seek, sitting in blissful silence with the Lord. But if the Lord is not yet seeking such prayer from us, the mantra becomes forced, a frustration. In my own case, I have discovered that I do better just looking at Jesus, trying to make myself aware of his intense love for me. I might sit there and emit the occasional 'Lord' or 'Jesus' or 'Friend' but for a little while, late at night, I can arrive at some moments of genuine, undistracted silence in his presence.

However, deliberately inculcating the silence of contemplation is hard work. I am drawn to Cantalamessa's four-part approach to prayer ... a little bit of everything. I find that I can comfortably and easily pass a quiet forty-five minutes like this, vocalising, reading, meditating briefly on what I read, and then, finding that the 'silence' seeps in unobtrusively at some point and, even if only for a little while, I know, and very occasionally I even experience, that 'I am the Beloved'. I guess that will have to suffice for the time being.

April 2003
We have to go back to Edinburgh in a few days. I had been ringing Ian on and off to let him know we are coming and to arrange for our usual get-together. I had not been able to get him on the phone despite several attempts. All we got was his answering machine. I had left several messages for him to ring me but received no response. This evening I told Sadie that I was worried about him and that I was going to ring one of the co-ordinators at the Transplant Unit to see if they knew anything about him.

'He might have got his new liver,' Sadie suggested. 'We'll be able to visit him when we go over there.'

Donna answered the phone.

'Hi, Donna, it's Brian.'

'Oh hi! Everything all right, I hope?'

'Ah yes! No problems. I'll tell you why I am ringing. Do you remember Ian Cross? I've been trying to get in touch with him but …'

'Didn't you hear?' Donna cut in. 'He got his new liver a couple of weeks ago but …'

'Oh great!' I interjected.

'Brian,' she said slowly, 'it didn't take. It rejected after a couple of days and we were not able to get him a new one in time. He died last week.'

I was shocked then, and I am totally shattered now. I still cannot believe it. His death has affected me very deeply, perhaps due to the suddenness of it, or to the loss of a new and valued friend, or to the implication that exactly the same thing could have happened to me or, indeed, should have happened to me. I don't know what the reason is, but I have rarely experienced such a violent and debilitating reaction to the news of a death as I have to this one. Sadie too is shocked. All I can think is, 'He was a good man; he always brought flowers to his church. I must pray for his soul; I must pray for his soul.'

May 2003

It is taking me a while to come to terms with Ian's death. I read somewhere that Jesus not only expects us to pray for the souls of the dead but to talk to them also. I have been trying to talk to Ian and have derived some comfort from my efforts. Somehow I have been getting the idea that what has happened to him is not so bad. When I tell him how much I hope that he is happy in heaven and how shocked I was by his death, I get the feeling that he is telling me that of the two of us he has had by far the better part of the deal. But perhaps that is just me trying to make myself feel better about the sad event. Nonetheless, if he is, in fact, happily ensconced in the loving company of Jesus, and I have no reason to doubt that he is because he was a church-going man who talked to me more than once about prayer, then it is difficult to perceive his death as a tragedy. I am unhappy; Sadie is unhappy; but how does Ian feel? I have the feeling that he is smiling and beaming and roaring in his resonant voice, 'Brian, everything is great. Be happy for me.' So, I will continue to pray for him but I no longer intend to grieve.

Joan has had her last of her sessions of chemotherapy. They have been generally very severe and she has suffered a great deal because of them. I have been to see her for a little while today. She is pale, drawn, and wearing a wig to cover her total (temporary, I am told) baldness. She is, however, in good spirits and delighted to be done with the whole business. She cannot say with certainty that there will be no more 'chemo' but the most recent scans have been extremely positive and everyone – doctors, nurses, Joan – is optimistic that a cure has been effected. We continue to pray.

Briege was not there today. Apparently she and Rose have taken on the mantle of site-foremen (forewomen?) and spend a lot of their time making sure that work is progressing. The main contractor is a man who has filled them with confidence but they have had some problems with the chap who has been sub-contracted the responsibility for digging and preparing the site. His work is good but he tends to drift off to work on other sites, causing delays at Faughart. Nonetheless, things are progressing slowly and the nuns are generally content. They have now left my nieces' house and have acquired larger premises in a country district outside Newry. They love the peace. And the house is big enough for them to have set one room aside as a small oratory containing a little gold tabernacle within which the Divine Jesus permanently resides. I have been kicking myself all evening. I passed that 'oratory' on my way in to see Joan; I passed it again on the way out. Neither time did I pay a visit to the Blessed Sacrament. I'm mad at myself.

June 2003

I have been thinking off and on over the last day or so about that last remark. Just about everyone connected with my spiritual life – Father Niall, Father Martin, Sister Julie – would be quick to tell me that I am being my old scrupulous self again, that there is no need at all to feel like that. I probably agree with them; it is just that I had a chance to call in and spend a few moments with a good friend … and forgot! If I did that even to a human friend, I would be annoyed. It is a moment of togetherness, of friendship, that might have been and wasn't. I know Jesus is not annoyed at me; I suppose it is just … me being me!

Enough of introspection! I am down to seven small tablets a day now. Over the past couple of months the doctors have been weaning me off some of the short-term tablets, the steroids, the painkillers, the tablets for gastro-intestinal protection. All that I am left with are the immuno-suppressants. These are needed to keep my immune system from growing too strong and rejecting the liver as a foreign body. I will have to take these for the rest of my life, but I have become habituated to them already … a small price to pay for what I have in return. I am back at golf and, as I walk the green fairways again and feel the soft, springy grass beneath my feet, the young summer sun on my face, I cannot resist throwing my arms wide and yelling how good it is to be alive, to be enjoying the scenery, the company of good friends, and to thank the Lord that I once again have the great health to make the most of it. My friends are still at the stage of smiling indulgently at these shenanigans but if I continue to distract them from their golf, they may soon be reminding me of the rules on the game's etiquette. But it is wonderful. It is truly wonderful and, so far, the boys are delighted to have me back and are amazed at my fitness. Indeed, so am I. I am back to playing comfortably off a single-figure handicap and I can only assume that I have been carried along on the wings of prayer from the moment I got on to that small plane until now. It has been a period of the most inexplicable trouble-free progression, inexplicable, that is, if one discounts the Holy Spirit. I do not. Neither do I recall a time in my life when thanking God for anything was any kind of priority but nowadays I cannot stop doing it.

August 2003

Ten months after my transplant I was permitted, against the normal run of such things, to go off to France for my usual three week summer holiday. As a general rule, a transplantee has to wait a minimum of one year before being allowed to leave the country but I have been doing so well that, when I tentatively suggested that Sadie and I would like to join our children in France again this year, there was no demur at all. I was simply warned not to lie for too long in the sun since, if I got burned, my immune system would be unable to cope with it and skin cancer would be a possibility. I was told, however, that I could swim as much as I liked so long as I wore plenty of high-factor sun cream and got out of the sun fairly quickly afterwards.

The holiday was great. Sadie loved it. To be back to total normality again – no sick husband to worry about, no lonely walks at night, no clouds of nameless anxiety hanging over her head – she truly loved it and made the most of it. Apart from this electric undercurrent, this 'high', it was a holiday like any other holiday and there is not much I need to say about it. We had our time with our children and grandchildren, barbeques, evening meals out, drives to new places of interest, time on the beach – normal family stuff!

There was one little incident, I suppose, that I might mention. It is one Sadie likes to recount occasionally when we sit with guests enjoying an after-dinner glass of wine.

I could begin by saying that the French are a strange race. I have heard it said that they are like their bread, crusty and hard on the outside, soft and malleable on the inside. Because of this, the veneer of standoffishness occasionally slips and we are given a look at what lies beneath. One Sunday morning at Mass, an elegant lady, approaching her seventies (if not already there), old-thin but carefully made-up and well preserved, read the Readings. She was appropriately articulate, devout, and occasioned no comment from either Sadie or myself.

Later that evening Sadie and I were passing through a little cobbled square, surrounded by restaurants and alive with the bustle and chatter of the many diners on the pavements, eating *al fresco* in the soft, warm air. In the centre of the square was a Ukranian folk-group, dressed in full traditional costume – red jackets, black trousers and riding boots for the men, and a colourful peasant dress for the sole woman who was ululating in a language unfamiliar to me. The men were playing a variety of instruments, including a huge balalaika, an accordion, a violin, drums, and a guitar. The music was gloriously evocative of the Russian Steppes, of gypsy peasantry, of love and gaiety, of loneliness and loss. These people could play! Unsurprisingly, Sadie and I ensconced ourselves in a corner and sat down to watch, to listen, to enjoy.

Shortly after that, the lady who had read at Mass that morning emerged from a street opposite us and perambulated regally into the *place*, eyes demurely cast down, concentrating not on seeing but on being seen. Catching sight of the musicians, she stopped and, as she stood solo in the middle of the square, her wide-brimmed straw boater with its red silk ribbon, her colourful wide-skirted dress and her little golden shoes became inevitable objects of scrutiny from the ringed spectators.

As she listened to the music, the top half of her body began to sway and, shortly after, her entire body began to undulate. With her eyes fixed firmly on the musicians, she began to move her feet in little steps – a little step to the side, a little step forwards, a little step backwards. Moments later, she took the chiffon scarf from her neck and, with both hands stretched above her head, she began to dance, making musically inspired configurations in the air with the scarf. Soon she was whirling, reversing, spinning, weaving, and occasionally stretching out one leg, toe pointed elegantly to the ground, in sudden dramatic pauses ... and this lady, remember, was at least seventy! Smiling at the band, she continued her amazing performance until the music ended. For a moment she bowed and, eyes looking groundwards, she held her hands apart to receive the applause, the whistles, the cheers, of her 'fans', before regally resuming her interrupted stroll out of the lighted square and on into the surrounding dusk. Sadie stood up to speak to her as she passed us, complimenting her on her performance and telling her how much she had appreciated it.

'*J'aime la dance,*' she responded grandly. '*J'aime beaucoup la dance!*'

I thought the whole episode was hilarious but Sadie enjoyed the lady's performance immensely. She later surmised that the lady had been 'on the stage' at some point in her life and had lost none of her old skills. As I said, the French are a strange race.

August 2003
While we were away, Joan's recovery had continued positively, perhaps not with the amazing disregard for the normal pace of healing that my own body has shown, but steadily and satisfactorily nonetheless. I visit once a week now. Briege is often away at the site but I am on my honour to limit my visit time to one hour. The hour flies. It might seem, given my constant wrestling with issues spiritual in these pages, that I must have arrived at a point where I can now move on to other subjects. But when Joan and I get together, I barely even remember to ask how she is before we are, yet again, in the middle of some question about spiritual life. It is always like that. In fact, I once had to admit to Joan that the only reason I take time to ask how she is doing each week is simple avoidance of the telling-off I would get from Sadie if I went home with no information about her condition. Today most of the hour was spent discussing a letter in a spiritual journal that I had brought with me. The writer, a priest, was sympathetic to divorced couples in a long and loving second marriage who were not permitted to receive the Eucharist. As usual, I trotted out the letter and exactitude of 'the Law' and castigated the priest for creating unrealistic aspirations in the minds of people who might read his comments. Joan was less rigid and asked me to consider the nature of God's love and forgiveness in the context of the issue. What I thought was simple suddenly became very complicated and I came home with less hard certainty about the issue than I had when I first read the priest's letter.

We did have time to discuss the progress of the new monastery. It is at that dead stage when little seems to be happening despite the fact that workers are digging, and marking, and laying pipes, and shifting earth. Work is definitely going on but, to the untutored eye, not a great deal seems to be happening. Joan tells me, however, that Briege's reports to the group are leading them to anticipate that, when this slow preparation phase is complete, the skeleton of the new building will leap suddenly from the ground. All are looking forward to this more tangible evidence of their dream's realisation.

September 2003
We went back to Lourdes again earlier this month or, to be more exact, on another one of Michael's pilgrimages. He had arranged to take a busload of Scottish pilgrims on a tour similar to the one we had joined a few years ago and told us that he had five empty seats. Three others from Lurgan, as well as Sadie and myself, flew across to the Charles de Gaulle airport in Paris and met the tour bus there.

The tour was substantially the same as before except that this time we circled in the opposite direction and visited one or two new places. It was wonderful to revisit St Bernadette at Nevers, St Thérèse at Alençon and Lisieux, St Jean Marie at Ars, and to try again to experience the real spirit of Lourdes.

The Scottish pilgrims were outgoing and friendly and, while I have rarely come across a group that could pray so intensely, I have equally rarely come across a group that could laugh so heartily and for so long. One evening, early in the tour, I noticed one group of pilgrims at a dinner table. It was difficult not to notice them. Their laughter was uproarious and their various comments were probably audible to anyone back home in Scotland who might want to listen. In the middle of this cheerful, if noisy, group one pilgrim stood out. His laughter was louder than anyone else's, his contributions to the conversations longer (although, to me, virtually incomprehensible because of his Glaswegian accent), his bodily movements energetic as he twisted and turned to include every member of the group in his tales. I am not sure what designation that I, the inveterate 'watcher', gave him. 'Ringleader' may not be a far cry from what I was thinking. In any event, that was my first introduction to Father Matthew.

Father Matthew Despard can best be described as 'singular'. Late thirties, stocky, strong and cheerful, he hails originally from Glasgow and, after some travel and work in other climes, he is now back in Glasgow working as a curate in St Bride's parish in East Kilbride. He has scant regard for ceremony and while on the pilgrimage he eschewed clerical garb, preferring for the most part to wear jeans, a comfortable sweater and a huge pair of 'trainers', the laces of which were invariably undone. I have never heard anyone describe him as retiring. He is an extremely convivial man who is happy in company and who clearly enjoys a laugh.

I was, however, to discover a very different man behind the laughter. The quiet-spoken, contemplative priest who said Mass for us every morning was unrecognisable as Father Mathew, pilgrim. More than once I heard the comment, 'Isn't he a saint on the altar?'

We had another priest on the tour, a retired priest in his mid-seventies, whom I came to know as Father John. Unlike Father Matthew, who was the tour's official chaplain, Father John was, like the rest of us, a humble pilgrim. He was reserved, gentle, very much a priest of the 'old school', who tended to spend most of his time talking quietly with his brother who had accompanied him on the pilgrimage. He was not entirely reclusive, however. I enjoyed conversation with him on a number of occasions and he often concelebrated Mass with Father Matthew. He was thus able to say to me once, albeit in a bemused, perhaps even mystified, manner, 'Well … he has a good heart and he does know his theology.'

I do hope the picture that I am painting of Father Matthew is not too mischievous. It is just that we have become such good friends, and his personality and *joie de vivre* are such, that I find it difficult to speak of him other than with my tongue fastened firmly in my cheek. Ours is a strange friendship, at least on the surface. Like the 'older' Father John (I think of him thus to distinguish him from the younger Father John Bermingham) I, too, tend to be reserved in company, preferring the seriousness of the *tête-a-tête* to the conviviality of the group. Yet for some reason, despite our obviously different personalities, Father Matthew and I became firm friends, going for walks together, sharing the occasional lunch, and sitting with each other, and Sadie, of course, at the evening meals. It took little time for me to discover in him a serious side, a side that revealed an intense love of the Eucharist and a no-nonsense theology that is grounded, he told me, '… in the magisterium and the gospels.' He has, too, a strong determination to do and to say what is right, to declare his views and principles regardless of the consequences. I gather, from one or two comments he made, that this propensity may well have resulted in conflict, perhaps even more than once in his life. But it is a conflict he never shirks. 'Y' have tae do what is right! Y' cannae walk away frae it.'

Father Matt's serious side appealed to me. We had many discussions on our walks about issues I had already broached with Father Niall and Father Martin and the two nuns, but which have layers upon layers of meaning that need frequent peeling. I remember on one occasion discussing in intense detail the will of God, the extent to which he imposes, or does not impose, his will upon the world. Both of us, caught up in argument and counter-argument, could only end up laughing at our inability to arrive at a conclusion. Father Matt, however, always wins these arguments. His final judgement never fails to floor me.

'Lighten up, Brian. Y're too intense.'

Funny thing, though! He only says this when his back is against the wall.

I once asked him, 'Why … for want of a better phrase … the aggressive bonhomie with the other pilgrims?'

He told me that if he went to them with a long face and a mouth full of theology, he would lose them in ten minutes. Maybe there is a lesson for me in that. I know I enjoy a laugh with my friends in the golf club but when it comes to issues of religion and spirituality I become intense, serious and prone to rigidity in my views. This is doubtless a reaction to my long years in the wilderness and my currently developing fervour. But Jesus too, if I understand the gospels correctly, enjoyed a laugh with friends, attended feasts and parties, and could be equally at ease with sinners and saints. I am going to have to think about this. Every time I am forced to head-on recognition of kinks like this in my character, I know that I am only seeing the tip of the iceberg. I need to get down into the murky depths to see what is there and what changes need to be made. That takes a while ... sometimes even longer than that!

September 2003
The Stations at Lourdes, *Le Chemin de Croix* (the Way of the Cross), provide the pilgrim to Lourdes with opportunity to respond to the call to penance and conversion that issues from the meeting with Our Lady at the grotto. The Way winds up into the hillside behind the great Basilicas, a rough, beaten path that demands effort and continues for some one and a half kilometres before leading back downwards again from about the twelfth or thirteenth Station. The various figures that make up each Station – the soldiers, Jesus, the women, and others – are beautifully sculpted in cast-iron by Raffl of Paris and coated in a kind of bronze metallic paint. They are slightly larger than life-size and evoke a response that is a mixture of religious awe and wonder at their impressive majesty and beauty.

Sadie and I decided to pray the Stations and we started together. But the track and the gradient are quite arduous and the distance between each Station is often more than a hundred yards and soon I found myself forging on alone. I arrived at the recently added Fifteenth Station, a kind of cave near which, leaning against a rock, is a large circular stone with a sun-burst emblazoned on it. This clearly represents the Risen Christ, and the Station undoubtedly symbolises the Resurrection. There is an inscription in Latin on a rock nearby which says, if my schoolboy Latin serves me correctly, 'He is risen as he promised, alleluia!'

I sat beside this empty cave and pondered the Resurrection as I waited for Sadie. In what way would Jesus, the human being, be different from the Son of God when he rose to heaven? Did the Son of God, an intrinsic element of God, remain in heaven all the while Jesus was on earth? Theologically that cannot be correct. Or maybe it is. God is ubiquitous; he can be everywhere at once. The old *Apologetics* I studied all those years ago was very specific about what was termed 'the hypostatic union', i.e. Jesus was both God and man. So whether or not the Son remained in heaven, he was definitely on earth. In a rather fanciful way, I began to consider the problem from the point of view of human logic as opposed to the point of view of faith. In a little while I had written down four syllogisms which I presented to Father John after dinner that evening. I stated them one at a time and asked him for his opinion. In fairness to him, I must point out that I hit him with them cold, without giving him any time to think.

I began my conversation by asking him if he remembered the Sacred Logic studies of his clerical student days.

'Indeed I do,' he laughed. ' They nearly put me astray in the head, all those universal negatives, major and minor premises, syllogistic reasoning … it still doesn't bear thinking about. Why do you ask?'

'Well … it's just that I have a couple of syllogisms here that seem perfectly in keeping with the rules of Logic and yet they can't be.'

He was intrigued.

'Try me,' he said.

'OK. Here's one. Major Premise: God is divine! You OK with that?'

'Oh yes!'

'Minor premise: Jesus is God. No problem with that?'

'None at all.'

'Conclusion: Therefore Jesus too must be divine. OK?'

'Absolutely! I can't see what your problem is.'

'My problem is that when I apply exactly the same pattern to other syllogisms, the conclusions are wrong. They are logical … but they are wrong.'

'Give me an example.'

'OK! Jesus is God. Right?

'Uh huh!'

'Jesus is human. OK?

'Yeeess!'

'Therefore God is human.'

Father John was immediately on the defensive.

'You can't say that!'

'If I were to present this syllogism to an intelligent atheist, he would fully agree with the conclusion.'

'But it's wrong!'

'I know. Try this one. God is divine, not human.'

Father John just stared at me. I went on.

'Jesus is God. Therefore Jesus cannot be human.'

'That's heresy.'

I had to laugh.

'I know…but it is logical.'

'There is something seriously flawed in these syllogisms, Brian. What was your other one?'

'I'll take you through it. Major premise: Father, Son and Spirit share the same essence. Agreed?'

'Yes.' Wearily.

'The Son has a human essence. Right or wrong?'

'Right, but …'

'Therefore the Father and the Spirit share a human essence.'

'I knew you were going to say that. And you're wrong again.'

'I know,' shaking my head and laughing. 'But why?'

'Write them down for me and I will think about them tonight.'

Next morning after breakfast I went over to Father John's table.

'Go away,' he said. 'I am not talking to you.'

'Did you think about …'

'Yes, I did,' he interrupted, half laughing, half exasperated. 'I think there is something wrong with the premises but I can't for the life of me see what it is. Have you figured it out yourself?'

'As a matter of fact, I believe I have. The difficulty lies in our acceptance of the hypostatic union. Theologically it makes perfect sense but to an atheist it would be totally illogical. One third of a single God becomes human and the other two thirds do not. It is this incomprehensible mystery that renders our conclusions fallacious … in theological terms. The syllogisms are perfectly logical in human terms because God is, of the necessity of logic, perceived as a single entity; but they are theologically unsound because God is, in fact, a trinity as well as a unity and that is the mystery that human logic simply cannot encompass. In human terms, one is one; one cannot be three.'

Father John was relieved.

'I told you, you were wrong, ' he said.

I nodded, smiled, and left him still pondering the mystery.

I tried to inveigle Father Matthew into the same trap a little while later.

'Lighten up, Brian,' he responded. ' Y're too intense.'

End of discussion!

That night I went back to the grotto and sat with my Holy Mother. I did not pray much. I sat quietly pondering the events of my life since the last time I had been there, reflecting on the gifts to the spirit and to the body that have been given to me. The more I pondered them, the more I realised how extraordinarily blessed I have been. I have always thought of myself, of my life, as ordinary and yet (I seem to remember a phrase from some-where) during the past few years I have lived 'a life less ordi-nary' than most. I have been on a most adventurous journey, an odyssey, that lives deeply in my psyche. Not one minute of it would I exclude or reject. Each minute has been a part, and an essential part, of the amazing whole. Each of these minutes seems to have been carefully planned, carefully measured out, and gifted to me with an ineffable kindness. And I can see, hazily perhaps, something of the pattern that has led to my present state. I even look back on my 'ten months in limbo' with nothing but affection and gratitude. Those months, too, were a gift. They are part of me now; they always will be. And they culminated, in bodily terms, in the greatest gift of all, the gift of life. And I have to ask 'why?' Does the Lord have something in mind for me or are his gifts just the over-pouring of love from his besotted heart? Obviously I cannot answer that. But I can try to keep the promises I made to the unknown lady whose death brought me life. I can try to live my life for God and in God. I do not believe that I need to do anything really special. I will just be an ordi-nary Catholic with my eyes focused a little more sharply on eter-nity, my heart fastened a little more firmly on the command-ment of love, and my behaviours fixed a little more resolutely in the consciousness of 'witness'. I can do nothing less.

CHAPTER EIGHTEEN

Loose Ends

July 2004

Just south of Banbridge there is a little townland called Loughbrickland. As you drive through it towards Newry, you will notice on the left of the dual carriageway, a large and scenic lake, a couple of houses built on its far banks and behind them, lush green countryside stretching into hazy distance. Leading off from the main road and around the back of the lake is a narrow road which, if travelled, leads into the heart of the country – few houses, even fewer farms, just wide-open countryside. When the sun shines, the whole is gloriously picturesque. About three miles along this narrow road, a yet smaller road cuts off at right angles. About five hundred yards along it, on the left, is a large, rambling, single-storey country house with ample car-parking spaces in front and to the side. This is 'The Brontë Steakhouse', so called because it is situated in the heart of the land where the Brontë sisters were born and lived part of their childhood. The restaurant is literally in the middle of nowhere, decorated in nineteenth century rustic style, with photographs of the Brontës adorning its walls. Despite its isolation, it is impossible to get a table at this restaurant without reservation, usually requiring at least a week's notice, so creative and delicious is the menu.

It was to this restaurant that Sadie and I brought Father Matthew, with Briege and Joan, one evening in January, to savour its gastronomic delights and to enjoy a companionable evening in its historic ambience. Father Matthew had come to spend a week with us and this evening out, as he was to tell us in a subsequent letter, was one a number of highlights in a holiday that he truly enjoyed.

We had also taken him, with Breige as our guide, to look around the almost completed monastery at Faughart. Father

Matthew was fascinated by the visit, by the shape and design of the building, and particularly by its connection with St Brigid, since his own parish, St Bride's, is the Scottish version of the same saint's name. The monastery had progressed very well by January although the plastering, painting, decorating and furnishings still had to be completed. Father Matthew loved the area, its beauty, its peace, and asked the nuns to reserve a place for him in one of the visitors' hermitages where he hopes to spend a few days in solitary prayer and contemplation. The nuns are delighted to have him, especially since he would be able to say Mass for them each day of his stay. He is intending to undertake his retreat in late September.

Joan enjoyed her conversations with Matthew, finding that spiritually and theologically they were very much in harmony. By January, Joan had been restored to an extraordinary level of health, energy and cheerfulness. She still has to walk with a stick but that is something she expects to jettison before the end of the autumn. Her hair, too, has grown back but, amazingly, it is now a dark colour most unlike the red hue she previously shared with Briege. At one point her X-rays were so worrying, even after her cure, that her consultant was seriously discussing a hip-replacement. The speed and excellence of her hip's regeneration, however, have rendered that particular surgery unnecessary. Her doctor and his team are mystified at her progress, delighted of course, but still mystified. It is beginning to seem as if the members of the O'Hare family can defy normal recuperative requirements and go straight to normal health.

Father Matthew had actually been a member of the Alexian Brothers before going on to the priesthood and he used to live in their community house in Warrenpoint over twenty years ago. Nothing delighted him more at that time than to travel to Newry to attend Mass in the cathedral. During his stay with us, Sadie cooked a meal one evening, inviting Father Niall and Sister Julie to join us. The evening was pleasantly companionable, especially since Sister Julie, too, hails from Glasgow and found that she and Matthew had many acquaintances in common. In addition, Father Niall, hearing Father Matthew's reminiscences about attending Mass in the cathedral, promised to arrange for him to say Mass there, a promise that he kept. Father Matthew told us afterwards that it was a great thrill for him to celebrate Mass in the cathedral that had so impressed him all those years ago.

Sadie enjoyed having Father Matt stay with us and tended to mother him. Early in his stay, at breakfast one morning, she insisted that he eat a bowl of cereal with plenty of milk, something that was not a part of his dietary routine.

'You should be taking this all the time,' she scolded. 'You need the calcium in the milk for your bones.'

Later that afternoon, Father Matt came into the lounge and said to Sadie, 'Mon, mah bones feel terrific after that cereal this morning. I can feel the milk doing them a world o' good.' It was a refrain he was to repeat more than once during the rest of his stay. Sadie just stared at him. He was lucky. If it had been me, I probably would have had something thrown at me. It was great to have him. When we returned home from leaving him to the airport, Sadie said that the house seemed strangely empty and quiet. We are looking forward to his next visit.

July 2004

The nuns moved into their new monastery in the middle of February 2004. It had not been fully completed – the ground was still very rough and required considerable landscaping; outside work on the timber walls and fencing still had to be done; the drive needed a tarmac overcoat – but the inside, in the main, was habitable and even with their saintly patience, they could no longer resist the lure of living in the new home that was as much a part of their hearts and their spirit as it was a dwelling place. When I called to see them, their delight and happiness were tangible. Support still arrives on a regular basis, various charitable organisations are supplying them with furniture, carpets, and other basic necessities to make the place habitable, and a group of friendly citizens from nearby Dundalk have formed themselves into an unofficial 'support group'. This group has been a godsend in all sorts of ways, particularly in organising and preparing for their grand inauguration on 1 May, a day-long ceremony involving bishops, dignitaries from various orders and organisations, wealthy patrons from America, Australia and even from the Philippines, members of their own and other religious orders – in all, some one hundred and twenty guests.

I still visit them every couple of weeks but it is getting to the stage where I will have to check with their diaries before I go. The spiritual guidance rooms are constantly in use and the locals, who are coming to a realisation of the great boon this monastery is in their midst, are beginning to place greater and greater demand on its services.

A month after the inauguration, the nuns held a family day to which the relatives of all five nuns were invited. It was a lovely day and I met a number of interesting people, including a relative of May's who told me that her grandson, not quite two years old at the time, had recently had a liver transplant and was now doing great. We talked for a while about him. The poor little fellow, Baby Dylan she called him, had all the same symptoms I had. God help him! The itch must have been a dreadful torture. He could not even have known what was going on, one advantage at least that was given to me. I could rationalise, pray, reach out and seek all sorts of support and comfort, but this poor little child must have lived in an agony of discomfort with no recourse whatever to the balm of understanding. Both his grandmother and myself were in tears at one point as she recounted the details.

One particularly special feature of the day was that Breige used it to launch her new CD – *We Adore You* – songs of Eucharistic adoration based very specifically on the writings of St Francis and St Clare on the Eucharist. I took a copy home and the following evening in my study I sat down to listen to it. Before doing so, however, I prayed to Jesus and asked him to sit with me while I played the hymns. The music was beautiful, Marie Cox's singing was wonderful and, with Jesus sitting there beside me, his presence so real, and my gaze all the while locked on his in a harmony of our own, it was one of the most emotion-filled experiences I have had since my epiphany. I was in tears after only two or three tracks.

Each day after communion I am often incapable of finding the words I need to express my feelings to Jesus about his gift of the Eucharist to me. But these hymns, these words of Francis and Clare, this music of Briege's, this sweet and lovely voice of Marie, give affirmation and expression to apprehensions in my soul of which I am scarcely aware. One hymn, in particular, filled my heart and has remained embedded there. In the simple introduction we are invited to

Look and gaze with wonder
At how humble is our God ...

something that we read so often about in the gospels yet seldom truly apprehend. Here St Francis is reminding the members of his order, and us, to realise that the God of all creation comes to us each day, not in power and might, not trailing clouds of glory, but in a humble and unimpressive wafer. The refrain of this hymn begins quietly with an extraordinary oxymoron, redolent of amazement and adoration,

Oh sublime lowliness ...

But then Marie's voice lifts to a high, sustained 'Ooooh...' of unutterable sweetness, a drawn-out, melodious sound that contains in it a dawning of realisation, a sudden understanding, that is reflected in the slow, tumbling cadences in the next word ... 'hu...mil...i...ty'. Then, in the steady, deliberate pacing of the last line of the refrain, the notes wander down to a low pitch and each word, even the humblest preposition, given equal value, to ensure that our minds have time to encompass the startling truth,

The ... Son ... of ... God ... in ... this ... ordinary ... bread.

Beautiful, evocative, gloriously melodic, intensely spiritual ... is it any wonder that I was moved? Is it any wonder that I was deeply affected?

I was so struck that I had to excuse myself to Jesus (Imagine! I asked Our Lord to sit there and wait for me while I went to make a phone call!) and run to the phone in order to tell Briege how much I loved the hymns. But when she came to the phone, I could not get the words out; they were stuck in my throat along with a lump the size of an egg. I could hear Breige repeating over and over, 'Are you all right, Brian?' Eventually I was able to tell her why I phoned. She was pleased to hear what I had to say and understood why I would have felt as I did. She explained that the words were not her own but were lifted directly from letters written by St Francis and St Clare and that, if listened to in a particular frame of spiritual awareness, they could be very moving indeed. I have listened to them many times since and I never tire of them. It seems to me that Jesus doesn't either.

July 2004

I think it must be obvious from the style and nature of these past few pages that I am simply tying up a few loose ends, that I consider my own story already to have been told. However, given that I had introduced Joan's cancer and the nun's story into the equation, I could not very well have left them hanging in limbo. Sadly there was one additional, and totally unexpected, loose end that came to light a couple of evenings ago. Sadie unfailingly reads the obituary column each day in the *Irish News*, a Northern Ireland provincial newspaper, although sometimes it is evening before she gets to it. The evening before last she read out to me, in shocked tones, that a Bernadette O'Hare from Banbridge had been buried that afternoon. She was sure that it was our Bernadette although we did not recognise the address in the newspaper. We were saddened by the news although not as shocked or, perhaps, not as surprised, as we had been at Ian's death. Bernadette had never seemed fully to recover and on the occasional times we met her at clinics she always appeared fragile and insecure. I recall, with regret and shame now, once saying to Sadie that Bernadette 'still thinks she is an invalid' and that if she wanted to improve she would have to come away from that mind-set. Clearly she was a great deal more ill than either of us realised. The following day we went to the address given in the newspaper. The house was empty but a neighbour was able to tell us that the dead young lady had recently had a liver transplant. Sad news indeed, and news that puts even more into perspective my own extraordinarily blessed condition. It is most strange but I do not remember the names of any other of my fellow patients; I can scarcely remember faces. Yet the two people with whom I did form a strong bond, people who, like myself, received liver transplants, are now both of them dead. What am I to make of that? I have no idea. All I can do is to continue to thank God each day for his gift of life to me and never forget how precious it is. To seek anything more would be to seek the mind of God.

And so I live my life in a state of what I can claim to be total contentment. I am still an ordinary Catholic, of course, with my human failings, my weaknesses. I still make mistakes, I still fall, but through the grace and love of Jesus my orientation is towards God, however halting my steps. Nothing in my life causes me pain; everything in my life demands my deepest gratitude.

I play golf with my doctor, Ian McVerry, on his (very) occasional days off. He was watching me hit a ball the other day and said, almost in mystification,

'You are a great advertisement.'

'What for?' I asked.

'Pick something … anything,' he replied, shaking his head.

'Prayer?' I suggested with a grin.

He laughed.

'OK! That too.'

'What were you meaning?'

'Strength, fitness for age, how hard you hit that ball, liver transplant, not the remotest sign of any after-effects. You're a walking miracle.'

That I am, Ian! That I am! And I shall be eternally grateful for it.